Social Information

CHANDOS
SOCIAL MEDIA SERIES

Series Editors: Geoff Walton and Woody Evans
(emails: g.l.walton@staffs.ac.uk and kdevans@gmail.com)

This series of books is aimed at practitioners and academics involved in using social media in all its forms and in any context. This includes information professionals, academics, librarians and managers, and leaders in business. Social media can enhance services, build communication channels, and create competitive advantage. The impact of these new media and decisions that surround their use in business can no longer be ignored. The delivery of education, privacy issues, logistics, political activism and research rounds out the series' coverage. As a resource to complement the understanding of issues relating to other areas of information science, teaching and related areas, books in this series respond with practical applications. If you would like a full listing of current and forthcoming titles, please visit our website www.chandospublishing.com or email wp@woodheadpublishing.com or telephone +44 (0) 1223 499140.

New authors: we are always pleased to receive ideas for new titles; if you would like to write a book for Chandos in the area of social media, please contact Jonathan Davis, Commissioning Editor, on jonathan.davis@chandospublishing.com or telephone +44 (0) 1993 848726.

Bulk orders: some organisations buy a number of copies of our books. If you are interested in doing this, we would be pleased to discuss a discount. Please email wp@woodheadpublishing.com or telephone +44 (0) 1223 499140.

Social Information
Gaining competitive and business advantage using social media tools

SCOTT BROWN

CP
CHANDOS
PUBLISHING

Oxford Cambridge New Delhi

Chandos Publishing
Hexagon House
Avenue 4
Station Lane
Witney
Oxford OX28 4BN
UK
Tel: +44 (0) 1993 848726
Email: info@chandospublishing.com
www.chandospublishing.com
www.chandospublishingonline.com

Chandos Publishing is an imprint of Woodhead Publishing Limited

Woodhead Publishing Limited
80 High Street
Sawston
Cambridge CB22 3HJ
UK
Tel: +44 (0) 1223 499140
Fax: +44 (0) 1223 832819
www.woodheadpublishing.com

First published in 2012

ISBN 978-1-84334-667-8 (print)
ISBN 978-1-78063-327-5 (online)

Chandos Social Media Series ISSN: 2050-6813 (print) and ISSN: 2050-6821 (online)

British Library Cataloguing-in-Publication Data.
A catalogue record for this book is available from the British Library.

Typeset by Domex e-Data Pvt. Ltd., India.
Printed in the UK and USA.

Contents

List of figures and tables

Figures

Tables

List of examples

Acknowledgments

As almost every author says, a book is not possible without the contributions of many people. I can't begin to count all the discussions I've had about these topics with colleagues, friends, students, and all of the people that I regularly rely on for making sense of these tools and their evolving dynamics.

I do want to say a special thanks to my many colleagues in the Special Libraries Association (SLA) and the Association of Independent Information Professionals (AIIP). Not a day goes by without learning something new or gaining a new insight from these amazing groups of people. All of you have shared your insights, sent me articles, and helped me to understand social tools in a broader and deeper context, and I am grateful for your help.

I would like to thank Dianna Wiggins for her expertise and insight into social sentiment, and her sharing of her expert knowledge in this area. She is also the originator of the term "social sleuthing," the original working title of this book.

Thanks to Graeme Byrd and Christian Gray for our ongoing discussions on the nature and future of social tools.

My editor at Chandos Publishing, Jonathan Davis, has made this foray into publishing a book an extremely pleasant one. I'm grateful for his guidance, patience, encouragement, and suggestions throughout this process. I also want to thank Geoff Walton, the series editor and the man who recruited me to write this book. If we hadn't met at the 2010 SLA Conference in New Orleans, this book might not have been!

Finally, I want to thank my wife and my daughter, who supported me during this entire process. They graciously allowed me the time and space to complete the hours of writing required, especially as the final manuscript date approached.

For all of you who have interest, passion, and enthusiasm about these tools and their potential – I hope you find this helpful.

About the author

Scott Brown draws on over 20 years' experience in library and information organizations (including public, academic, and corporate settings) to bring an extraordinarily broad range of expertise to his information work. Scott is founder and president of Social Information Group, an information practice focusing on the effective use of social networking tools for finding and sharing information. He has helped libraries, Fortune 500 companies, startups, government organizations, and individuals understand and effectively use social tools to achieve organizational goals.

In his previous position at Sun Microsystems, Scott developed, implemented, and managed information services and ongoing information training programs. In that position, he also conducted research and competitive intelligence for many business units in the company, covering technical, market, operational, human resource, and business topics.

A frequent speaker nationally on many areas of information work, Scott also teaches adjunct for the San Jose State University (San Jose, California, USA) and University of Denver (Denver, Colorado, USA) LIS programs, and has mentored students from those programs. He has taught on topics including the use of social tools for competitive intelligence, professional branding online, and career transitions, among others. He also provides professional coaching services.

Scott is an active member of the Special Libraries Association (SLA) and the Association for Independent Information Professionals (AIIP), where he has held several leadership positions. He has served on the advisory board of the Emporia (Kansas, USA) LIS program and the Corporate Library Advisory Board for Springer Publishing.

Scott received his MLIS from San Jose State University and his Masters in Counseling from Regis University (Colorado, USA).

Introduction: the impact of social media and the approach of this book

The impact of social media on business and competitive information

We "tweet," we blog, we post updates on Facebook and Google Plus. Our colleagues invite us to connect with them on LinkedIn, Orkut, Plaxo, Mixi, MerchantCircle, and any variety of other social networks. Social networking has had a profound global influence on how we connect with each other globally, and has, in fact, influenced our language.

Even if you don't use Twitter, Facebook, or LinkedIn, you likely have heard news stories about Twitter being used during elections and uprisings in Egypt, Tunisia, and Iran, and the blockage of social networking sites in China. You've probably seen video online, posted by individuals not affiliated with any "traditional" news outlet. Social tools have not only impacted on our connection to each other, they are impacting on our societies and our politics.

It's staggering to remind ourselves that in 2000, none of today's highly influential tools existed. Twitter came into being in 2006. LinkedIn started out in the living room of one of the company founders in the autumn of 2002, and officially launched in 2003. As of April 2012, LinkedIn boasts more than 150 million users and participants in over 200 countries worldwide – a growth of 60 million users just since January 2011. Twitter gained over 95 million users in just five years.

For some perspective, compare this with the time it took the following technologies to reach 50 million users:

- radio: 38 years
- television: 13 years.

For an even more dramatic illustration of the adoption of social tools, Google launched Google Plus, its own version of a social network platform, in June 2011. Though opinion on the number of actual Google Plus members and level of engagement varies, as of April 2012, it is reported that there are over 170 million people who have a Google Plus account – from zero to 170 million in ten months.

The adoption of LinkedIn (and the even swifter adoption of Google Plus and Facebook – 50 million users in only two years) illustrates the exponential growth of social media tools. Even more astounding is the fact that using LinkedIn or Facebook is not a "passive" activity. "Using" a television simply means buying one, hooking it up and turning it on. LinkedIn requires active participation. Users fill out their employment and professional information, and connect with colleagues, friends, and professional contacts. The successful use of LinkedIn also requires ongoing attention and updating. Using LinkedIn is far from a passive activity.

While there are large segments of users who register for social tools and rarely look at them again, why do so many people get involved in tools like LinkedIn and Facebook, and devote so much time to them? Like all successful social tools, LinkedIn provides a forum for connection, based around a shared interest. In LinkedIn's case, the shared interest is professional connection and networking. Because of its focus, LinkedIn provides an outstanding resource for business and competitive information for the savvy searcher. Other professional networking tools, like Google Plus, Xing, and Plaxo, can be rich sources as well.

What this book is about

The spectrum of social networking tools offers a broad variety of business and competitive information that can complement your research. If you are interested in understanding these tools and using them effectively – whether you are a business or competitive researcher, searching for information on a new career or industry, completing an assignment for a business or career class, doing investigative work, or simply curious – then this book is for you.

The landscape of social networking tools and online resources shifts and changes regularly. To be honest, every time I log in to a tool like LinkedIn or Google Plus, I discover changes and additional features that

I haven't used before. Often times, these changes add new functionality, which is delightful. Occasionally, the changes can be irksome.

The main point I wish to emphasize is that, to be a successful searcher in social tools, you need to be aware that you will need to continually adjust and adapt your searching skills. You can learn to search LinkedIn today, but, if you don't search it for six months, you will likely need to retrain yourself. This is simply the nature of these tools. They are not static "databases." The information, participation, and functionality change constantly.

Because of the changing nature of social tools, I've tried to take a dual approach in this book. I provide concrete search examples and focus on specific tools, and the information currently available in those tools. At the same time, I also attempt to provide the reader a strategy and approach for searching social tools that is *adaptable* to any tool that may be out there today, or that may change or emerge tomorrow. I will provide some perspective on these tools, and a framework from which to approach them, with the goal that, no matter how today's tools may change, you can quickly develop new search strategies as new tools and features emerge.

I encourage you to follow the examples in the book, and to explore and develop your own approaches to finding information in social tools.

I've attempted to provide the most current screenshots and statistics for the tools and examples covered in the book. However, due to the rapidly changing nature of social tools, the screenshots may not reflect the current state of the tool. Please bear this in mind as you compare the screenshots in the book with the tools online.

There is a high element of creativity in how people use social tools. The creators of Twitter, for example, likely never imagined that Twitter might be used to spread information to people affected by wildfires in the Southern California area, or be a part of political change. In the same way that the users of social tools find new and creative ways to use the tools, your job as a searcher in these tools is to be just as creative in finding and understanding the information. Social search can be quite fun, and ultimately, I hope that's a part of what you take away from this book.

A note on usage: I generally try to use the term "organization" when referring to any kind of entity, whether a for-profit company, a non-profit organization, a higher education institution, or any other kind of business entity. I have tried to maintain that phrasing consistently, except when a particular tool uses "company" as part of its nomenclature, or if the example I'm illustrating is a for-profit company. In these cases, I may refer to the entity as a "company." However, whenever you see the term "company," please keep in mind that these tools apply to any kind of business entity.

A final note: for readability and style purposes, the URLs of the tools and resources covered in this book are listed in the appendices and are therefore not listed in the main text.

A brief history of business and competitive information, and the rise of social tools

Abstract: This chapter briefly examines the history and availability of business and competitive information. The chapter contrasts the difference between information available in "traditional" sources (such as business databases) and social sources. A history of social tools is presented. The chapter outlines common features of social tools, including connecting with others and sharing information. The chapter concludes by outlining ten categories of social tools: networking tools, publishing tools, social search engines, RSS and news feeds, video/audio/image sources, collaboration tools, communication tools, location tools, games and lifecasting tools.

Key words: History of social tools, traditional information sources, social information sources, categories of social tools.

A brief history of business and competitive information

In some sense, business and competitive information has been important to humans since the beginning of society. How much grain is my neighbor growing? What price is he asking for it at the market? What price was he asking last year?

Prior to the information revolution, and the advent of "personal computing" in the 1980s and 1990s, business information was typically paper based and accessible only by either physically getting information or talking with other people. People read the newspaper, or visited the county recorder, the hall of records, the patent office, or the library to find information. The records held the "official" business information, which was certainly important to have. Libraries held the back issues of newspapers and business magazines. The gossip and discussion among people often held the "softer" information: what was the business owner thinking of doing next? Whom did he know? Whom was he dealing with? Where did people think things were going? This information was just as important, and it complemented the information available through the "official" channels of records and news.

While there does not seem to be one definitive history of competitive intelligence (CI) – the practice of specifically looking at business competitors so you could figure out their strategies and the market, and how you fit into it – it is generally agreed that the beginnings of CI practice in organizations began in the 1970s (although the practice of intelligence by government agencies started well before then). Michael Porter's publication of his book *Competitive Strategy* in 1980 signaled the foundation of modern-day business practice of CI. The establishment of the Society of Competitive Intelligence Professionals (SCIP) in 1986, and subsequent codification of the practice of CI, has made twenty-first-century CI practice a thriving and essential part of many industries and organizations.

Some early CI practitioners had roots in military intelligence and counter-intelligence, giving the practice of CI a "cloak and dagger" feel. Visions (and sometimes the actual practice) of "dumpster diving" for information, and other ethically questionable information-gathering activities, sometimes clouded the practice of gathering competitive information. With the advent of the Internet, and more readily available information online via the web, databases, and subscription services, a lot of competitive information can be more easily gathered without verging into the area of espionage.

"Traditional" business and competitive information sources

When I talk about "traditional" sources for business and competitive information, I think of these as the "official" sources I referenced earlier. These sources might include the paper-based resources that we've had for centuries: county records, required business filings with the government, etc. They also include online resources that provide *verified*, *reliable* information. These are either sources that have the blessing of an official governing body, such as the EDGAR records from the US government Securities and Exchange Commission that provide access to the official filings of US public businesses, or sources that have established themselves as credible and reliable, such as OneSource, Dun & Bradstreet, and Hoover's. These sources have been used for decades, and have come to be regarded as reliable and authoritative.

The intersection of "traditional" and social information

"Traditional" sources can provide information that forms the basis of business and competitive analysis. Business information such as sales, revenues, profits, cash flow, and debt helps to provide a picture of the financial health of an organization, and gives some idea of the competitive positioning of a company in the market. Financial analyst reports, provided by investment firms such as the US firm J.P. Morgan, can provide a perspective on the strengths and weaknesses of an organization, and its opportunities and vulnerabilities in the market. News articles from major media outlets provide a picture of the market forces at play for any given industry. All of these contribute to the picture of an organization and its market, as well as some sense of the broader industry.

The information a researcher can gather through social tools can help paint a richer picture of the organization and its market positioning. Through social tools, one can potentially discover such things as:

- **Employee movement:** How and whom is the organization hiring? Who is leaving the organization? Where are they going?
- **Customer sentiment:** Is the organization well regarded by its customers, or vilified? Is the organization having any issues with its products?
- **Company structure:** What titles do the employees have? What kind of structure does the organization have? How "social" is the organization – in other words, how active is it online?
- **Organization initiatives and growth areas:** What talents and skills is the organization looking for in employees? What titles do new hires have? How is the organization shifting its focus?
- **Market disruptors:** Is the organization being challenged by other entrants into the market? What kinds of products or services are potentially rivaling the organization's products and services?
- **Strategic direction:** How is the organization talking about itself? What is the leadership talking about? What events is the organization targeting? What does that say about the direction of the organization, and the shifting market?

In this book, we'll explore these aspects and more, and how social tools can help uncover this type of information.

The growth of social tools

Social networking tools are called "social" for a reason. They are, at their core, about connection. In this sense, social networking as a concept goes back to the beginning of history. We, as a species, get together and share information. We tell stories. We hear stories. Our society has a long oral and written tradition. If we look at "networks" that we've used in the past for sharing information, we can point to libraries, educational institutions, and postal services as examples.

A next wave of "networks" might begin with the telegraph. The telegraph gave us the ability to electronically send information long distances with relatively little "transit time." Radio, telephones, and television further increased this ability to transmit information. These tools sometimes provided an element of having an interaction or conversation, such as the telephone; sometimes they only transmitted information in one direction.

The introduction of online information-sharing utilities like ARPANET, in the late 1960s, and USENET, in the late 1970s and 1980s, may be considered the earliest forms of social networking as we know it today. These tools electronically connected different groups of people for the express purpose of sharing information and interacting. The development of ARPANET ushered in an era of computers communicating with each other (with humans obviously being involved in there somewhere), and established at least the conceptual basis of the Internet as we know it today.

The earliest forms of social networks as we know them today can be traced to Bulletin Board Systems, or BBS, in the 1980s. These online communities would be accessible only if you could use your telephone to dial in, via a modem, to a computer running the BBS software. You could send text-only information to other interested parties – and typically, the other interested parties would be other hard-core techno-geeks like you. If you weren't in the same local calling area as the computer, you also had to pay long-distance fees (in addition to tying up your phone line with a screechy modem signal).

It wasn't until CompuServe and, later, America Online (or AOL) came along (in 1979 and in 1989–91 respectively) that more interaction was possible online, and that these technologies began to be used more widely.

Using these services, members could participate in thousands of online forums about a variety of topics (from sex to health to environment to cooking). People also started using a new tool called "email." Because of AOL, many people have embedded in their brains the upbeat announcement of "You've got mail!"

As the Internet became more and more robust and user friendly, and more and more people had faster connections to the Internet, the usage of online networks expanded. Social networks came and went quickly. One of the few networks that lasted, created in 2002, is Friendster. Friendster was initially a way to connect with people, and to see how they were connected with other people – very similar to Facebook in concept. Friendster still exists, but today has more of a social gaming focus.

Facebook was started at Harvard in 2004. Within two years, Facebook had 50 million users. As of April 2012, it has more than 800 million active users.

While Facebook, at the moment, seems to be the largest "personal" online social network, a variety of other types of social tools have emerged. Google launched Google Plus in June 2011 in response to Facebook, and quickly gained millions of users. LinkedIn has emerged as a premier online network for professional use. Blogs have transformed the way we write, and the way we share online. Twitter has become a tool not just for telling others what you had for breakfast, but for sharing timely and critical information in a variety of settings. Journalists have spent shorter times in jail because of Twitter.[1] Twitter has been used in Iran, China, Egypt, Tunisia, the USA, and other countries as a way to communicate outside of traditional communication channels. Video is constantly being recorded and uploaded to YouTube and other video-sharing tools, so that more information is available to more people through more channels than ever before.

What does all this mean? The availability of "tacit" knowledge through social tools

Why do we want to share our information? How is it that people continue to overcome their increasing fear of online identity theft, spamming, phishing, and other online fraud, and continue to share details of their lives in social networking tools?

I think there are a variety of reasons that contribute to this: the need for connection, the fun inherent in using a lot of these tools, and an aura of experimentation. The communication and sharing that happens in social tools is really just an extension of our natural human need to connect with others. Social tools provide a fun and unique way to connect, and they also provide a way for us to stay connected with the people in our lives on an ongoing basis. No matter where we are, if we can connect to the Internet somehow, we can connect with our networks. To share a personal example, my family and I recently moved from Colorado to Oregon. While we all miss the friendships we made in Colorado, we still have the ability to stay up to date on and connected with those friends via tools like Facebook. Of course, it's not the same as being "in person," but it allows us to stay connected with friends, family, and colleagues.

Looking at professional usage of these tools, I believe that the current wave of social networking use is helping fulfill some of the original aims of knowledge management (KM). The initial KM "wave" in the late 1990s and early 2000s was driven by the need to capture the "tacit" knowledge in people's heads, especially within organizations. For example, retiring employees leaving the company take great amounts of organizational and specialized knowledge with them. Employees simply shifting from one position to another take a wealth of "inherent" knowledge about their old position with them.

In early KM efforts, companies often spent hundreds of thousands of dollars to implement organization-wide KM systems to try to capture this type of "tacit" information. While some of these initiatives certainly succeeded, many of them did not achieve their goals. One of the biggest problems was getting employees to actually put their knowledge into the systems – and then getting employees to use the systems to leverage the knowledge within them.

Social tools, in many ways, have solved this problem. By providing fun and engaging ways to interact online, social tools are overcoming some of the struggles of these early KM initiatives. Experts, employees, thought leaders, business leaders, and industry pundits are willingly and actively sharing their knowledge and expertise via LinkedIn, YouTube, Facebook, blogs, Twitter, and social bookmarking services, among other tools.

The knowledge and information is increasingly available; the challenge now is to harness and make sense of that knowledge. This is where research skills in using social tools can be invaluable.

Getting started with social tools

Social tools are different than "traditional" research tools in three ways.

1. Some tools, especially social networking tools, require you to sign up for the tool and provide some type of information about yourself, often in the form of "profile" information, before you can start using it.

2. Some strongly suggest that you connect with others using the tool. Often, you cannot get access to the rich information in the tool without creating a network in the tool.

3. All social tools provide access to "social" information – information shared or created by others. News and other "traditional" information, such as sales, may be integrated into social tools, but social information is a key part of social tools.

Most of the currently popular social tools and sites allow you to sign up and start using the tools for free. Many also offer subscription pricing that will allow you to leverage advanced features of the tools. In the examples in this book, we'll primarily examine the features and information available in the free versions of the tools, but we will also highlight important features of the paid versions.

For many people, providing personal information and "connecting" with others online feels a bit risky and unsafe. Especially in this age of online identity theft, many people are hesitant to provide even a birth month and date when registering for a tool, much less a full birth date, place of employment, and other potentially sensitive information. For people using these tools for researching direct competitors, the idea of sharing information and, potentially, connecting with, and risking exposure to, competitors can be daunting.

As we look at these tools, keep these considerations in mind. Depending upon the sensitivity of your work, and the information available without registering, you may decide to not register at all. You may decide that you want to create a "dummy" account, using an email name and information that are not easily traceable to you. We will highlight potential issues and explore them as needed.

That said, in order to use these tools effectively – or at all – you will need to register and create a basic profile for some of them. For many tools, you literally can't use them for research unless you register. I believe that, unless your work is competitive or sensitive in nature, the more transparent you can be online, the better. I'm not saying that you should share or expose your personal information indiscriminately. But I do believe that the more you are willing to register, share some of your information, and connect with people authentically and safely, the more benefit and enjoyment you will get out of these tools.

For each tool, I will share both "caveats" and some tips on protecting your information. "Caveats" can cover both considerations in determining the reliability of the information available in the tool and safety measures specific to the tool. In the final chapter, we will also take another look at the issues of online safety.

Connections: finding expertise

As I've mentioned, one of the ways that social tools are different than traditional tools is that they are about connecting, and sharing information with people. When you use a tool or database like Hoover's or LexisNexis, you're not required to create a profile, or to connect with other users. Typically, all you need is IP authentication or a user ID and password, and you can search for information relatively anonymously.

Social tools are called "social" for a reason. They are social because you share information about yourself and you connect with others. Again, while there are good reasons for keeping your information confidential, especially in doing competitive and sensitive research, I encourage you to approach these tools with an open and positive perspective.

Networking and connecting online, in many ways, mirrors networking and connecting in person. When you meet someone in person, you can tell pretty quickly whether that person is open to sharing information and creating a relationship with you. Conversely, you can tell if a person seems untrustworthy or closed to creating a relationship. Others can observe that about you, too. If you approach online networking and social tools from an open and positive position, you will find that your connections, just like in "real" life, can be strong and beneficial.

One of the astonishing characteristics of social tools, especially networking tools like LinkedIn, is that you are able to connect with experts in all areas of business more easily than ever. It used to be that you might need to rely on directories, pay for company information, make calls, and try to get a hold of organizational charts in order to find out whom to connect with in an organization, or to find experts in particular topic areas. Of course, there are certainly instances where you still need to do that. However, because millions of people are using social networking tools, you are able to find and connect with more expertise more quickly and easily than ever before.

As an example, a colleague of mine was interested in getting involved in a specific segment of the healthcare industry, but he had no connections at all with that segment of the industry. By searching LinkedIn, he was able to find contacts within that segment, connect with them, and start to build his new network. In fact, he was able to secure a meeting with a person who was doing the exact job he wanted to do in the future.

We'll cover how to connect with experts, and the best ways to build your networks, specifically for each tool.

Common characteristics of social tools

There are literally thousands, if not hundreds of thousands of tools out there that could be considered "social" tools. How do you make sense of them all?

We'll look at categories of tools in the next section, but first, let's look at the main characteristics of all social tools. The following characteristics outline levels of engagement in social tools, from simple connection to building community.

- **Connection.** We've discussed this aspect of social tools a bit already. No matter what tool you're talking about – blogs, wikis, or social networks – these tools are about connecting with people. While you may not have "direct" connections in some tools – for example, connecting with people directly in LinkedIn – these tools allow you to find people who are sharing information online, and, if you are using the tools, they allow people to find you.
- **Sharing.** Once you've connected with or identified people through these tools, professionally or personally, often you can find information that they have shared, and you start sharing information.
- **Participation.** The step beyond sharing is participation – the active sharing of information and communication back and forth. Another way to think about this is as conversation. In addition to sharing, people begin to have active conversations in these tools.
- **Community.** Ultimately, the most successful social tools become online communities, with leaders, moderators, content contributors, occasional participants, and "lurkers." The community actively engages around the topic areas of the community – again, whether that community is around a blog, a Facebook or LinkedIn group, or a Twitter stream or hashtag.

As people share, participate, and begin to form a community, *serendipity* begins to happen. People discover information from other participants that is valuable, but that they didn't know existed. The phenomenon of serendipity adds to the value of the community, making it stronger.

Categories of social tools

Another way to help make sense of social tools is to categorize them into areas of functionality. These categories are not definitive, but hopefully they will help you to make sense of the world of social tools.

Networking

The primary focus of these tools is connecting with others. These are the most social of social tools. Examples include:

- Facebook
- LinkedIn
- Google Plus
- Mixi
- Orkut
- Xing.

Publishing

These tools allow single or multiple authors to publish their writing. Typically, entries are written in a personal or journalistic format and style. Examples include:

- **Blogs,** which allow you to write entries as long or as short as you like. Often, you can include video and images in your post, and link to other sites and blog postings. Examples include:
  - WordPress
  - Blogger
  - Typepad.
- **Microblogs,** which typically have a limit on the length of your entry. For example, Twitter limits you to 140 characters for your entry. Similar to blogs, you can link to images and other sites. One way you can think of microblogs is as text messaging online (because of the limited length). Examples include:
  - Twitter
  - Yammer.

An interesting category of publishing tools are tools that combine features of blogging and microblogging, such as Tumblr and Pinterest

(Figures 1.1 and 1.2). These types of sites allow users to post quick updates – text, images, audio, URLs – which give them features of both blogs and microblogs. There is often not an easy way to comment on entries, but it is relatively easy to share or repost others' content. The blogs created in these types of tools also are often more design oriented and visual in nature.

Figure 1.1 Example of a Tumblr blog. This particular Tumblr blog is from IBM Global Services. Although this looks like a blog entry, all the administrator has done is post a link to an article – the text is drawn entirely from that article

Figure 1.2 Example of a Pinterest "pinboard." The topic is IBM servers, and the administrator has "pinned" four photos to this topic

Social search engines

Social search engines primarily pull information from social sites, though most will often include information that isn't "social." These engines will pull results from microblogs, blogs, social networks, and video and image sources, among others. Often, they will include links to documents found online as well, such as PDFs and Microsoft documents (Word, PowerPoint, and Excel). Examples include:

- SocialMention
- Addictomatic
- Samepoint
- CrowdEye (focuses specifically on Twitter search)
- Pipl (focuses on information on individuals in social sites)
- YoName (also focuses on information on individuals in social sites).

Some social search engines also attempt to provide "sentiment" analysis – a gauge of the tone of any particular post or piece of content. Sentiment is typically characterized as positive, negative, or neutral. We will discuss sentiment in more depth in the chapter on social search.

RSS and news feeds

RSS is generally accepted to be an acronym for "Really Simple Syndication." In practice, RSS feeds provide an automatic way to get the latest news from a site or a resource. RSS feeds provide "real-time" updates on news from an information resource, a website, blog postings, and many other online sources. For many sites and resources, you can create an RSS feed from a saved search, so that you can customize the information you receive, and receive updated search results automatically.

You can collect the information from RSS feeds on a website, such as NetVibes, or you can have them delivered to you via email via a feed aggregator, such as Google Reader.

A few examples of RSS feed pages include:

- New York Times RSS feeds (*http://www.nytimes.com/services/xml/rss/index.html*)
- CBC (Canadian news) (*http://www.cbc.ca/rss/*)
- NPR (National Public Radio) (*http://www.npr.org/rss/*).

Examples of RSS aggregator sites and tools include:

- NetVibes
- Google Reader
- FeedBlitz.

Video/audio/images

These tools primarily provide places to share and find video, audio, or images. Usually you can search these sites for particular content, people, or organizations.

Video examples include:

- YouTube
- Blinkx
- DailyMotion.

Audio examples include:

- iTunes podcasts (through iTunes)
- Podcast Alley.

Image examples include:

- Flickr
- Picasa.

Collaboration

Collaboration tools help people work together. While many social tools naturally have collaboration features, these tools focus primarily on facilitating collaboration in sharing information. This category includes social bookmarking tools and wikis.

- **Social bookmarking tools** allow you to tag articles, links, websites, and other online sources with keywords to make them more findable. As these tools evolve, they are actually providing easy-to-use and robust tools for capturing and organizing a variety of content, including images and video. Many tools are incorporating the ability to bookmark and capture information via mobile apps as well. Examples of social bookmarking tools include:
  - Digg
  - Diigo

- Instapaper
- Evernote
- Delicious – acquired by Yahoo! in 2010. There were indications that Yahoo! would shut the service down. As of this writing, the service is still up and running.

- **Wikis** provide a simplified interface for a group of users to create online pages of resources. They usually allow users to create a hierarchy of and structure for information, create web pages on the wiki, and to include both online links and documents. Many people use them for managing projects, or collections of documents. Most wiki tools these days have an easy-to-use interface that allows users to do editing, formatting, and embedding of information, images, videos, and links. Examples of wiki tools include:
  - PBworks
  - Zoho.

Some collaboration tools are starting to incorporate social networking features, so that users can not only share and organize information, but also communicate and manage workflow and tasks. These types of tools are starting to be used more frequently within organizations. One example of this kind of tool is FMYI.

Communication

These tools help users communicate via text, voice, and/or video. Often times, multiple users can communicate at one time, and many tools allow the sharing of documents and multimedia files (such as video and photos). Examples include:

- Skype
- AOL Instant Messenger
- Windows Live Messenger
- Yahoo! Messenger
- ooVoo.

Other social tools, of course, have communication features built into the tool, but this category is distinguished by a primary focus on communication.

Location

These tools have an emphasis on location. You can share your location with others through "location-based services." Typically (though not always), you would use these applications on a mobile device that has GPS or location capabilities, so you can "check in" wherever you are, and share your location with friends. Not only are you able to share your location, but you can also share your insights, photos, and information about that location. Examples include:

- FourSquare
- SCVNGR
- Path – a more limited, personal networking tool
- Yelp (food-based).

Many social networking tools are also incorporating location features. One example is Facebook, which, similar to FourSquare, allows you to check in at a location as part of your status update.

Games and virtual worlds

These are primarily just for fun! Games may be embedded in other social tools (such as the games available through Facebook); they may be location based or available through a mobile application (such as the currently popular Angry Birds); or they may allow you to play with other players in diverse locations online.

Included in this category are 3-D virtual worlds, such as Second Life. While Second Life is not a game in itself, it and other virtual worlds sometimes have gaming elements within them.

Examples in this category include:

- World of Warcraft
- Second Life
- Friendster.

Lifecasting

Lifecasting can encompass live video streaming, and can be taken to the extent of "always on" broadcasting of your life. You can think of lifecasting as the extreme end of the social networking spectrum: continuous broadcast of a person, a room, or a life. Examples in this category include:

- UStream
- Livestream
- Justin.tv.

As you can see, these categories are not always clearly delineated, and likely will become less so in the future, as social tools incorporate more cross-functionality. For example, DailyMotion, the video site, also provides live streaming video from several sources – which also means it falls into the Lifecasting category. Facebook has gaming elements, as we've already discussed. It also has location functionality like Foursquare, as well as microblog capabilities, like Twitter. Google Plus currently has a feature called Hangouts, which allows for a group of up to ten people to have a video conference.

The purpose of the above categorization is not to provide definitive categories for each tool, but to help you think about the primary functionality of each tool, so that you can understand them and choose the right ones for your research.

While we will look at tools that have features from several of these categories, we will be focusing primarily on the following categories of tools:

- networking
- publishing
- blogs and microblogs
- social search engines
- video/audio/images.

These tools provide some of the richest resources for business and competitive information.

Review

We've covered a very brief history of traditional business and competitive information and sources, and the disruptive influence of social tools in the information space. We've taken a look at how social tools have evolved, and how more expertise and tacit knowledge is available online than ever before. We've talked about the different types of social tools, and narrowed down the ones we will emphasize in this book. We're ready to begin looking at our first set of social research tools: social networks.

Note

1. In April 2008 an American journalism student was arrested in Egypt for photographing a demonstration. He immediately tweeted his plight to his followers and was released the next day. See M. Arrington (2008) Twitter saves man from Egyptian justice. *Techcrunch* (16 April). Available from: *http://techcrunch.com/2008/04/16/twitter-saves-man-from-egyptian-justice/* [Accessed 25 April 2012].

2

Social networks

Abstract: This chapter looks specifically at finding information in social networks, such as Facebook, LinkedIn, Google Plus, Orkut, and others. Common characteristics of social networks are explored. For Facebook, LinkedIn, Orkut, and Google Plus, the chapter outlines the different kinds of information that can be found in these tools, and provides examples for each tool to illustrate search techniques and results. Tips for searching each tool are provided. The chapter also explores ways to protect your personal information, and cautions on using each tool. The chapter concludes with a list of additional social networks, and a review of the content covered in the chapter.

Key words: Social networking tools, Facebook, LinkedIn, Orkut, Google Plus, Google+, G+, searching social networks.

What are they?

As we've discussed, the primary focus of social networking tools is connecting with others. You can think of these tools as online versions of in-person networking. Because they are primarily about connecting with people, I think of them as the most social of social tools. Examples include:

- **Facebook:** As of April 2012, Facebook has over 800 million users. While Facebook is increasingly being used by businesses, it is still widely used by individuals for personal networking rather than professional networking.

- **LinkedIn:** As of April 2012, over 150 million people in 200 countries use LinkedIn as a *professional* network, distinguishing it from more personal networks like Facebook. LinkedIn is also available in 17 languages, including English, French, German, Italian, Portuguese, and Spanish.

- **Google Plus:** Google launched its own version of a social network, Google Plus (or Google+ or G+) in June 2011. As of this writing, anyone who has a Gmail account can sign up for and participate in Google Plus. Google Plus has grown very rapidly. Though the opinion on the number of actual Google Plus members and level of engagement varies, as of April 2012, it is reported that there are over 170 million people who have a Google Plus account. Google Plus originally offered only individual pages, but in November 2011, it launched the ability for organizations to create pages.

- **Orkut:** Orkut is another online social network operated by Google. Because it is operated by Google, like Google Plus, it is integrated with your Google accounts. Like Facebook, it is primarily used for personal networking, though professional use is also growing. As of April 2012, the top countries using Orkut are Brazil, India, and the United States.

- **Mixi:** Mixi is a social network that is currently very popular in Japan – much more popular than Facebook. As of April 2012, over 25 million people in Japan use Mixi, primarily as a personal social networking platform. Mobile Mixi, a way to access the Mixi network via mobile devices, is growing in popularity.

- **Xing:** Xing is a professionally focused social network. As of April 2012, Xing boasts more than 11 million members. Xing is most popular in Germany, with over 4 million German members. Like LinkedIn and other social networks, participants can join interest groups.

- **Ning:** The Ning platform allows you to create specific social networks and groups, and invite people to participate in those groups. This is what makes it different from many other social networking sites: It has an almost exclusive focus on groups. The group is created first, and then people join the group, rather than the other way around. Ning has changed recently so that it's more difficult to find Ning groups, but there are Ning groups that can provide great information on industries.

- **Plaxo:** Plaxo is a bit different in that it promotes itself as an online address book. You can connect with others using Plaxo, and participants primarily use it as a way to keep their contact information current, and to keep track of others' contact information. As of April 2012, Plaxo claims to manage over 50 million online address books.

Social networks, and social networking tools, can come and go quickly. The specific sites mentioned here may be around for several more years, or may disappear soon. You can be assured that all of these tools will continue to change focus, as well as add, delete, and modify features. The important thing to understand is how these tools work in principle, so that you can always develop an approach to searching them for important information, no matter what the tool.

How do they work?

As already mentioned, the primary characteristic of social networks is connecting with other people. Most social networking tools have five common components and steps to using them:

- **Free registration.** You can begin using almost all of the popular social networking tools without any charge to you, and without any restriction on who can register. Some social networks can be accessed only by invitation from an existing member of the network. More exclusive social networks continue to emerge, but generally, most of the larger social networks continue to be accessible and free to everyone, at least at a basic level.

- **Access to additional features with a paid subscription.** In addition to the free access level, almost all of the popular social networking tools will also provide one or more paid subscription levels, which typically give you more features, or greater access to network members, or both. The network may charge a monthly or an annual fee. Some features you might get with a paid subscription include being able to email any member in the network, being able to access more information about those members not in your direct network, or having an "enhanced" profile, with additional features and promotion capabilities.

- **Your profile.** All social networks require you to provide some information about yourself. Depending upon the network, you may be required to provide only minimal information, such as your name, industry, and contact information. Other networks may require more information. Some networks, such as LinkedIn, allow you to provide large amounts of information about your career history, education, awards and honors, interests, and a variety of other information.

- **The ability to connect with others.** This is the distinguishing characteristic of this type of tool; social networking tools are, first and foremost, about connecting with people. Usually you are able to search for people in the network using a variety of keywords. Often times you are also able to utilize other tools to connect with people, such as importing your email contacts.

- With almost all social networks, when you connect with others, or when others connect with you, the connection is not automatic. Each person has to agree to the connection. For example, if you receive an invitation to connect, you have the ability to approve that connection, or to ignore or refuse the connection. (Note that this is *not* true for Google Plus, which offers a "following" model more than a connection model.)

- **Interest groups.** This feature adds to the ability to connect with others. Almost all social networks have interest groups, based on topic, industry, geography, events, or interest. These online groups allow you to connect more easily to others with similar interests. Often, the online groups will have features such as the ability to start and participate in discussions, connect with other members of the group, and post information or job listings, depending upon the tool.

Many social networks, of course, have other features to complement these components, and those features will vary, depending upon the tool. However, almost all social networking tools will share these common features.

LinkedIn

What is it?

LinkedIn is an online professional social network. In contrast to a social network like Facebook, LinkedIn has a primarily professional focus, and allows businesses, professionals, customers, and clients to interact. You can think of LinkedIn as a "supercharged" resume or curriculum vitae (CV) for individuals.

LinkedIn officially launched in 2003. As of April 2012:

- LinkedIn has more than 135 million participants in over 200 countries worldwide. More than half of LinkedIn participants are outside of the United States. The top non-US regions and countries using LinkedIn are Europe, India, Canada, Australia, and Brazil.

- In 2011, users conducted almost 4.2 billion people searches.

- As of April 2012, LinkedIn is available in 17 language interfaces, including English, French, German, Indonesian, Italian, Japanese, Korean, Malay, Portuguese, Romanian, Russian, Spanish, Swedish, and Turkish.
- Executives from every Fortune 500 company are on LinkedIn.
- You can find over one million company pages on LinkedIn.

What kind of business and competitive information can be found there?

LinkedIn is a rich source of employee and organization information. Examples of the type of information that you can find include:

- **Executive and employee information:** What titles do the executives and employees have? What degrees do most employees hold? How many years of experience do they have? From which universities or schools did they graduate? How are those employees regarded? What skills do they bring to the organization? Where did they work before?
- **Employee movement:** Whom has the organization recently hired? Who has recently left the organization? To which organizations did they go next?
- **Organizational initiatives and growth areas:** What talents and skills is the organization hiring in employees? Have employees changed job titles recently? What does that say about a shifting organizational focus?
- **Organization and employee location:** Where is the organization's headquarters? Where are there large geographical concentrations of employees?

How do you get started using it?

Anyone can register and start using LinkedIn at no cost at *http://www.linkedin.com*. As with all social tools, you provide your name, email and password to get started. Once you sign up, LinkedIn will walk you through a few steps to help you get some minimum information into your profile, and to help get you connected.

As of this writing, LinkedIn allows you to import an existing resume into your profile, which can help you get a start on filling out your profile information. Even if you do import your resume, you will still need to verify, correct, and update that information.

LinkedIn allows you to fill in a lot of information, well beyond a typical resume or CV. Some currently available content fields include:

- summary information
- website links
- experience or positions held
- education
- awards and honors
- publications
- interests
- recommendations from others
- membership in LinkedIn groups
- contact information.

Through plugins, you can also integrate and share your Amazon book-reading lists, slide presentations and documents, travel itineraries, and blog entries, among other things. LinkedIn currently offers some features specific to certain industries, such as the legal industry. Additionally, LinkedIn allows you the ability to tag your profile with a broad set of skills tags. These tags allow others to search for people by one or more skills. You can identify your profile with up to 50 skills tags.

LinkedIn also currently has features that allow you to import your email contacts so that you can more quickly identify and connect with people you already know on LinkedIn.

In addition to a free account, LinkedIn does offer subscription accounts which provide you extra connection and search features. With a paid account, you can get access to additional advanced search features such as seniority level, years of experience, company size, and whether the person is associated with a Fortune 1000 company. You also get access to expanded profile views for everyone on LinkedIn, including people outside your network. These features may be worthwhile to you, depending upon your research needs.

Whom should you connect with?

Many users who first join LinkedIn hesitate to start connecting with people. Users sometimes feel that they might be annoying other people by sending other LinkedIn users invitations to connect. Alternatively, users sometimes draw a blank – who would I connect with?

First of all, don't hesitate to connect with others on LinkedIn. Anyone who has been on LinkedIn for any time at all expects that they will get invitations to connect. It is actually quite delightful to receive an invitation to connect with someone you know!

As to where to start, some initial connections you might want to make include:

- work colleagues, current and past
- professional colleagues, current and past
- friends
- clients, if you have had a business or a consulting business
- people who invite you to connect (but be sure to take a look at their profile if they're someone you don't know).

There are many ways to build your network thoughtfully on LinkedIn. Again, think of networking on LinkedIn as similar to networking at a conference or a meeting. You may make a plan to connect with people in a new industry in which you're interested. You might want to connect with people in a certain company in order to find out more about that company. You may wish to get "up to speed" on a particular industry, and so decide to join some LinkedIn groups focused on that industry.

In searching for information on LinkedIn, the broader your network, the more information you can find and the more connections you can find. If you are interested in building your network quickly, try connecting with the following types of people on LinkedIn:

- human resources professionals and recruiters you know
- people you know who have 500+ connections.

HR professionals and recruiters utilize LinkedIn for their work, and so typically have very large networks. Likewise, people who have 500+ connections can expand your network exponentially. You can take advantage of these networks in order to be able to research and reach people and experts more easily.

Additionally, becoming a member of a few large LinkedIn groups will help build your connection network quickly. For example, the Consultants Network on LinkedIn has tens of thousands of members. If you have any interest in consulting – or are a consultant yourself – this group can provide great discussions on the topic, as well as provide a connection to tens of thousands of people in one click. While many groups require approval to gain acceptance into the group, many groups are also moving to "open" formats, where anyone can join without approval.

As you continue using LinkedIn, you'll find yourself connecting with more people, and people reaching out to connect with you. You may be surprised how quickly your network can grow!

Some initial tips for getting the most out of LinkedIn

If you are using LinkedIn for sensitive competitive search, you may be hesitant to share so much information about yourself or your current and past employment. Because of the nature of LinkedIn, some competitive professionals may choose not to join it at all, or may create a "dummy" account in order to protect their identities.

Even if you don't sign up for LinkedIn, you can leverage some of the information available in individual profiles in LinkedIn by using Google and adding "LinkedIn" to your search terms. For example, if you search for "Barack Obama LinkedIn" in Google, you'll be able to access the public LinkedIn profile for Barack Obama. Depending upon the privacy settings of the individual, you may be able to see almost all of the information on the profile, or a limited amount of profile information. Unless you are registered with LinkedIn, however, you will not be able to access group or company information.

If your research and work is not highly sensitive, the benefits of using LinkedIn are highly compelling, both for visibility and for research reasons. To get the most out of your use of LinkedIn from a research perspective, I offer the following suggestions.

- Actively build your LinkedIn network, both by connecting with people and by joining LinkedIn groups. Connecting gives you easier and broader access to people and to information in LinkedIn. As we've discussed, you can start by connecting with people you know, current and past colleagues, professional colleagues, professional groups, and industry interest groups.

- Conduct yourself openly, honestly, and ethically. As we've already mentioned, social networks are about community. To build a strong community, you have to show up, conduct yourself responsibly, give to others, share what you know, and look out for other people. If you are a responsible participant in your online communities, your communities will notice, and will be willing to connect with you, help you, share what they know, and do their very best for you. This is the heart and the reward of participating online.

Example 2.1: Business and competitive use

Let's get into the search. From the main LinkedIn page (*http://www.linkedin.com*), you'll see a link at the top for Companies. When you click on that link, you will land on the main Companies page (Figure 2.1).

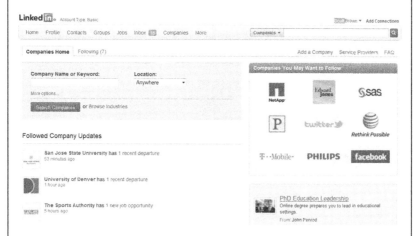

Figure 2.1   Main Company page on LinkedIn

You'll see that you have a simple search box in the upper right of the screen, as well as a central search box (Figure 2.2). You can select more options for company searching, including company size, location, and industry. You also have an option to browse industries.

To get an idea of the type of information available on companies, you might want to try the LinkedIn suggestions of "Companies you may want to follow" on the right.

Let's choose the company Philips (*http://www.philips.com*) (Figure 2.3).

On the Philips Company page in LinkedIn, you'll see a brief description of the company, as well as a short list of the industries associated with that company. As you scroll down the page, you'll see people associated with Philips who are also a part of your

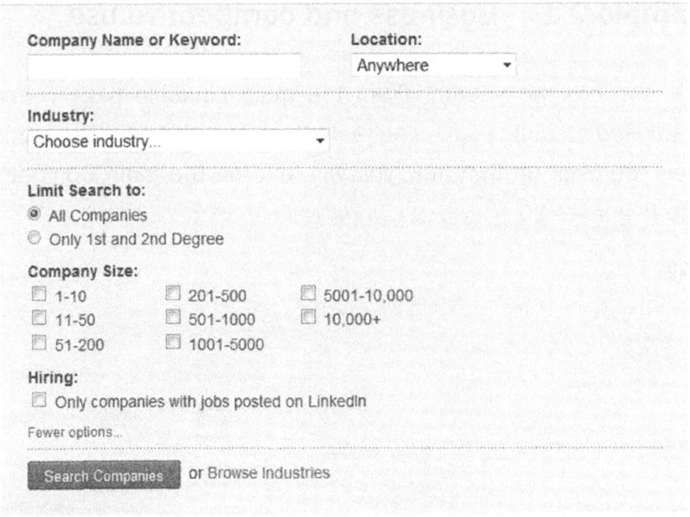

Figure 2.2 Company search options in LinkedIn

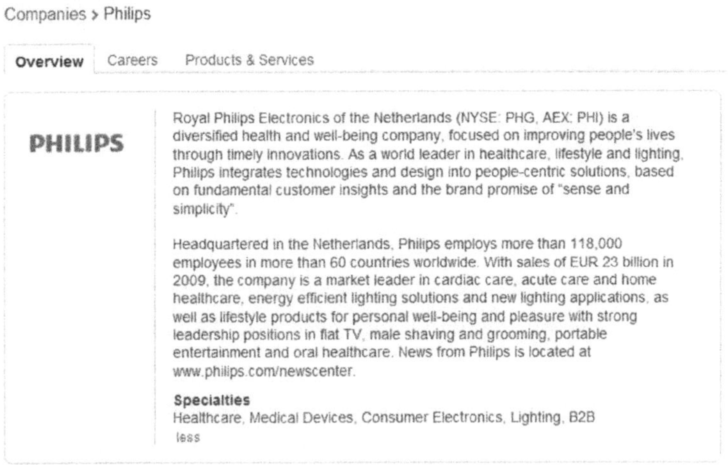

Figure 2.3 Main Philips Company page on LinkedIn

network (Figure 2.4). If you are relatively new to LinkedIn and don't have a large network yet, you may not have many people show up in this category.

On that same list, you'll also see separate tabs indicating New Hires, and all employees on LinkedIn. As of this screenshot, over 32 000 Philips employees, past and present, are on LinkedIn.

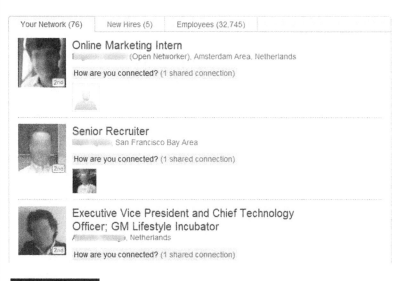

| Your Network (76) | New Hires (5) | Employees (32,745) |

Online Marketing Intern
(Open Networker), Amsterdam Area, Netherlands
How are you connected? (1 shared connection)

Senior Recruiter
San Francisco Bay Area
How are you connected? (1 shared connection)

Executive Vice President and Chief Technology Officer; GM Lifestyle Incubator
, Netherlands
How are you connected? (1 shared connection)

Figure 2.4   **Philips employees in my network on LinkedIn**

This number is indicative of the current number of present and past employees whose LinkedIn profile is linked to the company page – whether or not they are in your network.

As you further explore the page, you'll find recent "activity" for Philips employees, which may be Tweets, status updates, and other postings from Philips employees. Through this information, you have a view of the "buzz" among Philips employees on LinkedIn. What are they talking about? What are they thinking? What are they doing? LinkedIn provides a view into that activity – and, at this point, all without you actually doing any search.

On the right side of the screen, you'll find some other interesting information about the company and the employees. You'll find some summary information about the company: type of company (public/private), approximate company size, website, industry, and date the company was founded (if available) (Figure 2.5). You may also see a map of the company headquarters. (In this case, the company headquarters is in Amsterdam, The Netherlands.)

For any company page, you will also see an option or button to "Follow Company". When you follow a company, you will get

Type
Public Company

Company Size
10,001+ employees

Website
http://www.philips.com

Industry
Medical Devices

Founded
1891

Headquarters

 Breitner Center
Amstelplein 2
Amsterdam, Noord-Holland 1096 BC
NETHERLANDS

Figure 2.5 Company details: size, location, industry

regular email alerts as to LinkedIn changes associated with that company. For example, you'll get notified when new people are hired, when titles change, and when new employees join LinkedIn. It's important to note that, if you follow a company, others on LinkedIn will be able to see that you are following the company.

From the main Company page, you will also see a link to "Check out insightful statistics about Philips employees." Here's where things start to get really interesting. You can see company information on "job function composition," years of experience, "educational degree," and university attended (Figure 2.6). In other words, you can see the concentration of generalized job titles, how many years' experience employees generally have, what level of education employees have, and the most common universities that employees attended. This information is provided for the company, and also compared with the same information for other companies in the same industry and with a similar number of employees.

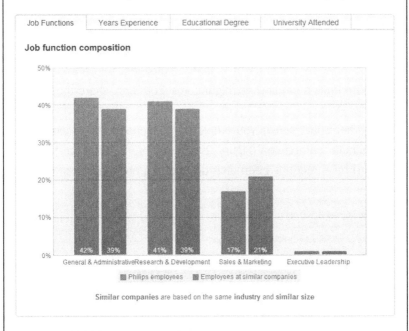

Figure 2.6 Job functions at Philips, as compared to other industry companies

A chart called "Annual Company Growth" looks at the number of employees joining LinkedIn, as compared with similar companies. This information is probably the least useful, as it is solely reflective of company employees' participation on LinkedIn. However, from this information, you can see if the company's employees have been joining LinkedIn recently, and how that compares with similar companies.

A great place to find competitor information is the "Also Viewed" information (Figure 2.7). Similar to recommendations on Amazon – "people who bought this also bought ..." – this feature shows you the other companies that people viewed after viewing the Philips company profile. This feature gives you an interesting, supplemental snapshot of some of the competitors of the company. In other words, you may find lists of competitors via "traditional" tools like Hoover's (*http://www.hoovers.com*) and Onesource (*http://www. onesource.com*). This feature in LinkedIn provides an additional view of competitors of any given company.

You'll also see a tab indicating which companies Philips employees connect to most. Typically, this indicates personal or professional connections of Philips employees, and another view to where Philips employees might come from and where they might go after Philips.

Another chart shows you employee title changes, as compared with similar companies (Figure 2.8). This information can tell you if there have recently been disproportionate changes in employee

Figure 2.7 **Other companies viewed by viewers of the Philips profile**

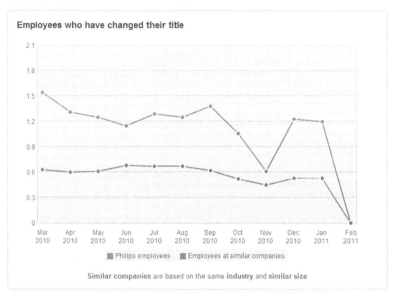

Employees who have changed their title

Philips employees   Employees at similar companies

Similar companies are based on the same industry and similar size

Figure 2.8   Philips employee title changes, compared to same industry companies

titles. Seeing a spike in title changes often can mean a restructuring or layoff. This information can provide you with clues for researching in other sources – for example, searching an article database for any news about layoffs, restructuring, acquisitions, etc.

Further down the page, you'll see a list of the Philips employees on LinkedIn with new titles (Figure 2.9). You'll also see a tab for "Departures" – people who have left the company recently – as well as "Most Viewed," which lists those Philips employee profiles that are viewed the most. Keep these "Most Viewed" profiles in mind – we'll come back to profiles in just a bit.

On the right side of the Philips page, you can see more information on the company. As of this screenshot, there are over 38,000 Philips employees on LinkedIn. Elsewhere on the Philips page, you'll see companies where Philips employees worked before coming to Philips, and then where Philips employees went after they left Philips (Figure 2.10). You can get a sense of the sources of

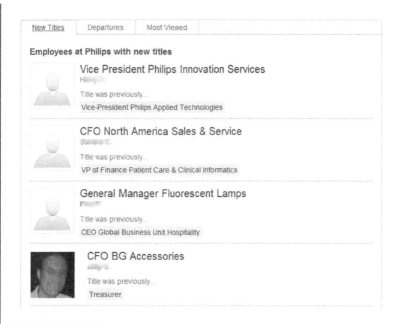

Figure 2.9   Philips employees with new titles

employees for Philips, as well as whether Philips employees go back to those same companies, or if they go elsewhere. Are those companies in the same industry or different industries? What might that say about the company?

You will also see other geographical groupings of employees (Figure 2.11). For Philips, the greatest concentrations of employees are in the Eindhoven area in the Netherlands, the greater Boston and Seattle areas (USA), China, and other locations.

You'll also find a short list of "Most Recommended" employees at Philips (Figure 2.11). As we come to this feature, it's time to take a closer look at profile information.

Viewing profiles

Let's take a look at one of our "Most Recommended" employees to see what information we can find in a profile.

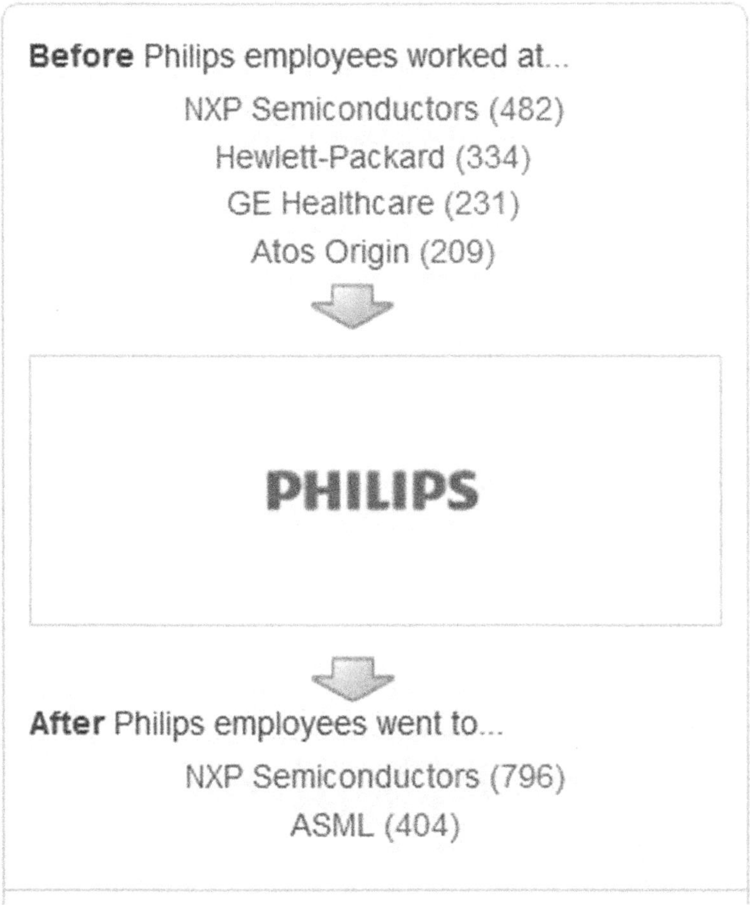

Before Philips employees worked at...

NXP Semiconductors (482)

Hewlett-Packard (334)

GE Healthcare (231)

Atos Origin (209)

PHILIPS

After Philips employees went to...

NXP Semiconductors (796)

ASML (404)

Figure 2.10 — **Where Philips employees worked before and after Philips**

If a LinkedIn user has given full viewing access to his or her profile, you'll be able to see as much information on the user as if you were connected to him or her. From the screenshot in Figure 2.12, you can see the employee's title, past titles and positions at the company (so you can find out a bit more about career paths at the company), education, and some of the employee's projects.

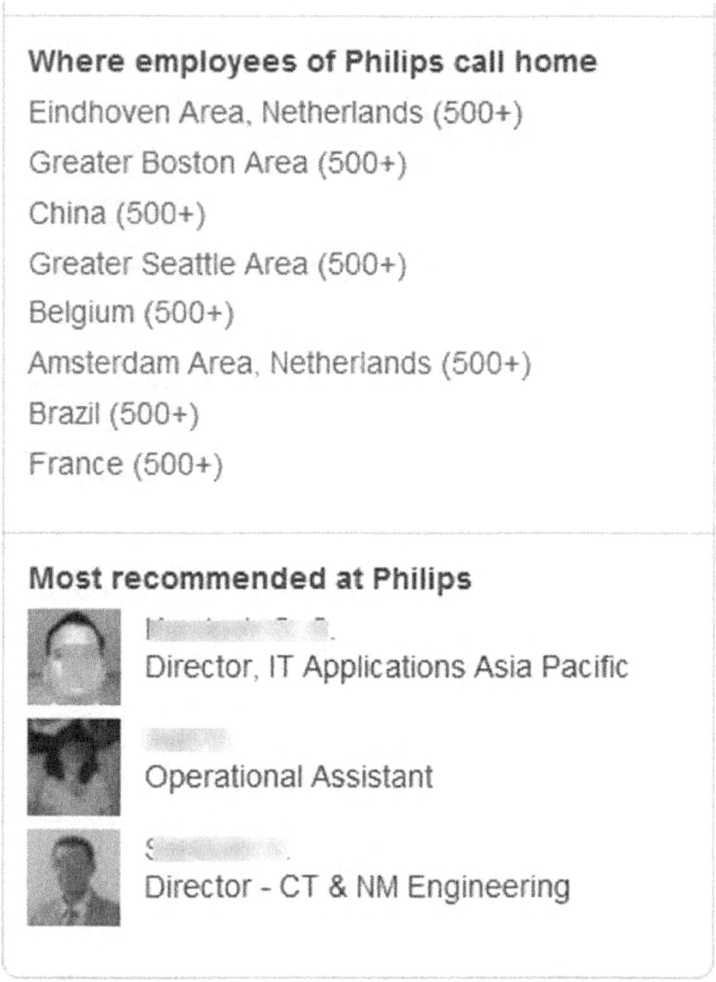

Where employees of Philips call home

Eindhoven Area, Netherlands (500+)

Greater Boston Area (500+)

China (500+)

Greater Seattle Area (500+)

Belgium (500+)

Amsterdam Area, Netherlands (500+)

Brazil (500+)

France (500+)

Most recommended at Philips

Director, IT Applications Asia Pacific

Operational Assistant

Director - CT & NM Engineering

Figure 2.11 Philips employee locations, and most recommended employees

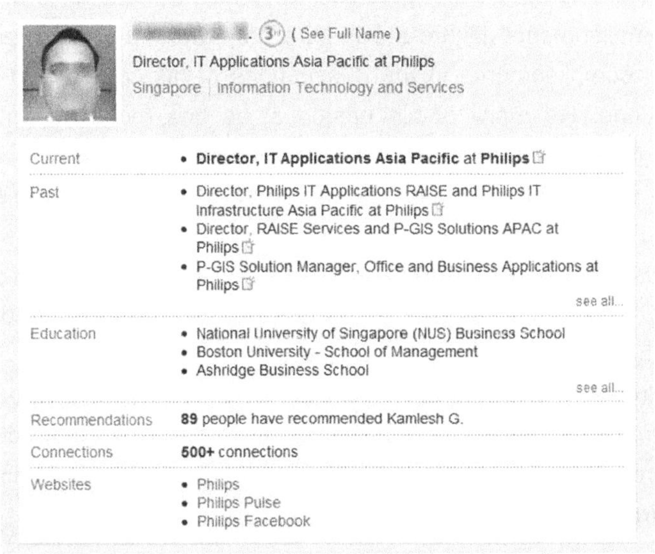

Director, IT Applications Asia Pacific at Philips
Singapore | Information Technology and Services

Current	• **Director, IT Applications Asia Pacific** at **Philips**
Past	• Director, Philips IT Applications RAISE and Philips IT Infrastructure Asia Pacific at Philips • Director, RAISE Services and P-GIS Solutions APAC at Philips • P-GIS Solution Manager, Office and Business Applications at Philips <div align="right">see all...</div>
Education	• National University of Singapore (NUS) Business School • Boston University - School of Management • Ashridge Business School <div align="right">see all...</div>
Recommendations	**89** people have recommended Kamlesh G.
Connections	**500+** connections
Websites	• Philips • Philips Pulse • Philips Facebook

Figure 2.12 One of the most recommended Philips employees on LinkedIn

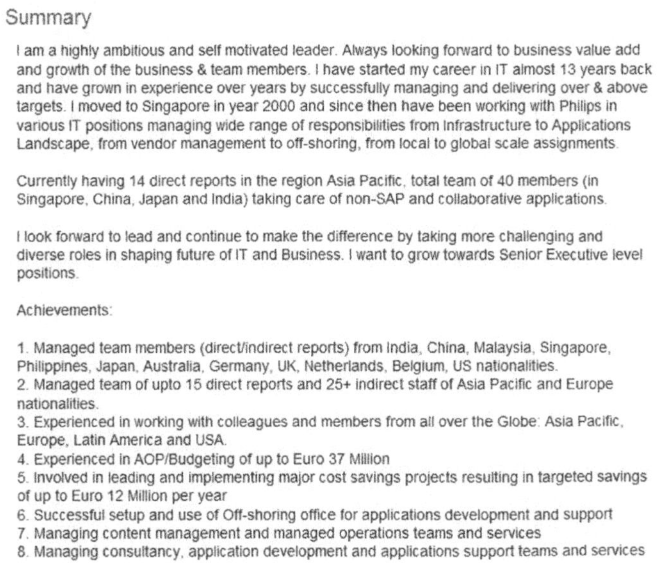

Summary

I am a highly ambitious and self motivated leader. Always looking forward to business value add and growth of the business & team members. I have started my career in IT almost 13 years back and have grown in experience over years by successfully managing and delivering over & above targets. I moved to Singapore in year 2000 and since then have been working with Philips in various IT positions managing wide range of responsibilities from Infrastructure to Applications Landscape, from vendor management to off-shoring, from local to global scale assignments.

Currently having 14 direct reports in the region Asia Pacific, total team of 40 members (in Singapore, China, Japan and India) taking care of non-SAP and collaborative applications.

I look forward to lead and continue to make the difference by taking more challenging and diverse roles in shaping future of IT and Business. I want to grow towards Senior Executive level positions.

Achievements:

1. Managed team members (direct/indirect reports) from India, China, Malaysia, Singapore, Philippines, Japan, Australia, Germany, UK, Netherlands, Belgium, US nationalities.
2. Managed team of upto 15 direct reports and 25+ indirect staff of Asia Pacific and Europe nationalities.
3. Experienced in working with colleagues and members from all over the Globe: Asia Pacific, Europe, Latin America and USA.
4. Experienced in AOP/Budgeting of up to Euro 37 Million
5. Involved in leading and implementing major cost savings projects resulting in targeted savings of up to Euro 12 Million per year
6. Successful setup and use of Off-shoring office for applications development and support
7. Managing content management and managed operations teams and services
8. Managing consultancy, application development and applications support teams and services

Figure 2.13 Summary of our most recommended Philips employee

This employee has provided a detailed summary of his accomplishments (Figure 2.13). He also provides further detail on his accomplishments in the descriptions of his current and past positions. For many of his positions, he has recommendations from others (Figure 2.14).

From recommendations, you can often find the employee's full name (if it is not available to you at the top of the profile), as well as further detail about the employee's projects, reports, and work style. In fact, if an employee has quite a few recommendations – which also provide the recommender's relationship to the employee – you could begin to get an idea of the reporting structure within the company. Who reported to this employee? Whom did he report to? Who were his peers? All this information can become clearer through recommendations.

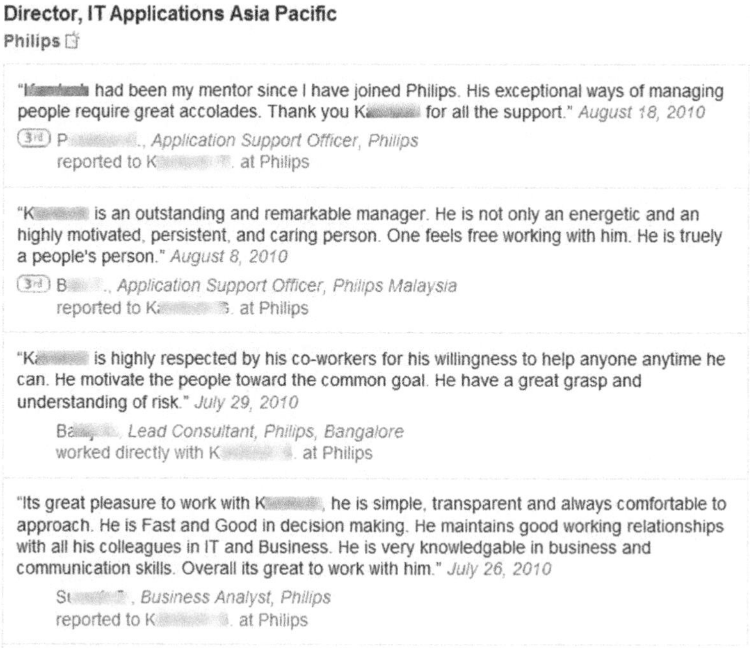

Director, IT Applications Asia Pacific
Philips

"M████ had been my mentor since I have joined Philips. His exceptional ways of managing people require great accolades. Thank you K████ for all the support." *August 18, 2010*
3rd P████., *Application Support Officer, Philips*
reported to K████ at Philips

"K████ is an outstanding and remarkable manager. He is not only an energetic and an highly motivated, persistent, and caring person. One feels free working with him. He is truely a people's person." *August 8, 2010*
3rd B████., *Application Support Officer, Philips Malaysia*
reported to K████. at Philips

"K████ is highly respected by his co-workers for his willingness to help anyone anytime he can. He motivate the people toward the common goal. He have a great grasp and understanding of risk." *July 29, 2010*
B████, *Lead Consultant, Philips, Bangalore*
worked directly with K████ at Philips

"Its great pleasure to work with K████, he is simple, transparent and always comfortable to approach. He is Fast and Good in decision making. He maintains good working relationships with all his colleagues in IT and Business. He is very knowledgable in business and communication skills. Overall its great to work with him." *July 26, 2010*
S████, *Business Analyst, Philips*
reported to K████. at Philips

Figure 2.14   Recommendations for our Philips employee

What other information is available in a LinkedIn profile?

- **Links:** Employees will often link to their company website, and they may also link to company websites specific to their projects or work with the company. These links can provide additional pointers to company information that might not be readily apparent from a company site. You can often find other interests of employees as well, if they link to their own personal blogs or websites.

- **Groups and associations:** Depending upon how the employee has set his or her privacy settings, you can often see the groups to which the employee belongs. Groups might include industry groups, alumni groups, professional association groups, or other groups in which the employee is active. Seeing an employee's groups can tell you more about the employee's work and how it relates to the company. By looking at an

Publications

Creating Information Communities with Twitter: Notes for Publishers and Content Providers

FUMSI · October 2010

Authors: Scott Brown, Christy Confetti Higgins, Cindy Hill

We analysed dozens of Twitter accounts from both publishers and content providers, and share our findings on best practices for publishers using Twitter.

How Do THEY Use Information? Investigating the user information process

FUMSI · July 2010

Authors: Scott Brown

In the second part of Scott Brown's real life case studies on using, reusing, and repurposing information we move into the real Bermuda Triangle. Where exactly does the information go that we, as professionals, provide for our clients/users? What 'use' do they make of it? We all need to show value in the services we provide with tangibility and outcomes being important. Scott also points out that... more

'Retreading', not Reinventing, the Wheel: How info pros repurpose content for increased efficiency and visibility

FUMSI · June 2010

Authors: Scott Brown

How do information practitioners repurpose, recycle and modularise information? I distill down and offer up tips and ideas to help in our daily and long term work efforts. The upshot - be prepared to work more efficiently and effectively to show your true value.

Figure 2.15   **Publications feature on LinkedIn**

employee's groups, you can also potentially get a sense of where that employee is focusing in his or her work, and strategic direction of the company. Is the employee a part of a group to gain insight on a new area of development? Groups can also lead you to other experts in that industry.

SlideShare Presentations
The Top 40: Best mobile apps for
4 days ago
Naked Online: How Naked Pizza and oth...
4 months ago
Future-ready: Thriving in times of tr...
7 months ago
More from your industry | More from connections | Customize this?
slideshare
PRO Generate leads on SlideShare. Upgrade to Pro.

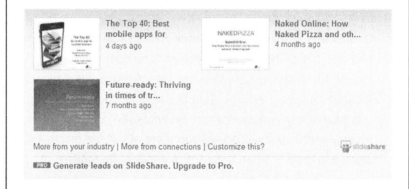

Figure 2.16 Slideshare feature on LinkedIn

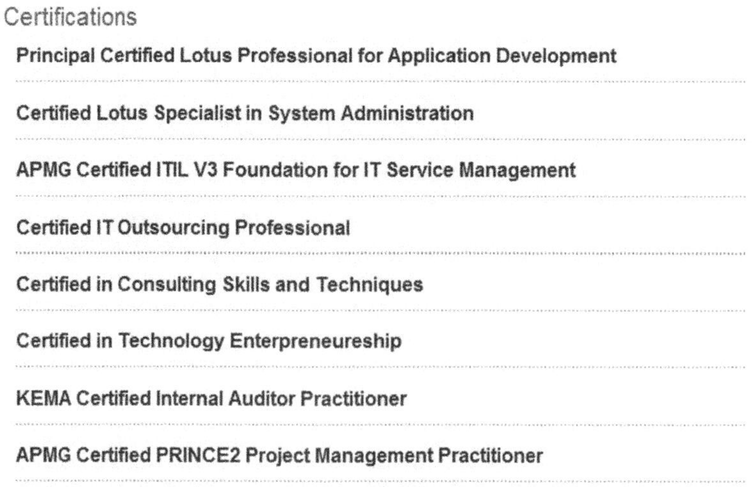

Certifications
Principal Certified Lotus Professional for Application Development
Certified Lotus Specialist in System Administration
APMG Certified ITIL V3 Foundation for IT Service Management
Certified IT Outsourcing Professional
Certified in Consulting Skills and Techniques
Certified in Technology Enterpreneureship
KEMA Certified Internal Auditor Practitioner
APMG Certified PRINCE2 Project Management Practitioner

Figure 2.17 Certification feature on LinkedIn

Many users of LinkedIn also integrate information about their publications, certifications, presentations and travel itineraries (Figures 2.15, 2.16, and 2.17).

While some of this information may seem frivolous, regarded from a strategic approach – what do an employee's past and activities say about the direction of the company's products, research, and focus? – it can start to make sense in very interesting ways.

LinkedIn Groups

For researchers and other practitioners conducting primary research – those interested in conducting interviews, or connecting with experts – LinkedIn can be a powerful online tool for locating and connecting with expertise. The powerful people-search capabilities of LinkedIn allow you to focus your search by location, title, company, education, industry, and language. In subscription versions of LinkedIn, you can also refine your search by company size, function, years of experience, and seniority level, among other things.

LinkedIn Groups are a powerful complement to finding industry expertise. If you simply change the basic search box drop-down to search Groups, you can start typing in your search term and see information fill in on the established groups within LinkedIn.

For example, if you start to type in "medical device," you see several group names come up, including Medical Devices Group (with over 50 000 members) and Medical Device Development, Marketing and Sales (with over 20 000 members). If you go ahead and do a search on "medical device," you get the full set of results (Figure 2.18).

For each group that comes up in your search results, you can see information such as number of members and activity over the last day. Active groups will be better choices for finding discussions and experts with whom to connect.

The Group search is not always very effective. A way to target similar groups more effectively is to search for a group that is close to what you need, and then click on the "Similar Groups" link. Using this link narrows down your search and brings up much more relevant group results.

Search Results (854)

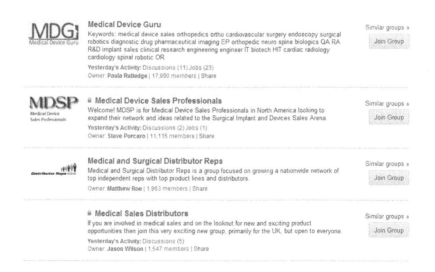

Biotech & Pharma Professionals Network
With 90,000+ members, we are the most active LI group in Biotech, Pharma, HealthCare and
Life Science. We welcome folk in diagnostics, medical device, research, QA, academics,
writers, job hunters, students, and recruiters. We have an active Forum with moderated
discussion: we keep jobs apart.
Yesterday's Activity: Discussions (67)
Owner: **Martin Blundell** | 99,273 members | Share

Similar groups »
Join Group

Medical Devices Group
Network exclusively with Senior Medical Device Professionals from around the world and
discuss the latest developments and best practices in our forums. Find help and advice and
access to specialised services together with events. Network your next career move
Yesterday's Activity: Discussions (39) Jobs (12)
Owner: **Christopher Taylor** | 59,465 members | Share

Similar groups »
Join Group

Pharmaceutical Jobs Biotech Life Sciences & Medical Devices
Career network job pharmaceuticals generic pharma healthcare biotechnology clinical
research device hospital sales regulatory affairs pharmacy engineering lab science R & D
nurses doctors HR recruitment writers physician communications drug health news marketing
finance STM publishing careers QA QC
Yesterday's Activity: Discussions (27) Jobs (18)
Owner: **Paul Healy** | 40,116 members | Share

Similar groups »
Join Group

Figure 2.18   "Medical Device" LinkedIn Group search results

In the example in Figure 2.19, I clicked on the "Similar Groups" link
for the Medical Device Development, Marketing and Sales group, and
found even more targeted groups in this area, including specific medical
device distributor and sales groups.

In the screenshot in Figure 2.19, you see a lock next to the name of the
Medical Device Sales Professionals group. This means that the group is

Medical Device Guru
Keywords: medical device sales orthopedics ortho cardiovascular surgery endoscopy surgical
robotics diagnostic drug pharmaceutical imaging EP orthopedic neuro spine biologics QA RA
R&D implant sales clinical research engineering engineer IT biotech HIT cardiac radiology
cardiology spinal robotic OR
Yesterday's Activity: Discussions (11) Jobs (23)
Owner: **Paula Rutledge** | 17,990 members | Share

Similar groups »
Join Group

Medical Device Sales Professionals
Welcome! MDSP is for Medical Device Sales Professionals in North America looking to
expand their network and ideas related to the Surgical Implant and Devices Sales Arena.
Yesterday's Activity: Discussions (2) Jobs (1)
Owner: **Steve Porcaro** | 11,116 members | Share

Similar groups »
Join Group

Medical and Surgical Distributor Reps
Medical and Surgical Distributor Reps is a group focused on growing a nationwide network of
top independent reps with top product lines and distributors.
Owner: **Matthew Roe** | 1,963 members | Share

Similar groups »
Join Group

Medical Sales Distributors
If you are involved in medical sales and on the lookout for new and exciting product
opportunities then join this very exciting new group, primarily for the UK, but open to everyone.
Yesterday's Activity: Discussions (5)
Owner: **Jason Wilson** | 1,547 members | Share

Similar groups »
Join Group

Figure 2.19   "Similar Groups" results

a "closed" group. You can request to join, but your request will be moderated and decided upon by the owner or managers of the group. If you don't see a lock, it means that it is an open group, and you can join without going through an approval process.

Why join professional or industry groups in LinkedIn? What advantage does that give to your research?

- **Track industry buzz.** By monitoring the conversations happening in LinkedIn Groups, you can easily see what's being discussed in the industry *right now*. LinkedIn Groups provide a "realtime" view of industry discussion on trends, challenges, and opportunities.

- **Find the experts you need to know.** By seeing who is participating in the group and the information shared, you get a sense of that person's expertise and areas of focus. You also can get an understanding of who may be willing to connect more readily with you, if you are interested in starting an individual connection and discussion with that person.

- **Share your knowledge and expertise.** From the perspective of marketing yourself and *your* expertise, you can demonstrate your knowledge by participating in the group. You can answer questions, ask questions, and provide your knowledge and insight on any of the discussions happening in the group. This visibility is powerful because you're not just *stating* your knowledge areas and capabilities; you're *demonstrating* that knowledge and ability.

An added advantage of being a member in LinkedIn Groups is that being a member of a group allows you to connect more easily with others in the group. When you want to send an invitation to connect directly with another person in the same group, you have an option to indicate how you know the person, and your common group will be an option on the invitation (Figure 2.20). This helps the person you're asking to connect with to know why they may want to accept your invitation to connect.

Before we leave the topic of Groups in LinkedIn, I want to touch on the Group Statistics feature. For any group – whether you're a member of that group or not – you can see some statistics on that group. In the example in Figure 2.21, I've landed on the Medical Devices Group. In the lower right corner, you see the Group Statistics feature highlighted.

The Group Statistics feature is particularly helpful because it provides insight on the composition of the group, which is very valuable in helping you determine the "fit" of the group to your needs. Group Statistics provides you demographics, growth, and activity of the group.

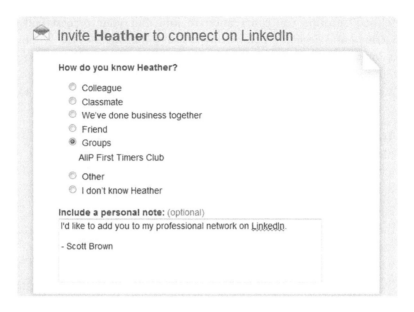

Figure 2.20   Connecting with someone in the same group as you

In the screenshots in Figure 2.22, for the Medical Devices Group, we see that there are almost 83 000 members, and lots of activity (192 comments in the last week). We also see that 25% of the group is made up of people holding senior positions. We see that the concentrations of the locations of the members reflect hotspots of activity in the medical device industry

Figure 2.21   Group Statistics feature for the Medical Devices Group highlighted on the right

Figure 2.22 LinkedIn group member statistics

in the United States (San Francisco Bay area, Greater Boston area, and Greater New York City area, among others) (Figure 2.23). Finally, we see that this group has grown steadily and continues to be active, and that jobs are being posted in good volume as well (Figures 2.24 and 2.25). Would this be a good group to join for industry information? The answer is, yes, definitely!

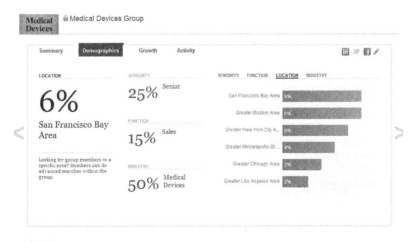

Figure 2.23 Location information in Group Statistics

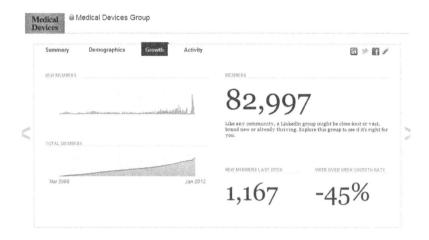

Figure 2.24 Group growth statistics

Figure 2.25 Activity statistics

Example 2.2: Other sample searches

We have looked at a basic for-profit company profile, and have seen how we can find business and competitive information about the company and its employees as well.

To round out our examples, let's conduct a few brief searches for information for a non-profit company, a university, and a government agency.

For our non-profit company, let's look at the American Red Cross (*http://www.redcross.org*), one of the largest emergency response agencies in the United States. We won't go through all of the basic features that I've already illustrated; we'll just look at some of the highlights.

If we look at the "Insightful Statistics" about the American Red Cross, we can see:

- The agency has a high level of administrative positions – which makes sense for a non-profit agency, and is similar to other agencies.

- Employees generally have many years of experience with the organization. Additionally, there is no information as to where employees come from before the American Red Cross, or where they go afterward. This helps support the idea that many employees stay with the agency for many years – turnover likely is relatively low.

- A majority of the employees are based in Washington, DC, and we also see many of the other central offices for the agency.

- Other agencies and companies that people view include the American Cancer Society and the American Heart Association, among others. Generally, we can infer that employees in this industry move to other non-profit organizations with a focus on human safety and health.

For our university example, let's look at the University of Phoenix (*http://www.phoenix.edu*). As indicated in its company summary,

University of Phoenix is one of the first accredited universities to offer an online, degreed college education. It is also the United States' largest accredited private university. As of April 2012, over 15 000 University of Phoenix employees are on LinkedIn, which makes sense for an online university.

There are some interesting pieces of information in looking at the University of Phoenix Company page.

- First, most University of Phoenix employees graduated from – you guessed it – University of Phoenix.

- Over 100 employees, prior to coming to University of Phoenix, were in the US Air Force.

- Afterwards, University of Phoenix employees tend to go to other online universities, suggesting that employees may use the University of Phoenix as an initial platform to move into other online university organizations.

For our final LinkedIn example, let's look at a government agency: Government of Canada (Figure 2.26).

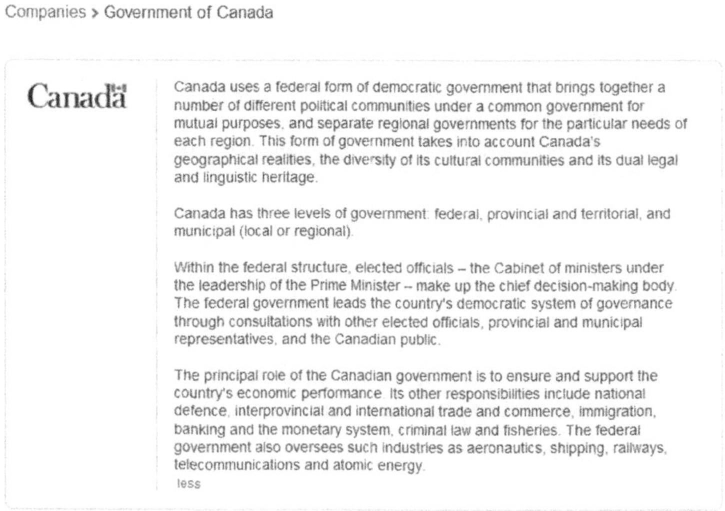

Companies > Government of Canada

Canada

Canada uses a federal form of democratic government that brings together a number of different political communities under a common government for mutual purposes, and separate regional governments for the particular needs of each region. This form of government takes into account Canada's geographical realities, the diversity of its cultural communities and its dual legal and linguistic heritage.

Canada has three levels of government: federal, provincial and territorial, and municipal (local or regional).

Within the federal structure, elected officials – the Cabinet of ministers under the leadership of the Prime Minister – make up the chief decision-making body. The federal government leads the country's democratic system of governance through consultations with other elected officials, provincial and municipal representatives, and the Canadian public.

The principal role of the Canadian government is to ensure and support the country's economic performance. Its other responsibilities include national defence, interprovincial and international trade and commerce, immigration, banking and the monetary system, criminal law and fisheries. The federal government also oversees such industries as aeronautics, shipping, railways, telecommunications and atomic energy.

less

Figure 2.26   Government of Canada page on LinkedIn

As with other organization or "company" pages in LinkedIn, you can find information on the degrees, education, and activity of Government of Canada employees. With universities and government agencies, it is particularly interesting to see how employees come into the organization and move out of the organization (Figure 2.27).

With Government of Canada, many employees have come from the telecom industry: Nortel Networks, Bell Canada, and Alcatel-Lucent.

Before Government of Canada employees worked at...

Nortel Networks (77)

Department of National Defence (15)

Bell Canada (13)

Alcatel-Lucent (11)

Canada

After Government of Canada employees went to...

CGI (8)

Government of Ontario (8)

Carleton University (8)

Figure 2.27 Where employees come from before and go to after working at Government of Canada

If you look at all the employee profiles for Government of Canada, many employees do have technical titles: product integration and testing, IT infrastructure integrator, business analysis, CIO. While this likely may be reflective of the type of employees or positions that would use LinkedIn – "techie" people – this concentration of telecom folks within a government agency might be worth investigating further. Does Government of Canada have a technical/telecom emphasis? What information could we find via an article search to help explain this trend?

With universities and government agencies, it's also interesting to look at the other organizations people viewed. For Government of Canada, some of the organizations include Foreign Affairs and International Trade Canada, Government of Ontario, and Canada Revenue Agency (Figure 2.28). Primarily, this is a way to quickly discover other similar agencies and organizations on LinkedIn.

While I've covered these other examples quickly, I strongly suggest that you search deeply in LinkedIn for any organization or industry you might be researching. In addition to gathering information on the organization and the industry, it's valuable to look at non-profit, governmental, and educational organizations from a competitive perspective in LinkedIn. For example, if I am a dean of a university program, I can gain some insight by looking at my university's LinkedIn page to see what kind of people are tracking my university, see what other universities people are considering, and track my "competitors." I can also use my page

Figure 2.28 Other pages viewed by viewers of Government of Canada on LinkedIn

as a way to further engage those coming to the page – by highlighting offerings and providing updates, among other things. While the discussion of using LinkedIn and other social tools to market an organization online is outside of the scope of this book, there is no doubt that finding competitive and market information via social tools is a critical first step in building a strong online presence.

Caveats

It's important to keep in mind that the organization information you find in LinkedIn is based *only* upon people participating in LinkedIn. It can be easy to fall into a false sense that the aggregated organization information available in LinkedIn is a complete and entirely true representation of the organization. It is not. However, this information does provide trend indicators and "leads" for further investigation.

One way to gauge the reliability of the aggregated information is to compare the number of employees of an organization with the total number of employees of the organization. In other words, to go back to our University of Phoenix example, if close to 15 000 University of Phoenix employees or past employees are on LinkedIn, and company size (according to the information pulled in by LinkedIn) is estimated to be up to 10 000 people, there is some indication that a significant number of current and past University of Phoenix employees are utilizing LinkedIn. If a smaller fraction of employees of an organization are using LinkedIn, we know that we have to regard the aggregated organization information with more skepticism.

Protecting your information

As you've seen with some of the profiles in our examples, you can often see quite a bit of information about a person on LinkedIn without being connected with them – indeed, without even being a registered user of LinkedIn. (To see some examples, try searching Google using the name of a person and "LinkedIn".)

You should review and use your LinkedIn settings to protect your information. Make sure you go through all of the settings and have an understanding of what they are. While LinkedIn offers a variety of privacy settings, the most important way to control what information is available to "the public" – those not connected with you in LinkedIn – is to change your public profile visibility settings. While the way you reach your public profile settings may change, you should be able to see a list of what is viewable on your public profile (Figure 2.29).

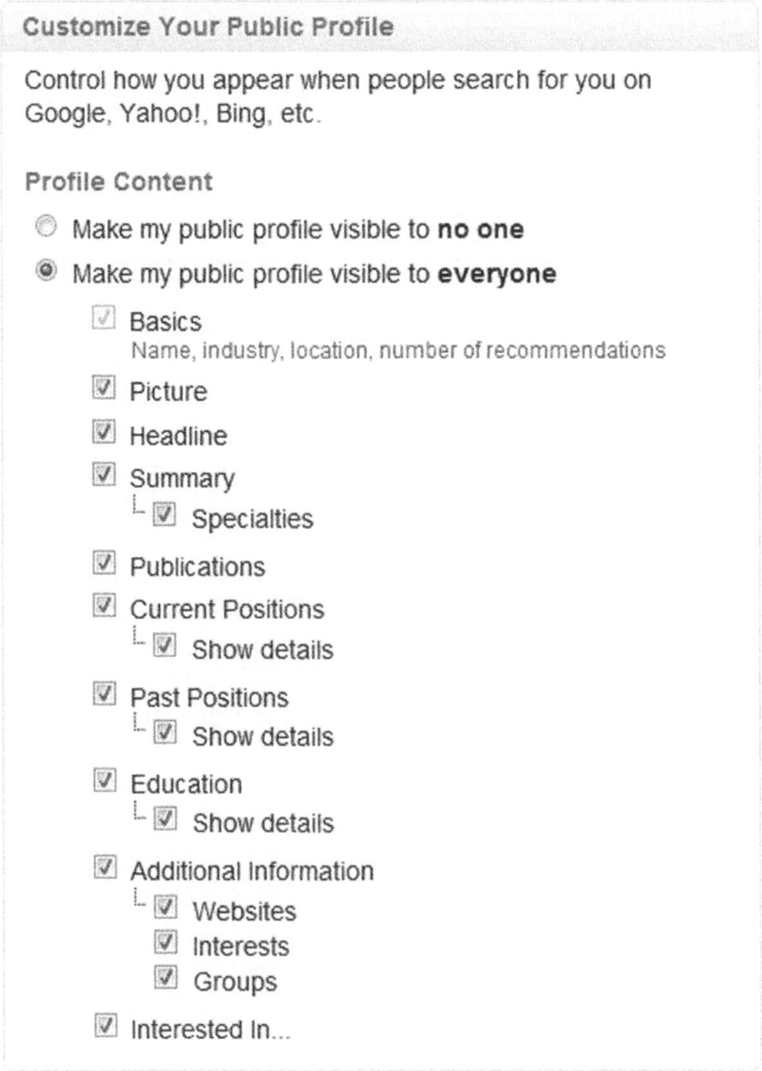

Customize Your Public Profile

Control how you appear when people search for you on Google, Yahoo!, Bing, etc.

Profile Content

- ○ Make my public profile visible to **no one**
- ◉ Make my public profile visible to **everyone**
  - ☑ Basics
    Name, industry, location, number of recommendations
  - ☑ Picture
  - ☑ Headline
  - ☑ Summary
    - ☑ Specialties
  - ☑ Publications
  - ☑ Current Positions
    - ☑ Show details
  - ☑ Past Positions
    - ☑ Show details
  - ☑ Education
    - ☑ Show details
  - ☑ Additional Information
    - ☑ Websites
    - ☑ Interests
    - ☑ Groups
  - ☑ Interested In...

Figure 2.29 Options for visibility of your public profile in LinkedIn

You have an option to have *no* information publicly visible. You can also customize your public profile so that only certain parts of your profile are publicly visible. You will also see a link so that you can view what your public profile looks like to others, so you can confirm that your settings are set to your satisfaction.

Google Plus

What is it?

As of this writing – and you'll hear me say that a lot, especially in writing about Google Plus – Google Plus positions itself as "real-life sharing, rethought for the web." Google Plus (which I'll abbreviate from here as "G+") is Google's version of a social network. Some Google watchers believe that G+ is an attempt to compete with Facebook – or to at least get at the type of information being shared on Facebook. Others have characterized G+ as a professional version of Facebook. In the months since it has rolled out, I am finding myself drawn to this second definition. G+ has very strong similarities to Facebook, and, in my experience, the type of sharing that happens on G+ is much less personally focused than that on Facebook. However, we'll see that G+ incorporates elements from different social tools in unique ways.

Launched June 2011, G+ quickly gained 40 million users – one of the most rapid adoptions of a social tool ever. When G+ launched, only individuals could participate, create profiles, share information, and "follow" other G+ users. In November 2011, Google launched business "Pages," which allowed organizations to create pages, just as organizations have created pages in Facebook.

Estimates are that, as of April 2012, G+ had over 170 million users, with hundreds of thousands of participants joining *every day*. While G+ is likely moving rapidly toward 100 million users, to provide some perspective, this is still not close to Facebook membership, which is more than 800 million users as of this writing, but G+'s growth has been exponential in a very short time.

As of January 2012, Google started integrating search results from G+ into the usual Google search engine results (Figure 2.30), and features are being added on an almost weekly basis.

G+ has elements of Facebook and Twitter, primarily. As in Facebook, users can post updates, articles, pictures, and videos. This creates a user

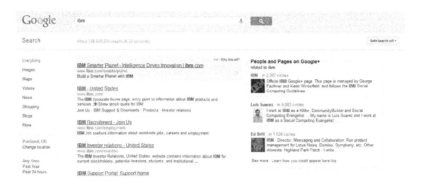

Figure 2.30 Google Plus (G+) results integrated into Google search results

"stream". As in Twitter, you can see and read other user streams by "following" them. In G+, "following" is done by adding users to your "Circles." Upon joining, you have a few standard Circles: Family, Friends, Acquaintances, and "Following" – just those users or pages that you want to follow, not necessarily interact with.

The Circles feature is one of the most striking and useful functions of G+, and another Facebook-like feature. Like Facebook "Lists," which allow you to create lists of Facebook connections for both receiving and sharing information, G+ Circles allow you to create "circles" of G+ users for receiving and sharing information. Unlike Facebook, however, you can add *any* page – individual or organization – to your Circles; you do *not* have to be formally connected to the individual, as you do in Facebook. This functionality of Circles, I think, is a distinguishing and important factor in using G+ for information and research. Because you can add any G+ user to your Circles, you have the potential for gathering information much more broadly than in Facebook.

Like other social networks, G+ requires you to provide some profile information – some of which is drawn from your Google account, if you have already set one up. However, your profile information can be quite detailed or quite spare. Mine, currently, is at about the minimum information a user can provide (Figure 2.31). Both personal and organizational accounts have similar profile features.

As you can see from the categories, your profile also shows information you've shared, as well as any photos and videos you have posted. You can also see anything you've "+1"ed.

The +1 feature is integrated in both G+ and Google search results (Figure 2.32). You can think of +1 as a kind of virtual "thumbs up." You

Send a message

Send an email

Scott Brown

Interested in watching G+ as it grows. Social evolution is fascinating!

Posts   **About**   Photos   Videos   +1's

Home	Email	⬤
Work	Email	scott@socialinformationgroup.com ⬤
Birthday		
Gender	Male	
Profile discovery	Profile visible in search	

Figure 2.31   My very minimal profile information on G+

North **Portland Veterinary** Hospital
www.northportlandvet.com/ [+1]
North **Portland Veterinary** Hospital. Serving the Greater Portland Community for Over 39 years. Gallery. web-pics-002. Our Mission. Our staff believes in the ...
Contact Us - Hours & Location - Meet Our Veterinarians - Appointments

Figure 2.32   An example of a +1 badge in a search result

click the +1 button to give something your public stamp of approval. While +1 is similar to "liking" a page in Facebook, +1 is much more widely applicable. You will find a +1 option for every search result you receive when searching Google. You also find the option to +1 any posting in G+. Even more interesting is that more businesses are adding a +1 badge to their websites (Figure 2.33) – again, similar to a "like" option on Facebook, but in the case of +1, the business doesn't need to have a G+ page in order to get a +1.

Then, if you want to share what you've +1ed right away, you can add a comment and send it to any combination of your circles on G+ (Figure 2.34).

Let's take a look at the Circles feature. On my profile, I can both see who's "in my Circles" – whomever I've added to any of my Circles – as well as who has added me to their circles. I can put anyone into any of my Circles, but I cannot see into which Circle other people have added me. In other words, I likely would never find out if someone added me to their "great people" Circle or to their "avoid this person at all costs" Circle.

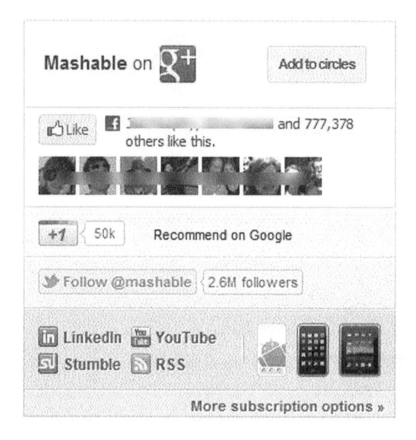

Figure 2.33 Mashable's main page, with the ability to +1 the page and add to your Circles

Managing your Circles is extremely easy. In the current Circles interface, you can see and manage who is already in your circles, as well as create new circles and search for people to add (Figure 2.35).

People and pages can be added to multiple Circles – and you can create a circle on any topic you like. This feature makes Circles easy to use and potentially very nuanced. We'll come back to Circles when we conduct our example search.

Let's take a look at my incoming stream in G+ (Figure 2.36).

This screenshot shows why I resonate with the idea of G+ as a professional Facebook. Both people and pages are posting in this example, and the sharing is very professional and businesslike – no one is complaining about how their morning went. This is not to say that people aren't personable on G+. I simply think the overall tone is more focused on business and professionalism.

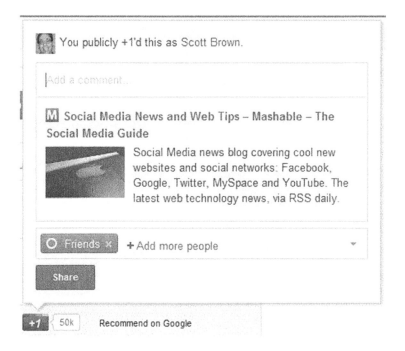

Figure 2.34 Example of sharing something you've +1ed

Figure 2.35 The main Circles dashboard. This view is suggesting people to add to my Circles, based upon my current Circles

To round out our look at basic features, Hangouts provide instant group web conferencing, based upon your connections in G+ who are online. You can instantly start up a web conference of up to ten people.

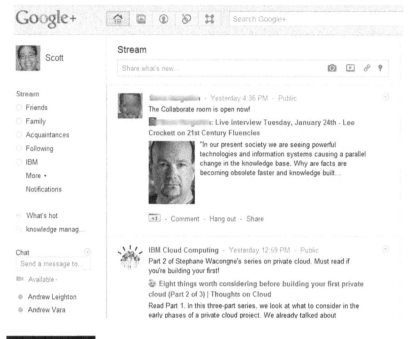

Figure 2.36 My incoming stream in G+

What kind of business and competitive information can be found there?

As we move into the type of information you might find in G+, let's take a look at two additional features. "Sparks" is a feature that allows you to narrow down your search results in G+ to web news (Figure 2.37). When you conduct a search in G+, you have the ability to filter your results to Sparks. Sparks is a nice integration of web news into the G+ environment, and it allows you to easily share that content within G+.

Sparks are interesting because, although they provide content similar to Google Alerts, the focus is on shared news, and the items are instantly "resharable."

The "Ripples" feature allows you to look at any content shared in G+ and see where the content has been shared. Ripples are interactive diagrams that show how a G+ post spreads as it is shared by users (Figure 2.38). You can find the Ripple of any public post using the dropdown menu to the right of the post. You can also look at the

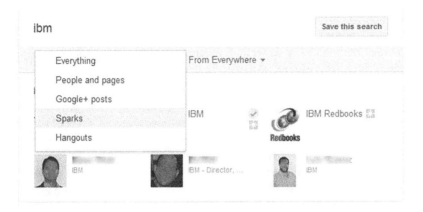

Figure 2.37 Narrowing results to Sparks

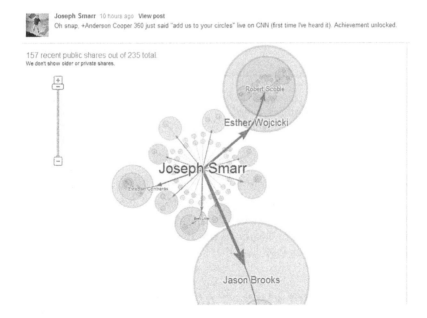

Figure 2.38 An example of a "Ripple"

"static" version and click down to anyone's profile, or you can actually watch a "movie" of how the Ripple spread. The Ripples feature currently provides both visibility to well-connected people on G+ and a time-lapse view of how the content propagated.

I think both Sparks and Ripples provide an interesting view of what content people find valuable and share on a topic.

A quick tip in passing: If you find interesting content on a particular topic, check out the Ripple of that piece of content to find other people whom you may want to add to your Circles.

Though I've shared a few ideas with you here, my primary focus in the example will be on using Circles to track information in G+. You can use Circles to track content and information being shared by:

- thought leaders and experts
- people working at an organization (you can search for and add specific people to a Circle)
- organizations, including competitors.

In terms of finding business and competitive information, because G+ is based on a "follow" model like Twitter, the type of information you may potentially find is more similar to what you might find in Twitter:

- "breaking news" and news developments about an organization or an industry
- organization or industry events
- product information
- sales and promotions.

However, I don't believe the list ends here. Because G+ is so new, especially for organizational use, people are still figuring out how and why to use it. As of April 2012, many organizations have claimed G+ pages, but have only just begun to use them. The business usage of G+ will continue to evolve very rapidly.

How do you get started using it?

If you have a Google Mail (or Gmail) account, you can join G+. Similar to other Google launches, like Google Voice and Google Wave, participation in G+ was initially by "invitation only." You had to either receive an invitation from Google, or receive one from someone who was already using G+.

Currently, you can search G+ without actually setting up a G+ account. However, you cannot use the Circles functionality without a G+ account. To get started on G+, Google does require you to create a public profile. Google indicates that your full name is the only required information that will be displayed on your public profile. You can set your other information to protect your privacy.

As I indicated earlier, you can get away with only providing minimal information on your profile. Similar to Twitter, you can be fairly anonymous in your participation on G+. However, keep in mind that the information you have in Google properties (such as your Gmail account) is connected.

Once you have a profile set up, you can start creating and managing your Circles. The really intriguing thing about Circles is the ability to manage your information – both incoming and outgoing. You can create any type of Circle to track any type of topic. You can also use them to share information with one or more Circles, and also choose to share beyond your Circles into "extended" Circles.

Whom should you follow?

Whom you follow – or add to your Circles – is entirely based on your interests and purposes. You can search G+ easily using the search box at the top. As you type in a search, the search box will automatically provide suggestions (Figure 2.39).

When you conduct a search in G+, you get results from individual posts, as well as page and profile results. When you find profiles or pages that you'd like to follow, it's extremely easy to add them to an existing Circle, or to create a Circle on the fly (Figure 2.40).

The types of profiles or pages you might follow include:

- thought leaders and experts in your area of interest
- people working at an organization – for example, you could add every employee of a competitor organization to a Circle
- competitor organization pages
- professional colleagues and peers, to keep up to date on your professional field.

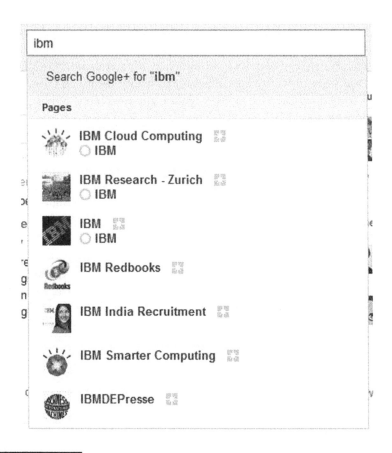

Figure 2.39 Auto-suggest feature on G+

Figure 2.40 IBM search results. As you can see, as you hover your cursor over a page, you have the ability to easily add it to an existing Circle, or to create a Circle on the fly

Some initial tips for getting the most out of Google Plus

Due to the quick evolution of G+, my suggestions here may sound old by the time of publication! However, I want to provide some ideas on using G+ to gather business, competitive, and industry information.

- First, take the leap and join G+. It really is evolving quickly, and I believe it is going to be worthwhile to be a part of it.
- Check back with G+ regularly. Frankly, it may look completely different within six months or a year.
- Consider using the +1 feature as a new kind of social bookmarking service. For your own visibility, you can utilize G+ as a way to highlight content that you find valuable and share that content with people who are following you.
- Consider the sharing capabilities of G+. What if you could put together a Circle of people – in your organization, or in your personal circle, or for your library or information function – and share appropriate information with that Circle? This feature is almost like having your own customizable listserv over which you could distribute information. People in your Circles could be inside or outside of the organization, or both.
- Continue to think creatively about how you can utilize Circles to target information available in G+.

Example 2.3: Company information using G+

Let's jump into an example, using the high-tech company Oracle (*http://www.oracle.com*). While we can use the auto-suggest feature in searching, let's go ahead and do the search and look at our results (Figure 2.41).

With the "Everything" results option, we currently see page results at the top, and post results after that. Before we take a closer look at the pages, if we scroll down our post results (Figure 2.42), we see an interesting mix of results: posts from Oracle pages, posts from others talking about Oracle, and Sparks news results.

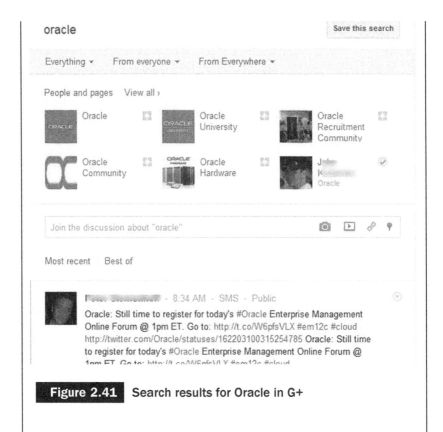

Figure 2.41 Search results for Oracle in G+

Before we limit our results to just people and pages, let's look at the current filter options at the top. Under the "Everything" tab, we can filter results by People and Pages, Google+ Posts, Sparks, and Hangouts. Under "From everyone", we can limit to posts "From everyone," "From your circles," and "From you" – so you have the option to search your own streams. Lastly, under "From everywhere," you can limit the results by location (Figure 2.43). You can either type in a location, or enter a postal code.

Let's choose to limit by People and Pages under the Everything tab (Figure 2.44).

What is striking in our People and Pages results is how many Oracle pages there are, and several Oracle people whom we would likely want to track as well.

Peter _____ - 8:17 AM - SMS - Public

TechCast Live Oracle Social Network in the Cloud TechCast Live
Oracle Social Network in the Cloud Senior Director of product
managment Andy Kershaw explains how the Oracle Social Network
works, the enterprise challenges it addresses, and its cloud -based
delivery model.

TechCast Live Oracle Social Network in the Cloud

youtube.com – Senior Director of product managment Andy
Kershaw explains how the Oracle Social Network works, the
enterprise challenges it addresses, and its cloud ...

- Comment - Hang out - Share

From the web
Oracle (ORCL) Approaches New Downside Target of $28.01
Financial News Network Online - 7:38 AM

Oracle (NASDAQ:ORCL) has opened bearishly below the pivot of
$28.50 today and has reached the first level of support at $28.26.
Should the shares continue to fall, the support pivots of $28.01 and
$27.52 will be of interest. Oracle (NASDAQ:ORCL) has potential upside
of 29.9% based on a current ...

- Share

Oracle Design - 6:26 AM - Public

Oracle Design - Recent Work & Clients (10 photos)

WE DELIVER BRAND IDENTITY,
GRAPHIC DESIGN AND DIGITAL
DESIGN WITH SOME OF THE
BEST BUSINESSES IN THE

Figure 2.42 Post search results for Oracle in G+

oracle   Save this search

Everything ▼   From everyone ▼   santa clara ▼

Join the discussion about "oracle"   ⊙ ⊡ ⌗ ⚲

Most recent   Best of

■■ ■■■■ - Jan 17, 2012 - Public
Judge William Alsup canceled the latest trial date due to Oracle's
exaggerated claims for damages. First Oracle attempted to claim over $6
Billion. Judge Alsup said it was more likely in the $100 Million range.
Oracle then revised their claim to $2 Billion. Obviously they are not seeing
eye-to-eye on this matter.

⟍ Judge attacks Oracle's 'stratospheric' damages claim against
Google, postpones trial

ORACLE   Everything we've heard about Judge
                William Alsup tells us he's a guy you
                don't mess with -- and yet Oracle
Google   seems bent on doing

Figure 2.43 | Example of limiting results by location in G+. In this example, you see in the bar that the location has been limited to Santa Clara

What kind of Oracle pages do we see? Not only is there a main Oracle page, but we also see Oracle University, Oracle Recruitment Community, Oracle Community, Oracle Hardware, and Oracle PartnerNetwork, among others. Each of these pages likely will have a whole set of unique information. Let's take a quick look at some of the unique content.

On the main Oracle page, we see a lot of events being shared – including invitations to webcasts with Oracle experts (Figure 2.45). In this one quick snapshot, we have quickly identified a source of Oracle news and events, and we also have a mechanism to track that via G+ Circles.

The Oracle University page also provides links to a multitude of webcasts and trainings focused on Oracle technology (Figure 2.46).

People and pages ▾

Oracle
With more than 380000 customers—including 100 of the ...
+1 130 people +1'd this
Add to circles

Oracle University
Oracle University has been providing education services for ...
+1 73 people +1'd this
Add to circles

Oracle Recruitment Community
Welcome to Oracle Recruitment's Google+ Community. This...
+1 31 people +1'd this
Add to circles

Oracle Community
For anyone interested in Oracle databases, applications and ...
+1 12 people +1'd this
Add to circles

Oracle Hardware
Oracle's complete portfolio of Sun servers, storage, ...
+1 15 people +1'd this
Add to circles

Product Manager at Oracle
I like breaking things and fixing them. @jkuramot, @...
Add to circles

Oracle Applications developer at UTi Worldwide
I am an Oracle developer, an Oracle ACE Director and the ...
Add to circles

Figure 2.44   Oracle search results in G+, limited to just People and Pages

This is a terrific resource for finding detail on Oracle technology, as well as information on certification requirements for Oracle technology. All of this information would be of great interest to any competitor tracking Oracle.

To look at just one more page, the Oracle Recruitment Community page is focused on recruiting efforts across the globe (Figure 2.47). The page provides information on Oracle jobs and careers, as well as a deeper view of the recruiting process at Oracle and in-depth information on the Oracle employee experience.

Figure 2.45 Main Oracle page on G+

Figure 2.46 Oracle University page on G+

Oracle Recruitment Community · Jan 6, 2012 · Public

Ali is a Business Development Consultant who moved to the Oracle office in Prague from Turkey. He studied in Istanbul and he is a fresh graduate from Bogazici University with a B.A. in Management, and he is a native Turkish speaker.

I approached him to ask how his life in Prague is going so far as he used to live in a completely different environment in every aspect: language, people, even the weather. I was not sure if he would be able to settle in. So I asked:

- Hi Ali, I was going to step by your desk later but had a chance now. How is everything going? ...

Check out our iPod Competition here: http://bit.ly/sNnO9g

A Quick Catch Up with an Expat in Prague (Oracle EMEA Campus Recruitment)
Blogs.Oracle.Com - Oracle EMEA Campus Recruitment

+1 · Comment · Hang out · Share

Figure 2.47	Oracle Recruitment Community page on G+. This post is about a recently hired employee in Prague

Again, I would not stop here – this is just the tip of the iceberg of the type of information being shared about and by Oracle in G+.

How would I go about managing and tracking this information on an ongoing basis? That's where the Circles come in. I can easily create an Oracle Circle for my own tracking purposes (Figure 2.48), and add any organizational Pages I like, as well as any Profile pages.

Once I've created a Circle and added some Profiles and Pages to it, I can now look specifically at that Circle to find all the posts associated with those Profiles and Pages (Figure 2.49).

Figure 2.48	Creating a Circle on the fly. I have the option of either adding this page to my existing Circles, or creating a new Circle

Figure 2.49   View of my Oracle Circle stream

Caveats

This has been a very quick view of the features and capabilities of G+. To be honest, I'm not going into too much detail, simply because G+ will continue to change rapidly. I do believe the information strategies I've introduced here, primarily based on Circles, will continue to be available to researchers. However, I am equally certain that new features will be added and some current features will change and disappear. Rather than try to cover much detail, I've tried to introduce you to the information perspective behind G+.

So the big question at this point is: If G+ is changing so rapidly, is it worthwhile using it?

My answer is yes, absolutely. Why do I say that?

- The adoption rate of G+ is unprecedented. I think enough people and organizations are using G+ that it demands attention. To some extent, the sheer force of the adoption rate will drive its momentum for a while. It will be worthwhile watching to see if more and more people continue to utilize G+.

- Information is being shared within G+ – and you can leverage it for both finding and sharing information. Just from the quick example I shared, you can see the type of information being shared by organizations. Organizations are still figuring out how to use G+, and they are dedicated – at least in the short-term – to making their time investment work.

- It's still evolving. My sense is that there is something different about G+ that could actually gain a lot of traction, and new features and capabilities are being added regularly.

In the end, will G+ succeed? Will it be worthwhile? As of this writing, no one knows. My guess is that yes, it will definitely be worthwhile. It already is.

Protecting your information

Google has positioned G+ partly as a more secure version of Facebook. While this may or may not be true, the main caveat in protecting your information in G+ is to manage your Circles carefully.

Be sure to go into your Google account settings and look for a category specific to G+. You have options to set who can see your posts. Note that, as of this writing, G+ automatically sets this to *all* of your Circles (except for your Acquaintances Circle) – including those Circles you created to track pages (Figure 2.50). Be sure to go in and set this to your own preference.

Do note that whenever you share something, you have the ability to pick and choose which Circles to share with (Figure 2.51). In addition to setting your visibility options as noted above, you may want to stop a moment and consider which Circles would be appropriate to each post.

Second, be sure to check your Profile and Circle visibility. Your G+ Profile is the same as your Google Profile, and you can customize which

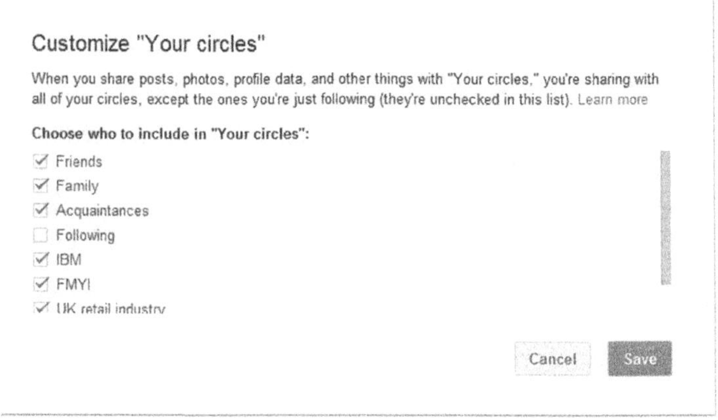

Customize "Your circles"

When you share posts, photos, profile data, and other things with "Your circles," you're sharing with all of your circles, except the ones you're just following (they're unchecked in this list). Learn more

Choose who to include in "Your circles":

- ✓ Friends
- ✓ Family
- ✓ Acquaintances
- ☐ Following
- ✓ IBM
- ✓ FMYI
- ✓ UK retail industry

Cancel   Save

Figure 2.50 Circle-sharing visibility options. Note that some of the Circles that I've created are able to see my posts

Share this post

Oracle originally shared this post:

Got questions about consolidation savings on private clouds? Ask Oracle experts Willie Hardie and Mark Townsend in a webcast Thursday, January 26, 10 a.m. Pacific as they explain the business case for a private database cloud; register now http://bit.ly/zSqAkA

Maximize ROI with Database Consolidation onto Priv

By completing this form and registering for this product and/or event, you will be providing information to UBM, a company located in the United States, for processing and use within the United States...

O Friends ×

- O Family (0)
- O Acquaintances (58)
- O Following (3)
- O IBM (3)
- O FMYI (3)
- 2 more circles...

Figure 2.51 Sharing options for my Circles. Note that I can choose many different options, and share with any combination of Circles I choose

parts are publicly visible. Specific to G+, you can also set the visibility of your Circles and the people who have you in their Circles. *If you are tracking any Pages or Profiles for competitive purposes, be sure to review these settings.* You can choose whether or not to show your Circles at all, and you can also select the ones that you want to show (Figure 2.52). You also can choose whether to show your choices publicly, or just to your Circles.

Lastly, it can be a bit unnerving to see that someone you don't know has added you to their Circles. Keep in mind that you always have the option to choose where you share your posts. However, there are certain

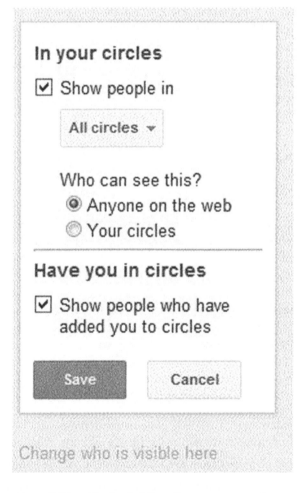

Figure 2.52   Editing Circle visibility. Be sure you understand your options here

parameters that apply to adding organizational pages to your Circles. Note the following:

- Pages *can't* track you easily unless you add them to a Circle or mention the Page. This means that, once you add a Page or Profile to a Circle, they *can* get visibility to you.
- Pages automatically drop you from their Circles if you drop them from your Circles.
- Pages can't even mention you unless you're connected via Circles.

All of which, finally, brings up the issue of "dummy" profiles and pseudonyms. As of April 2012, Google is actively discouraging pseudonyms – although it is allowing nicknames in G+. I won't advise you to create a "false" G+ account for tracking, just as I don't advise you to create a dummy LinkedIn account. I believe operating openly is the best way to go. Be aware of ethical dilemmas and the legal implications of your actions online.

Facebook

What is it?

Facebook is another example of an online social network. For many people, Facebook is their first introduction to social networking online. Facebook allows you to connect with other Facebook users, to share photos and "status updates," and to comment on other people's pages, photos, and updates.

As a general rule, people use Facebook for personal use, although organizations large and small are increasingly using Facebook for promotion, marketing, and connection with customers. You can also find many community organizations, such as public libraries, using Facebook to connect with their constituents.

Facebook officially launched in 2004. As of April 2012:

- Facebook has more than 800 million participants worldwide. More than half of those participants log in to Facebook every day.
- 70 per cent of participants are located outside of the United States.
- Participants are increasingly updating their Facebook pages and statuses via mobile devices.

What kind of business and competitive information can be found there?

Facebook is increasingly being used by organizations to connect with customers and interested parties. Some organizations are simply using it as a way to increase visibility with their customer base; some are using it as another channel to provide customer service, and for promotions and specials. Rather than a personal page, organizations typically use "fan" pages, which are more conducive to organizational use. Organizations can provide their business information, photos and video of their organization and projects, promotions, coupon codes, and other information. Individuals on Facebook typically can "like" a fan page (and therefore receive updates on the organization's activities), post comments, and share photos and videos.

Because organizations are increasingly using Facebook, it is becoming an excellent source for:

- **Customer sentiment:** What do customers post about? Are the comments positive or negative? How many "likes" does the organization page have? Are customers active on the page, or are all the posts from the organization itself?

- **Organizational responsiveness:** If someone posts to the organization's Facebook page, how long does it take for the organization to respond? Does it respond at all? Is the organization using its Facebook page as a customer service channel? If so, how does the organization handle it? Does it route the customer to another customer contact channel?

- **Organizational promotions and events:** Organizations use Facebook to promote products and events. Often, an organization will also post pictures or video of the event after the fact. Facebook allows you to track an organization's promotions, and to track what kinds of events the organization sponsors, as well as who attends those events.

How do you get started using it?

Anyone can register and start using Facebook at no cost at *http://www. facebook.com*. As with many social tools, you provide your name, email, and password to get started. Facebook also requires that you provide your gender and full birth date (although you can opt to not display your full birth date). Once you sign up, Facebook will walk you through a few steps to get some additional information into your profile (such as school and workplace information). As with LinkedIn, Facebook also provides you with some tools to help you get connected. You can import email contacts, or search for people you know on Facebook.

Whom should you connect with?

Opinion on whom you should connect with on Facebook varies widely, since many people use it strictly for personal purposes. Many people are simply not comfortable connecting with people they don't know well, since many people typically share more personal information about their lives and their families on Facebook. Your own use of Facebook is something you should consider carefully as you connect with people on Facebook.

That said, there is really no restriction as to whom you can connect with. Some you might want to consider are:

- friends
- school and educational colleagues – many people find they reconnect with old high school and university friends via Facebook
- work colleagues, current and past
- professional colleagues, current and past
- people who invite you to connect – but be sure to consider carefully before connecting with someone you don't know.

As with LinkedIn, as you continue to use Facebook, you'll find yourself connecting with more people, and more people reaching out to connect with you.

Some initial tips for getting the most out of Facebook

Facebook is different than LinkedIn in that you don't really need to connect with people to find business entity information. Business, non-profit, and other organization pages are typically open to anyone. The reason for this is because organizations use Facebook to raise their visibility, market themselves, or connect with their communities, so it is to their benefit to keep their Facebook pages open and accessible.

The search capabilities of Facebook are not nearly as sophisticated as those of LinkedIn. In fact, Facebook currently provides only a basic search box, though the search box does "auto-fill" as you type (Figure 2.53). This feature can help you to discover organization pages more easily.

An alternative good practice in searching Facebook is to type in part of the organization name, and then choose "See more results for [your search term]" (Figure 2.54).

When you get to your further results, you have an option on the left to limit the results. If you limit to Pages, you'll typically narrow your results to just organization and company pages (Figure 2.55).

Another way to more easily get to organization pages is via links in individual profiles. For example, in my own Facebook profile, I have direct links to my most recent business, as well as one of my university pages, Regis University (Figure 2.56).

Lastly, as a general rule, Facebook will usually be most useful for finding information on public, community, non-profit, and government

Figure 2.53 Auto-fill results for American Red Cross search

Figure 2.54 Auto-fill results for Australia. Note the option to "see more results" at the bottom

organizations. While many small, medium, and large businesses are using Facebook, the tool lends itself well to those organizations that rely on community connections and presence. By all means, it's always worthwhile to check Facebook for any business information. However, you may have more consistent success in searching for not-for-profit organizations in Facebook.

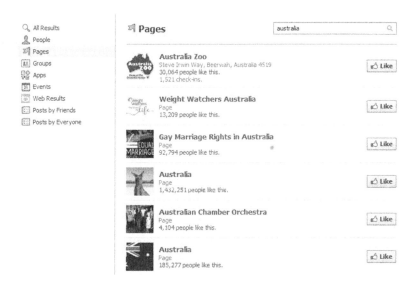

Figure 2.55 Australia search results, narrowed down to Pages

Scott Brown

🏢 Founder at Social Information Group 🎓 Studied Masters in Counseling and Psychotherapy at Regis University 🏠 Lives in ▓▓▓▓, ▓▓▓▓ 💗 Married 🎂 Born on ▓▓▓▓ 🏡 Add your hometown 🌐 Add languages you know ✏ Edit Profile

Figure 2.56 My profile information on Facebook, with click-through links to schools and workplaces

Example 2.4: Business and competitive search

Let's take a look at an international company on Facebook: Kraft Foods, which owns Cadbury, LU, Kool-Aid and other well-known food brands. You can find Kraft on Facebook at *http://www.facebook.com/kraftfoodscorporate* (Figures 2.57 and 2.58).

Many corporations are moving to a more sophisticated Facebook presence. Many have a "landing" site, as you see in Figure 2.58. The Kraft site is even more sophisticated, in that it functions

Figure 2.57 Facebook search suggestions for Kraft

Kraft Foods - Corporate 👍 Like

Food/Beverages

Figure 2.58 Kraft Foods on Facebook

almost as a mini-website. You can see some of Kraft's news about it initiatives: increasing sustainability, fighting hunger, and promoting a healthy lifestyle. Even more interestingly, you can see information about "our team": people employed by Kraft to run its social presence (Figure 2.59).

From this landing page, you can also find information about Kraft's initiatives in corporate social responsibility.

Hi, my name is Premal Spiegel. I'm the community manager for this page.

We'll be talking about news and interesting facts, community involvement, sustainability and a look back at our history. Some of my colleagues will also be joining us to talk about their own areas of expertise. And we want to hear from you, too. So, join our community.

introducing our team of experts

Name: Nicole Robinson
Position: Director Community Involvement
Year Joined Kraft Foods: 2006
Favorite Brand: *Planters* chocolate covered cashews

Figure 2.59 Kraft employees who help manage the company's Facebook presence

Let's move to the left side of the page, and walk through some of the links there. Though the links on this side will vary depending upon the organization, you'll typically find a link to "Wall" postings, information, discussions, and photos and video. For any organization, it's worthwhile looking through all the links present to see what information is available.

The "Wall" is where an organization will post news, and where others on Facebook will post comments or "like" posts. From the Wall, you can get an idea of:

- How active is the organization? Does it post a lot of news? Does it use Facebook only as a way to post news about itself, or does it post information from others? Is it only self-promotional, or does it truly practice community interaction?

- Does the organization respond to the comments and/or complaints posted on its Wall? Does it use Facebook as a way to provide customer service? If so, how well does it do that? Does it respond quickly to complaints, or does some time go by before it responds? Does it sometimes not respond at all? Does the organization seem to be able to resolve the complaints? Because of the time and date stamps on posts, you can get a pretty accurate sense of how responsive the organization is.

- How much interaction is happening on the site? How many people "like" the organization? (As of April 2012, more than 39 900 people "like" the Kraft corporate page.) How much interaction does each post get? Do people "like" the posts and/or comment?

The Wall is a great way to get a sense of how people and customers really perceive the organization. This type of information used to be available only by connecting with customers directly: calling them, conducting surveys, or simply trying to find customers to talk about an organization. With social tools like Facebook, this type of customer sentiment information is much more readily available.

From the Info link (Figure 2.60), you can often find out information such as organization hours, mission statements, social presence(s), and other web links and contact information for the organization.

Other useful Facebook links are the photos and videos links (if available). Let's take a look at an example, the United States Marine Corps (Figure 2.61).

The Marine Corps posts photos from Marine Corps events, as well as some pictures from training sessions. Under the organization's video channel, you can find several clips from Marine Corps commercials.

By viewing available photos and video of any organization, you may be able to get a sense of:

- what kind of events the organization participates in or sponsors
- who attends those events, and how big they are

Basic Information

About
: Welcome to the official Kraft Foods Corporate page. Join us for conversation about company news, global initiatives & corporate social responsibility. We're working hard to make a delicious difference around the world. Rules: http://on.fb.me/9nxvIY

Company Overview
: Welcome to the official Kraft Foods corporate global page!

Kraft Foods is building a global snacks powerhouse and an unrivaled portfolio of brands people love. With annual revenues of approximately $48 billion, the company is the world's second largest food company, making delicious products for billions of consumers in approximately 170 countries.

Kraft Foods (www.kraftfoodscompany.com; NYSE: KFT) is a member of the Dow Jones Industrial Average, Standard & Poor's 500, Dow Jones... (read more)

Mission
: Our higher purpose is to Make Today Delicious.

We understand that actions speak louder than words, so at Kraft Foods:

We inspire trust.
We act like owners.
We keep it simple.
We are open and inclusive.
We tell it like it is.
We lead from the head and the heart.
We discuss. We decide. We deliver.

Products
: We proudly market 11 brands with revenues exceeding $1 billion, including: Cadbury, Kraft, Jacobs, LU, Maxwell House, Milka, Nabisco and its Oreo brand, Oscar Mayer, Trident and Philadelphia. Approximately 70 additional brands generate annual revenues of more than $100 million. More than 40 of our brands are at least 100 years old.

Figure 2.60 Info section on Kraft's Facebook page

- how the organization advertises itself
- the types of promotional events the organization runs.

Again, depending on the organization, you may have additional links with further information. Be sure to take a look at all of it!

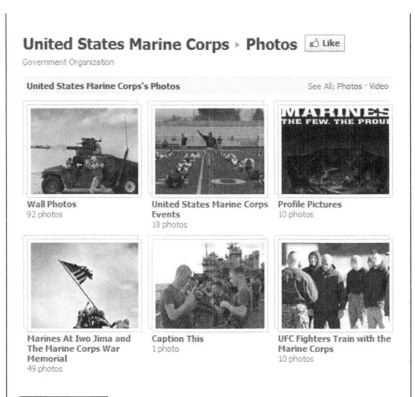

Figure 2.61 United States Marine Corps photos on Facebook

Example 2.5: Non-profit searches

Facebook is particularly good for finding information about non-profit, government, and community organizations. Because it is important to these organizations to be visible to and connect with their communities, they often share a lot of information via Facebook. You can also get a sense of how the organization relates to its community.

Let's take a look at The Wilderness Society on Facebook (*http://www.facebook.com/wilderness.society*), a not-for-profit organization dedicated to "protecting, promoting and restoring wilderness and natural processes across Australia for the survival and ongoing evolution of life on Earth" (Figure 2.62).

As of April 2012, the site has over 39 900 "likes." Just looking at the activity on the organization's Facebook page tells you that the community around The Wilderness Society is passionate and active. People are posting comments, conducting conversations on topics, and the people at The Wilderness Society are interacting as well. You get a strong sense that this is an engaged community.

The Wilderness Society uses Facebook to share news relevant to its community, and photos about events in which the organization participates, and also promotes other causes through its page. In addition to the type of information we discussed above, with a community organization, you can also find information such as:

- What causes the organization supports.

- What other Facebook pages the organization "likes." What can you surmise about how those pages and other organizations are related to the organization you're investigating?

Figure 2.62 The Wilderness Society on Facebook

> For example, The Wilderness Society is a page that the Australia Zoo "likes." Could you then take this information and investigate further as to how the two organizations relate to each other? Are they partners? Do they work together in other ways?
>
> By examining organizational Facebook pages, you can derive a lot of information about the organization.

Caveats

As with all social tools, you never know how much or how little information you will find in Facebook about an organization.

One of the challenges with Facebook organization pages is that there can be many pages listed that are related to the organization, making it difficult to discern which might be the "official" page. To complicate matters, Facebook has, in the past, automatically created organization and company "pages" on Facebook from posts and profile information on Facebook, and sometimes populated with information from Wikipedia. These pages have *not*, in fact, been created by the organization; yet, it is sometimes difficult to determine if a page is an "official" company page.

For just one example, let's look at the global company General Electric. If we do a search for General Electric, and narrow our results down to Pages, we get the results shown in Figure 2.63. In this screenshot, you can see at least three pages that have the GE logo, and that look official. So which is the official one?

After some investigation, the answer is: None of them! Screenshots from the three official-looking pages are shown in Figures 2.64, 2.65 and 2.66.

Especially in the first illustration, you might think this is an official page, because of all the interaction on the page. Seventy-four people "like" the page, and there have been multiple posts on the page, some within the last week. Yet, *none* of these is truly run by General Electric.

How do you determine if a page is "official"?

- Does the page have the recognizable, official logo, rather than an icon or something that doesn't look official? This is your first way to narrow down official pages.
- Next, take a look at the "Info" link. If there is no information posted in the Info section, you can bet that this is probably not an official page.

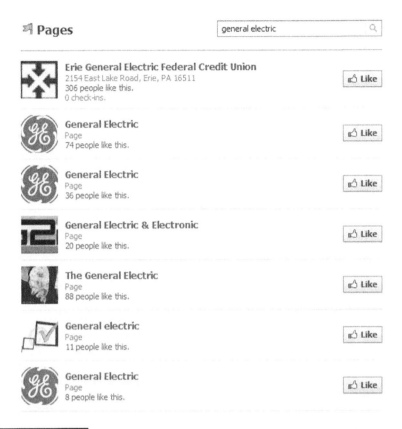

Figure 2.63 Search results for General Electric in Facebook

Why? Because only organizations that have created or claimed a page can update the Info page. Also, often organizations will include links to their websites, which helps to further validate the page as official.

- Another clue is to see how many people "like" the page. As we've seen, a lot of people will "like" a page, no matter what! Look for big numbers: thousands or hundreds of thousands of "likes." These types of numbers will help you to find official pages.

So why do people end up "liking" pages that aren't the official pages? Your guess is as good as mine. It may be that they "like" the page but don't look closely at it. Then their friends see that they "liked" the page, and so their friends "like" it too – and so on, and so on. Now, you have the knowledge to make sure you're "liking" and looking at the right

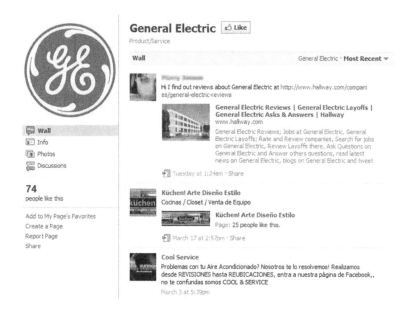

Figure 2.64 One example of a General Electric page

Figure 2.65 Another example of a General Electric page

Figure 2.66   Yet another example of a General Electric page. Which is the "official" page?

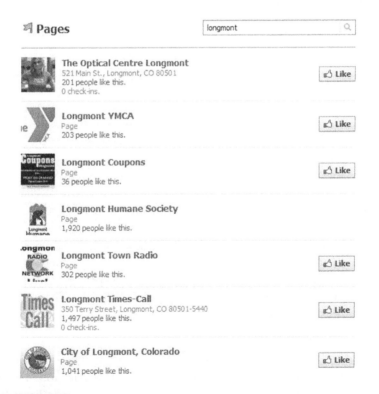

Figure 2.67   Page search results for Longmont (CO) in Facebook

page. Even with this guidance, it can still be difficult to determine if an organization has an official page, especially if it is a well-known, global company.

Is it useful to look at the "non-official" pages? Yes, I think it can be useful. First, you can often find people commenting about the organization on non-official pages – comments that the organization may not be aware of, and that might not show up on official pages.

When researching geographical areas, you can also often find interesting and related pages. For example, if I search for "Longmont" (Colorado, USA) in Pages, I pull up a variety of organizations on Facebook (Figure 2.67).

Though I may be looking for a particular organization in a specific location, it might be helpful to know what other organizations in that location are using Facebook, as they may have relationships to or perspective on the organization I'm investigating.

Protecting your information

Facebook is notorious for changing its privacy settings. Facebook has a track record of changing privacy settings without telling users, and changing them to be more open and exposed than most users want. Ironically, the way most users find out about privacy setting changes is through posts from friends on Facebook.

As with any social tool, it's important to go in and check your privacy settings regularly. With Facebook, this is especially true. I recommend going in and checking your privacy settings at least twice a year – maybe at the same time that you change the batteries in your home smoke alarms.

To get to your privacy and account settings, you can use the drop-down menu at the top of your home Facebook page (Figure 2.68).

I highly recommend checking Facebook security and privacy options regularly. Facebook has a tendency to "bundle" privacy settings in a very general way, as well as to frequently change how you set your privacy options. As of April 2012, the interface looks as shown in Figure 2.69.

What do the recommended settings allow?

- **Public:** "Public" means everyone, whether they know you or not, and whether they are a member of Facebook or not. Everyone can see your Facebook posts, your photos, your information, your favorite quotes, *and* your family and relationships that you've indicated on Facebook.

Home   Profile   Account ▼

Scott Brown

Edit Friends

Use Facebook as Page

Account Settings

Privacy Settings

Help Center

Logout

Figure 2.68   Account options on Facebook

Control Your Default Privacy

This setting will apply to status updates and photos you post to your timeline from a Facebook app that doesn't have the inline audience selector, like Facebook for Blackberry.

Public
○

Friends
◉

Custom
○

How You Connect
Control how you connect with people you know.   Edit Settings

How Tags Work
Control what happens when friends tag you or your content.   Edit Settings

Apps and Websites
Control what gets shared with apps, games and websites.   Edit Settings

Limit the Audience for Past Posts
Limit the audience for posts you shared with friends of friends or Public   Manage Past Post Visibility

Figure 2.69   Privacy dashboard on Facebook

- **Friends:** This sounds relatively safe, but can include people that you are not connected to, but that your friends are connected to. All of those people can also see photos and videos where someone else has identified you in that photo or video, your religious and political views that you've indicated in your profile, and your birth date.

I don't know about you, but I feel that both of these recommended settings share too much information, especially for people using Facebook for personal reasons.

Facebook allows you to customize your privacy settings for many specific components of your information and interactions on Facebook. I recommend that you choose "Customize settings," and set your sharing options to your comfort.

You'll see different levels of visibility available for various components (Figure 2.70).

What do the different levels of visibility mean? Let's start at the most restrictive level and go from there.

- **Friends only:** Only people you are connected to directly on Facebook.
- **Friends of friends:** Friends, as well as the people your friends are connected to on Facebook.
- **Friends and networks:** Friends, as well as all the people on Facebook in your network.

Figure 2.70 Some of the custom settings for sharing in Facebook. Be sure to review these regularly and set them to your liking

What is a network?

You can join a network of people in Facebook if you have an email address associated with that network. For example, if you are an employee of a company, and have an email address associated with that company, you can join that network on Facebook. You then have a connection, and can share information, with all of the other people on Facebook that are also a part of that network. That can be a lot of people!

To join or leave a network, go to your Account Settings, and choose the Networks tab (Figure 2.71).

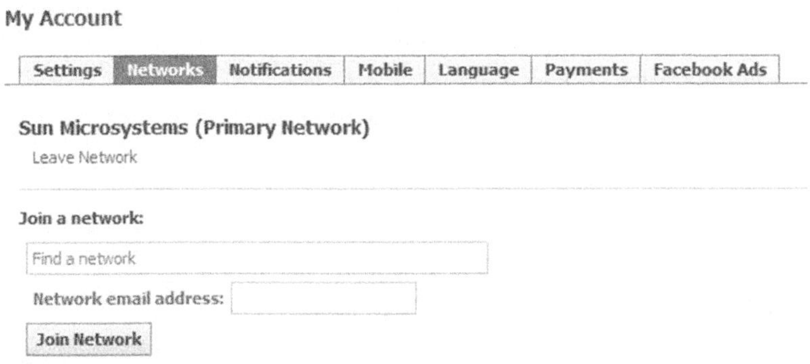

My Account

| Settings | **Networks** | Notifications | Mobile | Language | Payments | Facebook Ads |

Sun Microsystems (Primary Network)
Leave Network

Join a network:

Find a network

Network email address:

Join Network

Figure 2.71 Network settings in Facebook

- **Friends of friends and networks:** Friends, as well as the people your friends are connected to on Facebook, as well as all the people on Facebook in your network.

- **Everyone:** As mentioned above, "Everyone" means everyone – anyone who uses the Internet, whether or not they are a member of Facebook, or are connected to you or not. This is why, when you Google yourself or others, you'll often find Facebook search results for that person.

Again, be sure to check your privacy settings on Facebook often, as Facebook has been known to change them without notifying Facebook users. Facebook also seems to change privacy group settings regularly, as well – for example, you may or may not have a "Friends of friends" sharing option for certain parts of your profile. The settings can be very confusing; be sure you understand what they mean.

Orkut

What is it?

Orkut is an online social network similar to Facebook and LinkedIn. It was created and is run by Google. The name Orkut comes from the Google developer of the network, Orkut Buyukkokten. As of April 2012:

- The majority of users of Orkut are based in Brazil, India, and the United States.
- Orkut has been the social networking tool of choice for Brazilians and Indians for many years. Recently, more Brazilians and Indians have been migrating to Facebook.
- While the majority of users on Orkut use it for personal use, a significant percentage use it for business networking.

What kind of business and competitive information can be found there?

The primary advantage of using a social network like Orkut (or any other social network that is not as heavily US focused) is that you can find more non-US company and organization information. Through using Orkut, you can potentially:

- find organizational employees, locations, and groups outside of the US
- get a sense of trends and hot topics in other organizational geographies and topic areas
- see results of member polls.

How do you get started using it?

If you have a Google account, you can start using Orkut almost immediately. You supply your name, birth date, and gender – that's all you need to get started (Figure 2.72).

Figure 2.72 Account registration in Orkut

You have the option to put as much or as little information in your profile as you like.

Whom should you connect with?

One of the interesting things about Orkut is that you don't have to be connected to anyone in order to look at the detail in the online communities. You can also view quite a bit of detail on members' profiles without being connected. However, if a group is not an open group, you may not be able to join or view the group content without becoming a member of the group.

Since Orkut is both a professional and personal networking tool, you may want to connect with:

- friends
- school and educational colleagues
- work colleagues, current and past
- professional colleagues, current and past.

Some initial tips for getting the most out of Orkut

Compared to LinkedIn and Facebook, Orkut has a much more basic interface. You can browse communities by selecting the "Communities" button at the top of Orkut (Figure 2.73).

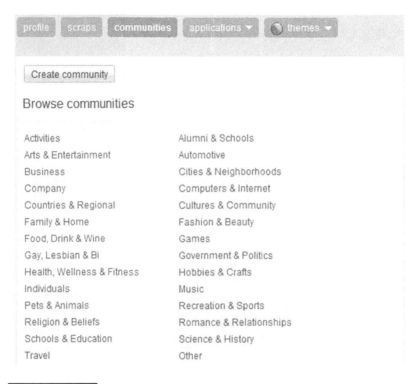

Figure 2.73 Community browsing on Orkut

However, browsing communities only allows you to look at the latest posts in those communities, making this feature mostly unusable. Your best bet is to conduct a search, which I will illustrate below.

Again, Orkut can be a powerful tool for finding non-US company, organization, and individual information.

Example 2.6: Business and competitive search

Let's try a search for the company IBM on Orkut. Rather than browse the communities, let's just search for IBM (Figure 2.74).

As you can see, we get a community group not only for IBM, but also for other specific groups, such as IBM DB2, IBM WebSphere, etc., along with the number of members in each group. If we click

---

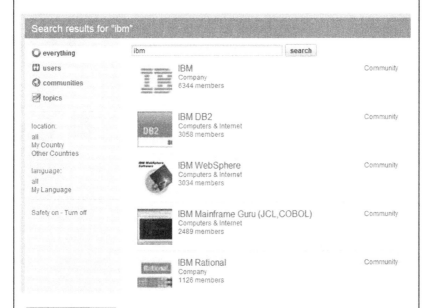

Figure 2.74 IBM search in Orkut

into the IBM group, we see a description of the community, some of the members, some of the forum discussions, and polls (Figure 2.75).

If you click into the Forums, you can not only see all recent forums, you can also search the forums for particular posts. Depending upon the forum, you may see a lot of "spam": offers for training, certification, and other products. However, you do have the ability to search through the forums to find specific keywords. From a competitive standpoint, you might search for "problem" or "issue" or "complaint" to see if you can find indications of issues with a company or product.

Under Polls, you can participate in any active polls, as well as see results of past polls. It's worthwhile to take a look at polls, as you can see the topic, the number of people that participated, and the results.

Figure 2.75 IBM community in Orkut

For one example, Figure 2.76 shows a poll on "Which IBM country unit do you work from?" from 2007. Over 700 people voted and provided comments.

While this is not a statistically sound sample of IBM employees, you can at least get a sense of where IBM employees are based, and in what proportions. Other polls may provide additional information.

Which IBM Country Unit do you work from?
Home > Communities > Company > IBM > Polls > Which IBM Country Unit do you work from?

Created by: Bijo

United States		72 votes (10%)
India		449 votes (63%)
Brazil		87 votes (12%)
China		15 votes (2%)
Russia		7 votes (0%)
United Kingdom		11 votes (1%)
Others (Please specify as comment)		64 votes (9%)

Only community members may vote on this poll   total: 705 votes

« back to polls   report spam   hide results and comments

Figure 2.76 Example of a poll in Orkut

While forums and polls are potentially useful, the Members piece of Orkut may provide the business or competitive researcher with the most value. You can search members, and view profile information. While you may not find an abundance of information, you often can find at least where the members are located geographically. Often times, as in the example in Figure 2.77, where I searched for "Scotland," conducting a search can pull up job-profile information in the search results.

When you click into the member profile, this information is not available – however, the search engine picks up this information and displays it.

Granted, depending upon your project and the size of the organization you are researching, you may not have the time or interest to go to this level of granularity in your search. Knowing that this type of information is out there – that, for example, you may be able to locate specific organizational personnel anywhere in the world – may come in handy for searches you conduct today or in the future.

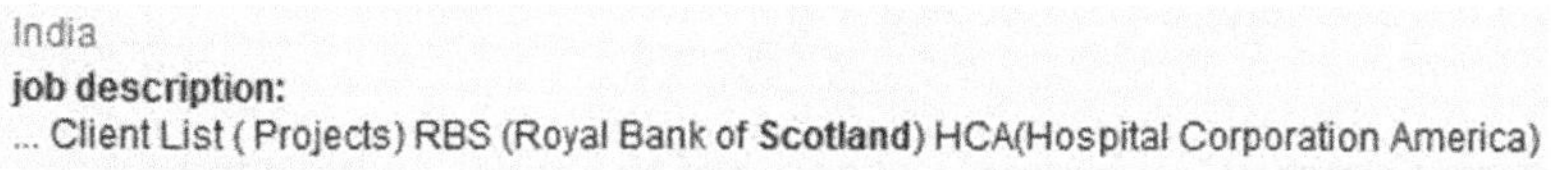

India
job description:
... Client List (Projects) RBS (Royal Bank of **Scotland**) HCA(Hospital Corporation America)

Figure 2.77 Search result for Scotland. This brings up an IBM client list in a user profile on Orkut

Caveats

As with all social tools, you never know how much or how little information you will find in Orkut about an organization. It's always worth checking.

As with Facebook, it's important to keep in mind that Orkut is both a professional and a personal network. While Orkut can provide some unique non-US information, my experience has been that you also have to sort through a lot of spam, non-essential, and personal information to find the "gold dust" (Figure 2.78).

oracle golden notes	rajesh
Get installed oracle R12 on PC or Laptopfor 2500/-	Basavaraj
Oracle DBA	shahid
Study in Germany with OESolutions	OESolutions
Oracle SQL and PL/SQL Training	Mariyan Clement
~ New Orkut Sex 2011 ~!	฿ũĐĐกÂÿāṆ
a new 3g website launched	aarush
Get certified to get Job	Raju
[-NEW-]ORKUT OFFICIAL SEX CHATROOM	Utsav Mukherjee
Web Designinig Material only RS:399/-	website
ONLINE TRAINING ON ORACLE DBA,INFORMATICA 8.6,BOXI	syed
new 3g website	aarush
Get certified to get Job	Raju

Figure 2.78 An example of some of the stuff you have to sort through on a company forum on Orkut

Even compared to Facebook, which is used by many people for personal use, Orkut seems to attract much more "junk" in organizational communities.

Is it worthwhile sorting through all of the personal information, spam, and dubious offers to see what useful business and competitive information you can find? It might be – and it might not be. Use your good judgment. If you haven't found relevant information on your target company relatively quickly, save yourself some time and move on to another resource.

Protecting your information

As you've seen, you don't have to be connected to anyone in Orkut in order to see a lot of information from their profile. This means that you should take extra care as to what information you provide in *your* profile.

When you go in to edit your profile, you can write a "headline" (a personal tagline), provide information about yourself socially ("what do you like to do?"), as well as professional and personal information (Figure 2.79).

In your settings, you do have the ability to limit who can see your information, but only by broad category (General, Social, Professional, Personal).

Orkut profile information is fairly rudimentary, compared with a tool like Facebook or LinkedIn. For example, you can enter only one place of employment.

My guidance for filling out your profile in Orkut is to consider what information you would want everyone to see – even if your settings are such that only your friends can see it. For example, you can enter your work email for your current position. In a tool like Orkut, I personally would not do that, simply because I don't know how often Orkut

Figure 2.79 Example profile template on Orkut

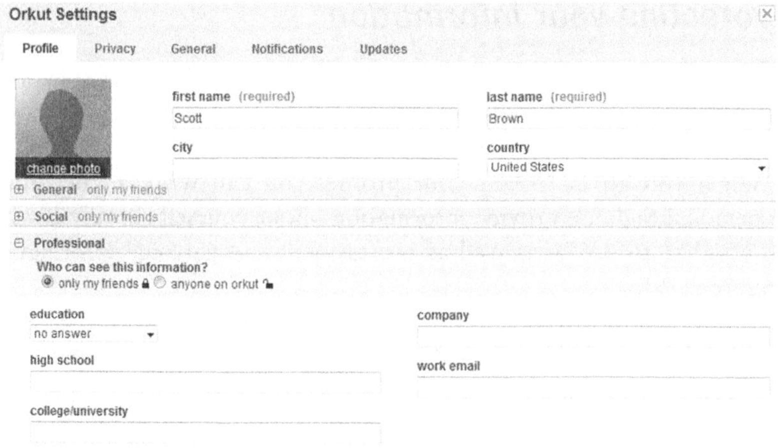

Figure 2.80 Privacy options in Orkut

changes its security settings. It's possible that my work email could suddenly be available to anyone using Orkut.

If you are using Orkut for professional purposes, I would also recommend either not providing a lot of personal information, and/or making that information available only to friends.

As with all social tools, think about your purposes for using the tool, what others might be able to find out about you, and what information you are comfortable sharing on that tool.

In addition to looking at your profile's visibility, be sure to look at the other settings. Under the "Privacy" tab, you can control who can view the content on your profile, as well as who can write to you, send you "friend" requests, tag you in photos, or find you via your email address (Figure 2.80).

The "Notifications" tab will also allow you to set from whom you receive notifications, and for what purposes.

Other tools in this category

At the beginning of this chapter, we mentioned some similar tools in this category:

- **Mixi**: Mixi is a social network that is currently very popular in Japan, primarily as a personal social network.

- **Xing**: Xing is a professionally focused social network. Xing is most popular in Germany. Like LinkedIn and other social networks, participants can join interest groups.

- **Ning**: The Ning platform allows users to create specific social networks and groups, and invite people to participate in those groups. Within the last two years, Ning has done away with a free option to create a group. If you want to create a group, you now need to commit to a paid subscription. Joining a group in Ning is still free, provided the group creator approves your request for membership.

  A tip on finding Ning groups: I've not found an effective way to search for Ning groups via the Ning site. However, you can use Google to find Ning groups. If you go to advanced search, simply type in your search terms, and in "Search within a site or domain," type in "ning.com". This will help you to easily locate Ning groups (Figures 2.81 and 2.82).

| Figure 2.81 | Example Google Advanced Search to search for Ning groups in healthcare |

Figure 2.82 Ning search results using Google Advanced Search

- **Meetup,** an online tool that helps people organize and meet in person locally. As of April 2012, Meetup boasts over 9.5 million members, and 280 000 "meetups" every month. Meetup is global, with participation in 45 000 cities worldwide. Meetup is quickly becoming another interesting and useful tool to search for local interest groups, by company, topic, or industry.

- **Plaxo:** Plaxo is a bit different from the social networks we've covered so far, in that it promotes itself as an online address book. You do connect with others using Plaxo, but participants primarily use it as a way to keep their contact information current, and to keep track of others' contact information.

- **MySpace:** MySpace states that it is "aimed at a Gen Y audience," and specifically geared toward "entertainment and connecting people to the music, celebrities, TV, movies, and games that they love." In June 2011, MySpace was acquired by Specific Media from News Corporation. While MySpace was quite popular for a while in the late 2000s, the site has become primarily a destination for younger fans to find musical artists and celebrity information, and for bands to easily and inexpensively raise their visibility. As of April 2012, over 30 million people visit MySpace every month.

Social networking tools that are more exclusive in nature are increasingly emerging. Business networking tools such as MerchantCircle allow businesses to connect with each other locally – a kind of LinkedIn/ Facebook for locally based businesses. For another example, within Facebook, some "sub-networking" applications are popping up, such as BranchOut. BranchOut allows Facebook friends to connect for career and employment purposes via Facebook, creating a "network within a network" (Figure 2.83).

Another example of these kinds of emerging networks is Path. Path is similar to Facebook, in that it allows you to connect with friends, but users are limited to a maximum of 50 connections. The network is based on research that indicates that humans can only meaningfully connect with a limited number of people. Path combines this approach with tools that allow a "life-streaming" kind of experience: your personal connections are able to see various parts of your day, your "path," and therefore have a more "emotional" connection with you.

For other social networks on the non-US side, check out:

- Qzone, popular in China
- Vkontakte, popular in Russia

Figure 2.83 BranchOut's Facebook site. BranchOut attempts to create a professional network within Facebook

- Netlog, based in Belgium and popular with European youth
- Multiply, a global shopping social network with a focus in the Philippines, Indonesia, Malaysia, Singapore, Thailand, and Vietnam.

Other social networks in operation as of April 2012 include:

- Bebo
- Gaming social networks, such as Hi5 and Friendster
- Badoo
- Perfspot
- Zorpia
- Tagged
- MyYearbook.

For an extensive list of social networking sites, check Wikipedia.[1]

Review

As you've seen, you can find quite a bit of information about people, organizations, and industries using social networking tools. To review, some of the information you can find includes:

- executive and employee information, including information on employee education, experience, and skills;
- employee movement, including where employees have worked previously, and where they go after they leave an organization;
- company initiatives and growth areas;
- company and employee location;
- customer sentiment;
- company responsiveness;
- company promotions and events;
- industry "buzz," current trends, and topics.

The more you are connected on social networking tools, the more information you can access. Be sure to explore regularly the tools we've discussed in depth, because features are being added and upgraded continually. Also be sure to explore some of the other tools, such as Ning and Meetup, to get familiar with other social networks and the types of information they can offer.

Note

1. Wikipedia (2012) List of social networking sites. *Wikipedia.* Available from: *http://en.wikipedia.org/wiki/List_of_social_networking_websites* [Accessed 25 April 2012].

3

Blogs and microblogs

Abstract: This chapter looks specifically at finding information in blogs and microblogs. For blogs, the chapter primarily looks at the use of Google Blog Search for finding individual blogs, posts, and bloggers covering a particular organization or industry. For microblogs, the chapter primarily looks at Twitter for finding organization information and for finding sources of industry information. Tools for managing Twitter are covered, as well as a few of the Twitter analysis tools that are currently available. The chapter concludes with a list of additional blog and microblog tools, and tips on verifying the information available in these tools.

Key words: Blogs, microblogs, Twitter, blog search, Twitter management, Twitter analysis tools.

What are they?

In this chapter, we will cover the use of blogs and microblogs for finding information. While these tools are somewhat similar in structure and function, the dynamics of blogs and microblogs can be very different.

- **Blogs:** One way to think of blogs is as a form of online publishing. These tools allow single or multiple authors to publish their writing. Typically, entries are written in a personal or journalistic format and style. Blog entries, or "posts," may be as long or as short as you like. Often, you can include video and images in your post, and links to other sites and blog postings. Examples of blog platforms available to the public include:
  - **Blogger:** Blogger was the first publicly available blog platform, introduced in 1999. Several blogging platforms, such as OpenDiary, Xanga, and Live Journal, were introduced in 1999 as well. Blogger was purchased by Google in 2003, and subsequently has integrated several features from Google. Anyone can sign up for a blog account for free.

- **TypePad:** Typepad was launched in 2003, growing partly out of Live Journal. TypePad does not offer free accounts, only subscription accounts. However, the subscription accounts offer users the ability to create multiple blogs, custom-design the look of the blog, and map domains. (Mapping domains means the ability to have a URL for your blog that is, for example, *http://www.myblog.com*, rather than *http://myblog.typepad.com*.)

- **WordPress:** As of this writing, WordPress is growing in popularity both as a blog platform (Figure 3.1) and as a platform for creating a website with blog-like properties (Figure 3.2). Also launched in 2003, as of April 2012, WordPress claims there are over 72 million WordPress sites.

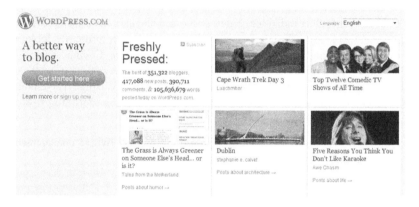

Figure 3.1   The WordPress.com site

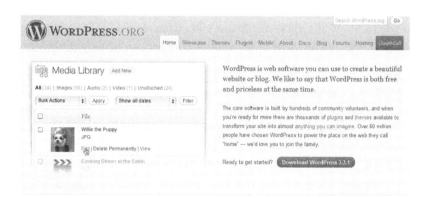

Figure 3.2   The WordPress.org site. WordPress.org is more geared toward creating websites based on the WordPress platform

Figure 3.3 shows an example of a typical business blog, and Figure 3.4 shows an example of a typical personal blog.

- **Microblogs** allow you to post text, links, and links to images, just as blogs do. The difference is that you typically have a limit on the length of your entry – hence the label "microblog." For example, Twitter limits you to 140 characters for your entry.

  Note that I wrote "*characters*," not "words." One way you can think of microblogs is as text messaging online (because of the limited length). Examples include:

Figure 3.3	Example of a typical business blog. This screenshot shows the New York Times Dealbook blog at *http://dealbook.nytimes.com*.

Figure 3.4 **Example of a typical personal blog. This screenshot shows an entry from the Crunchy Domestic Goddess blog at** *http://crunchydomesticgoddess.com.*

- **Twitter,** probably the most well-known microblogging platform; and
- **Yammer,** a microblog that allows only users with the same email address to be connected. In other words, if you signed up for Yammer with your work email (such as mary.smith@business.com), you would only be connected and could only share your posts with other users who had also signed up with their @business.com email.

How do they work?

The primary characteristic of blogs (and, by extension, microblogs) is the ability to easily publish text, photos, video, and other content in a journal-like, reverse-chronological format.

Most blogging and microblogging tools have common features. For blogs, common features include:

- **Free and subscription versions.** Many platforms will allow you to start at least one blog for free. (Note that not all blog platforms offer a free version.) In subscription versions, you often can have additional, separate blogs if you want to have more than one blog. Subscription versions often will offer additional features, such as expanded design templates, priority support options, and the ability to customize the look and features of your blogs.

- **A basic set of designs to establish the look and feel of your blog.** The good news for those of us who aren't web designers is that almost all blog platforms will provide you with some basic templates for your blog. You can choose a look that matches the content and tone of your blog, whether it's for personal or professional use. In subscription versions, you often have access to additional design templates, and often the ability to create your own custom look and features.

- **Ability to add metadata to your blog and to your individual posts.** Writing blogs can raise your visibility and search engine ranking, because the blog content makes it easier for search engines to find content associated with you. The more you blog on particular topics and use specific metadata descriptors, the more search engines associate you and your blog with those topics. Most blog platforms also allow you to add metadata and/or tags, both to your blog and to your individual entries. Doing this means that search engines can more easily find and prioritize your content, so that others searching for your topic areas can find you – and your blog rises in search results!

- **Use of search engine optimization (SEO) features.** Along with the ability to add metadata to your blog and entries, many blogging platforms also have other features to help your blog and your content be discovered by search engines. For example, a blogging platform may let you select options to make your blog "public" and visible to search engines, or to create a Google sitemap (Figure 3.5).

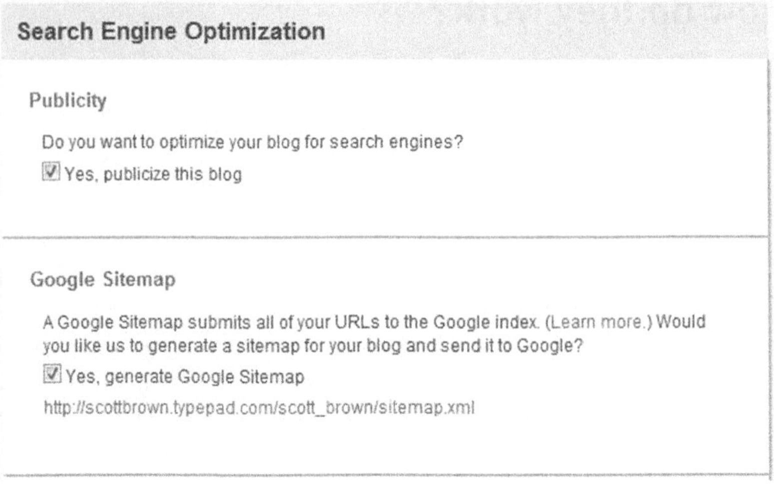

Search Engine Optimization

Publicity

Do you want to optimize your blog for search engines?
☑ Yes, publicize this blog

Google Sitemap

A Google Sitemap submits all of your URLs to the Google index. (Learn more.) Would you like us to generate a sitemap for your blog and send it to Google?
☑ Yes, generate Google Sitemap
http://scottbrown.typepad.com/scott_brown/sitemap.xml

Figure 3.5 Example of SEO features available in a blog

- **Widgets and blog features.** Some basic features you can often add to your blog include the ability to add a Twitter feed area onto your blog (using a widget), list other blogs of interest to you, and customize the tags you use in your blog.

- **Comments.** If you read or write blogs, you know that people can usually add comments to blogs. New bloggers sometimes worry that they will get negative comments on their blogs. The reality is that most blog comments are positive, and/or add to the "conversation" on the blog post. Comments are the "social" part of blogging. They provide a way to interact with your readers.

  Some newer blogging (or blog-like) platforms, such as Tumblr, do not provide an easy way to comment. In this sense, they are more like microblogs than blogs.

For microblogs, some common features include:

- **Free registration.**
- **Short messages or posts.** Twitter, for example, officially limits your messages to 140 characters. (Note again that I said "characters," not "words.") This means you need to be very succinct in your posts. It is often because of this character limit that newcomers to Twitter and other microblogging tools don't "get" them. What could you effectively say in 140 characters that anyone else would want to read? We'll explore this question when we look more closely at Twitter.

- **The ability to include links** – to articles, blog posts, videos, any kind of content – adds to the meaning and value of microblogging. Many people use microblogs as a way to share links, and to add a very short commentary or perspective on that link.

  The question is, why would you take up so many of your precious 140 characters with a long link? The answer is, link shorteners like bit.ly (*http://bit.ly*), which allow you to create very short URLs out of long URLs.

- **A "follow" model of connecting with people.** The "social" part of microblogging tools is connecting with other users. Unlike LinkedIn and social networking tools, microblogging tools usually have a "follow" model, which is a two-part process to connect with others. In the first part, you find other Twitter users, and "follow" them to receive their updates. Sometimes, the connection ends there. In the second part, Twitter and microblogging etiquette typically dictates that you follow those who follow you, thereby receiving their updates. However, in many instances, this is not the case. Because of this "follow" model, microblogging is a more "one-sided" connection model than tools like LinkedIn. I sometimes think of it as a "stalking" model.

Many blogging and microblogging tools have additional features, which vary depending upon the tool. However, almost all blogging and microblogging tools will share these common features.

Blogs and blog search

What are they?

The first versions of blogs were launched as early as 1994, though the term "Weblog" (later shortened to "blog") was not coined until 1997. Most early blogs were akin to online diaries, with the authors generally expressing their thoughts and opinions about their lives, their jobs, and the world around them. Blogs quickly evolved into platforms for one or more authors writing about a particular topic: the web, business, gossip, or technology, for example.

As of April 2012, according to NM Incite (which is part of Nielsen/McKinsey), over 181 million blogs exist, with tens of thousands of new blogs being created every day, on almost any topic. Individuals continue to create personal and professional blogs. Many experts, authors, and public figures, such as Ann Coulter (*http://www.anncoulter.com*), Bill

Gates (*http://www.thegatesnotes.com/*), and Will Straw (*http://www. leftfootforward.org/*), are using their blogs to share their thoughts and views in a very public way.

Additionally, Fortune 500 companies are increasingly using blogs as a way to talk to their customers, partners, and the world in general. According to Burson Marsteller, one-fourth of Global Fortune 100 companies are using more than one social media platform. As of 2012, Global Fortune 100 companies that are blogging typically have multiple blogs, not just one. While US companies increased their blog usage in 2011, Asian companies declined in their active blog use, and European usage remained roughly the same.

Though we've covered some of the platforms and functionality of blogs, the goal of this chapter is to utilize blog search tools. We will look at ways that you can examine and gather information from organizational blogs. We will also look at blog search tools as a way to find blogs and blog entries.

What kind of business and competitive information can be found there?

Company and organizational blogs can be a view into a "deeper layer" of an organization, providing information on organizational culture, strategy, approach, philosophy, products, and services. In our examples, we'll look at both the information provided by organization blogs, and the different information provided by "outsider" blogs (those blogging about an organization outside of that organization).

What kind of information are organizations sharing on their blogs?

- **Corporate culture.** Many organizations blog about what it's like to work at that organization. Organizations may highlight certain programs and initiatives, or highlight employees who have made an outstanding achievement in the organization. This type of information can give you a view of the corporate culture.

- **Corporate social responsibility.** Many organizations will share information about their initiatives that benefit the community and society as a whole. Organizations may share about how they are reducing their emissions, or about fundraisers or other events that benefit the community.

- **Organizational strategy, approach, and philosophy.** Through ongoing blog posts, you can get a sense of the focus of the organization. You'll hear about new initiatives and products, executive activities, and reaction to the larger industry. All of this type of information provides you a broader view of the organization's strategy and overarching philosophy.

- **An "inside" view to their organizations.** One of the distinctions between organizational blogging and, for example, press releases, is that blogs often provide a much more informal framework for sharing information. As a result, many organizations will share a much broader spectrum of information about the organization via blogs. Because the communication doesn't have to be as formal, you also get a sense of the "tone" of the organization. Are their posts fun? Serious? The tone provides some information as to what the corporate culture might be like as well.

- **Breaking news.** While certain information cannot be shared in advance on a blog, due to regulatory issues, you can sometimes get "pre-announcement" information via an organizational blog.

- **Executive perspective and personality.** If executives at the organization are part of the blogging effort, you will often see blog posts that provide some perspective on that executive's view and personality. True, some executives may not actually write their own blog posts – they may have someone else in the organization do it. However, a blog post that is posted as coming from the executive is always going to be worth reading, no matter who really wrote it.

- **Product news.** In addition to press releases and other traditional avenues for product news, blogs often provide an informal channel for an organization to share additional information about a new product. The advantage is, depending upon the magnitude of the news, an organization might make multiple posts on a new development, whereas it might provide only one press release. A series of posts on a new product may provide a much deeper perspective on the product, and the expectations and hopes of the organization for that product.

As I've emphasized, following an organizational blog can give you an ongoing perspective of an organization that simply is not available through "traditional" communication channels. You can get an understanding of how the organization thinks of itself and how it talks about itself to its customers, partners, shareholders, and other interested parties.

Alternatively, following organizational news and mentions through others' blogs can give you another view of the company.

- **Breaking news of a different kind.** What are the rumors coming out of the organization? Sometimes "outsiders" talk about organizational rumors and gossip on their blogs, and this can provide indicators and clues to potentially negative changes at the organization.

- **Issues negatively affecting the organization or its constituents.** Organizations do their best to minimize bad news. Bloggers outside of the organization can often more freely find and share the challenges and issues of an organization. Granted, bloggers are under no obligation to necessarily report fairly. However, you can often find more detail on organizational issues on blogs outside of the organization.

- **Customer, partner, and stakeholder sentiment.** "Outsiders" who track and report on an organization are often very passionate about that organization. You can get a sense of what really resonates with customers and stakeholders, and what issues customers and stakeholders see with the organization.

- **Alternative perspective on organizational announcements.** Especially when sharing news about themselves, organizations position themselves in the most positive way, and downplay any issues – naturally. Outside "reporters" and bloggers can provide some of the "missing pieces" in organizational news. They can often provide more information and analysis on the "downside" of organizational announcements and developments.

How do you get started using them?

On any organizational website, you may find links to one or more "official" blogs produced by the organization. This is often a good place to start in looking for official blogs. In the next example, I'll show you how you might locate official blogs via Google Blog Search. In this first example, we'll simply start with an organizational blog that we can find from an organization's website.

Example 3.1:   Organizational blog

If we take a look at General Motors' (GM) main web page (*http://www.gm.com*), we can relatively easily find a link to its FastLane blog (*http://fastlane.gmblogs.com/*) (Figures 3.6 and 3.7).

Figure 3.6   General Motors' main website, with a link to the FastLane blog

Figure 3.7   GM's FastLane blog

When you go to the FastLane blog, the site tagline that shows up in your browser tells you a lot about the approach that GM takes in its blog: "The FastLane blog is your source for the latest musings of GM leaders, like Bob Lutz, on the topics relevant to the company and the auto industry." This tagline tells you what to expect from the blog (and also, if you didn't already know, gives you a pointer to an executive to further research). In the current version of the blog, GM shares information across several categories, including auto shows, business, cars and trucks, concept cars, design, "FYI", "photo of the day", Volt (its new electric car), and web chats.

Just from the landing page of the blog, if you scroll down, you'll see a separate box on the right side called "Pages" (Figure 3.8). This box provides links to other pieces of the blog that may provide useful information, including "About this site," contact information, "Featured Comment," and, interestingly, "GM Impulsa una Comunicación Abierta", a link to a Spanish-language version of the blog.

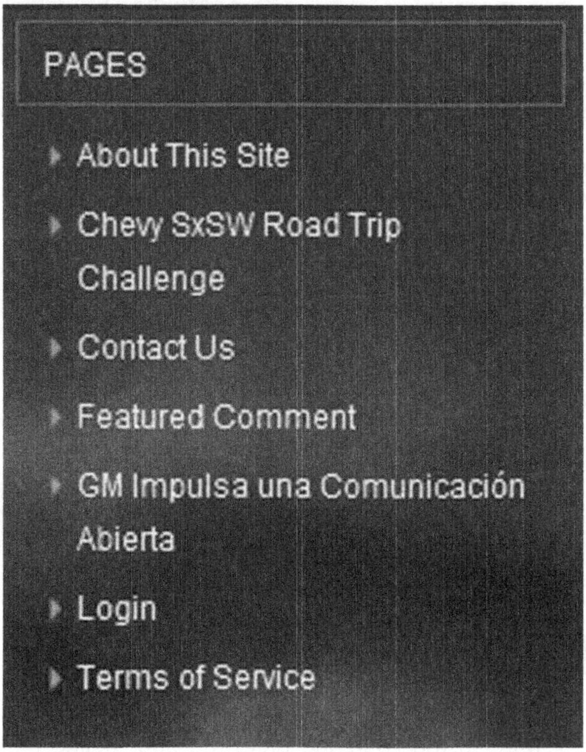

Figure 3.8   Some of the sections of the GM FastLane blog

If we follow the "About This Site" link, we get more information on the purpose of the blog: "GM's FastLane blog is a forum for GM executives to talk about GM's current and future products and services, although non-executives sometimes appear here to discuss the development and design of important products. On occasion, FastLane can be utilized to discuss other important issues facing the company." Two interesting things to note on this page are: 1) GM also outlines its blogging policy; and 2) GM links its Twitter postings here as well. (It would be worthwhile checking out GM's Twitter feed for further information.)

As with any social media presence, it's worthwhile to explore every part of it, whether or not you think it will provide relevant information. You simply never know where your valuable information will surface. However, some logical places to start to find out more about the business might be the categories "Business," "Featured," "FYI" (which stands for "For Your Information"), and "Web Chats."

A well-organized blog like the GM FastLane blog can quickly get you to the relevant information you're seeking. Again, explore the key categories, and pay particular attention to the unique features. In this case, let's look at the "Web Chats" section.

If we click into the section, we currently see an upcoming web chat with the Team Chevy Racing Team. However, we also see archived chats – particularly, archived chats about the Chevy Volt (Figure 3.9).

Looking at these archived chats, we see that experts from GM held an open discussion on the Chevy Volt – and that discussion continues to be available to us on the GM FastLane blog. This is the type of unique content that social tools allow us to access and utilize.

Before we leave the FastLane blog, note that in the upper right corner of the blog there is a search box. Unfortunately, on the GM blog, this search box is tied to the gm.com site, not specifically the blog.

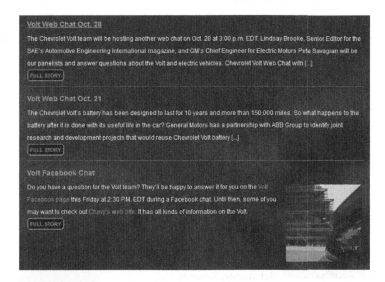

Figure 3.9   Archived web chats on GM's FastLane blog

An interesting alternative search strategy for any blog might be to search for executive names or keywords on the blog. Since the search box on the FastLane blog doesn't limit itself to the blog, let's take a moment and go back to Google to conduct an alternative search of the GM FastLane blog.

As of April 2012, Daniel F. Akerson is the Chairman and CEO of GM. If we go to Google Advanced Search, we can enter the search term "Akerson" and then limit our search to the FastLane blog by entering "fastlane.gmblogs.com" in the Domain search box (Figure 3.10).

Our search comes back with results only from the FastLane blog (Figure 3.11).

So, between exploring official organization blogs in depth, and utilizing search capabilities both on the blog itself and via Google Advanced Search, we are able to uncover quite a bit of information about organizational direction, strategy, executives, and subject-matter experts.

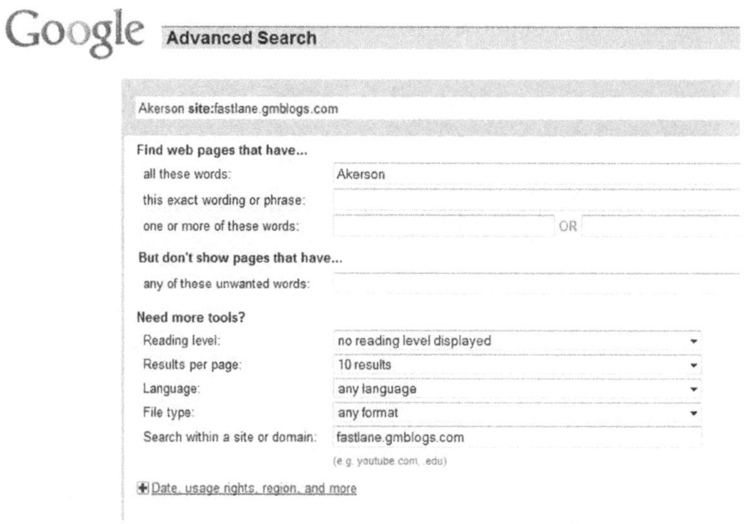

Figure 3.10   **Searching the FastLane blog using Google Advanced Search**

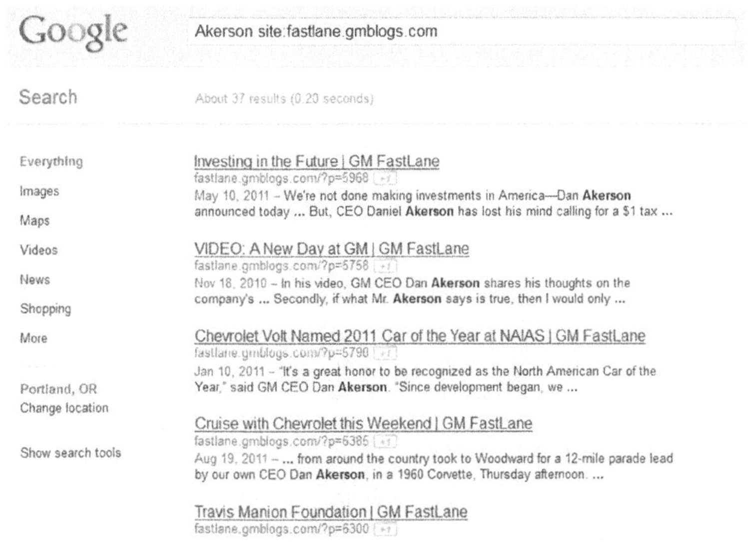

Figure 3.11

Figure 3.11 FastLane blog search results using Goolge Advanced Search

Example 3.2: Google Blog Search

Blog search tools help you to search across several different blogs for any topic of interest. Blog search tools continue to evolve, and are increasingly being bundled into "federated" social search tools that search across a variety of social media tools. (Social search engines will be covered in Chapter 5.) As of April 2012, some of the available blog-specific search tools include:

- Icerocket.

- Technorati. Though Technorati is focused on technology and business, you can still find a wide variety of information via this tool.

- Google Blog Search.

For this book and our example, we will take a look at Google Blog Search and how you might use this tool to search for organizational information.

For our Google Blog Search example, let's look at the German company Bertelsmann AG (*http://www.bertelsmann.com*), a global media company.

If I type "Bertelsmann" into Google Blog Search, the tool breaks the results into blog homepages and individual blog post results (though they are not labeled that way) (Figure 3.12).

From the screenshot in Figure 3.12, you can see the blog homepages section, which points you to blogs that may be produced by the organization. (Google makes its best effort to identify "official" blogs.) The results below the blog homepages section are search results where the organization is mentioned. Both of these sets of results are worth investigating.

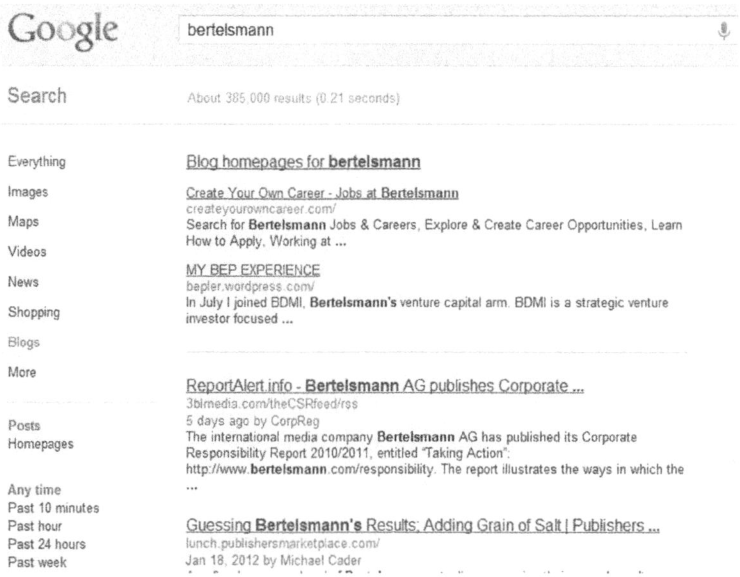

Figure 3.12   Google blog search results for Bertelsmann

Note that, on the left side of the screenshot, you can limit your results by posting time (past ten minutes, hour, 24 hours, etc.), as well as sort results by date. Note, too, that you currently have the ability to limit your search results by a date range. For example, if you were looking for blog posts about a company within a time-frame of a product recall, you could limit your results, say, to a six-month time block around the recall.

Let's start with the blog homepages results (Figure 3.13). I like to click on the Blog Pages link to get the full list of blog results.

As you see, Google Blog Search picks up blogs in multiple languages (Figure 3.13). This search found a career blog from Bertelsmann, a blog about the Bertelsmann Entrepreneurship Program (BEP), several German-language blogs (but none that immediately seem to be produced directly by Bertelsmann), and a blog called Bertelsmann Stiftung FutureChallenges (*http://futurechallenges.org*) (Figure 3.14).

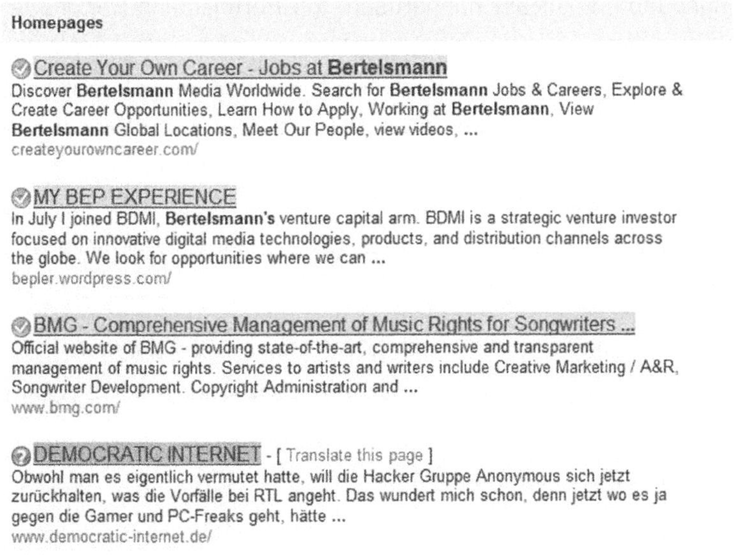

Homepages

Create Your Own Career - Jobs at Bertelsmann
Discover **Bertelsmann** Media Worldwide. Search for **Bertelsmann** Jobs & Careers, Explore & Create Career Opportunities, Learn How to Apply, Working at **Bertelsmann**, View **Bertelsmann** Global Locations, Meet Our People, view videos, ...
createyourowncareer.com/

MY BEP EXPERIENCE
In July I joined BDMI, **Bertelsmann's** venture capital arm. BDMI is a strategic venture investor focused on innovative digital media technologies, products, and distribution channels across the globe. We look for opportunities where we can ...
bepler.wordpress.com/

BMG - Comprehensive Management of Music Rights for Songwriters ...
Official website of BMG - providing state-of-the-art, comprehensive and transparent management of music rights. Services to artists and writers include Creative Marketing / A&R, Songwriter Development. Copyright Administration and ...
www.bmg.com/

DEMOCRATIC INTERNET - [Translate this page]
Obwohl man es eigentlich vermutet hatte, will die Hacker Gruppe Anonymous sich jetzt zurückhalten, was die Vorfälle bei RTL angeht. Das wundert mich schon, denn jetzt wo es ja gegen die Gamer und PC-Freaks geht, hätte ...
www.democratic-internet.de/

Figure 3.13   Blog homepage search results for Bertelsmann

Figure 3.14   BertelsmannStiftung FutureChallenges blog

According to the "About" page of the BertelsmannStiftung FutureChallenges blog, the blog "is an initiative of the Bertelsmann Foundation. Politically nonpartisan, the Bertelsmann Stiftung is a place where people come together to create forward-looking change. Our project work involves more than just developing compelling ideas. We are committed to 'helpfully improving the way things are,' to quote Reinhard Mohn, the Bertelsmann Stiftung's founder."

Simply browsing through these types of blogs could give you a better understanding of:

- community and philanthropic activities of Bertelsmann
- types of careers and jobs available at Bertelsmann, as well as a richer sense of the corporate culture and employee experience at the company.

Depending upon the company and the blogs that it offers, you may find much more information as well.

Now, let's go back and take a look at the blog search results, which search through blog postings for our keyword(s). Since we've done a general search with just a company name, the results we get are more "newsy." In this set of results, many bloggers are reporting on recent financial results announced by Bertelsmann (Figure 3.15).

Blog posting search results can be very helpful to find industry "buzz" and speculation about an organization. For example, in our search results, the third result talks about a Bertelsmann acquisition (Figure 3.15). If we go in and conduct another search using the terms "Bertelsmann acquisition," we get postings, both current and within the last several years, that discuss Bertelsmann acquisitions.

Could we get similar – and probably a greater volume of – information on Bertelsmann acquisitions through other means? Yes. The advantage of searching blog entries is that we have the

Bertelsmann Sees First Half Profit, Sales Growth - The Hollywood ... 🔍
www.hollywoodreporter.com/taxonomy/term/60/0/feed
1 day ago by edit@hollywoodreporter.com (Scott Roxborough)
Traditional TV advertising and digital sales buoy parent company of "American Idol" producer FremantleMedia and "Song of Ice and Fire" publisher Random House.

Content business drives **Bertelsmann** profits 🔍
www.digital2disc.com/
21 hours ago by Elizabeth Toppin
International media company **Bertelsmann** has announced an increase in the group's profit by nearly 10% in the first half of 2011 – from €243 million to €269 million. This, said the company, was due primarily to **Bertelsmann's** ...
More results from Digital2Disc

Bertelsmann CFO Says EMI Fits Company's Acquisition Strategy 🔍
musicindustryreport.org/
1 hour ago by admin
Bertelsmann AG CEO Thomas Rabe says that buying EMI would fit with the current music acquisition strategy of **Bertelsmann's** BMG Rights Management division. According to Bloomberg, after being asked if BMG could join a ...

In A Sign Of The Times, **Bertelsmann** Closes Its Book Clubs Division ... 🔍
paidcontent.org/
Jun 15, 2011 by Laura Hazard Owen
Over the past three years, Direct Group has sold off most of its international subsidiaries, including those in the U.S., UK, Italy, Spain, Australia, Asia, and France, and will fold the remaining ones into **Bertelsmann** or sell them ...
More results from paidContent

Random House eBook Sales Increase over 200% | 3D Tablet 🔍
www.3dtablets.ca/
4 hours ago

Figure 3.15   **Blog entry search results for Bertelsmann**

possibility of adding *perspective* to that news. If we look at one of the blog entries we uncovered with our search, from theCMUwebsite. com, we get the following perspective on Bertelsmann's interest in acquiring Warner Music and EMI:

> As previously reported, insiders at Warner have said that BMG's bid is unlikely to be successful because the major's current owners and bankers believe the German firm's offer price is too low given the amount of interest in buying the Warner Music company.

This type of information can be invaluable in looking at a market and its competitors.

In just this short example, we've illustrated some of the depth of perspective on an organization that is available via "official" blogs and outside blog postings.

Example 3.3: Non-profit organization

Let's try an example outside of for-profit organizations. Let's look at Net Impact (*http://www.netimpact.org*), an international non-profit organization that engages with businesses in the interest of a more socially and environmentally sustainable world.

If we do a search for "Net Impact" (with quotes) in Google Blog Search, again, we find blogs produced by Net Impact and related organizations, as well as blog post results from other blogs (Figure 3.16).

The listing of blogs created by the parent Net Impact organization is helpful, and it's interesting as well to find additional chapters that are blogging. In this instance, we have found blogs from the Seattle, Washington chapter, a Brandeis University chapter, the Net Impact "Bluegrass" chapter (and I'm not clear what that is!), and various other chapter blogs. If I'm interested in this organization and its activities, finding the various chapter blogs is going to:

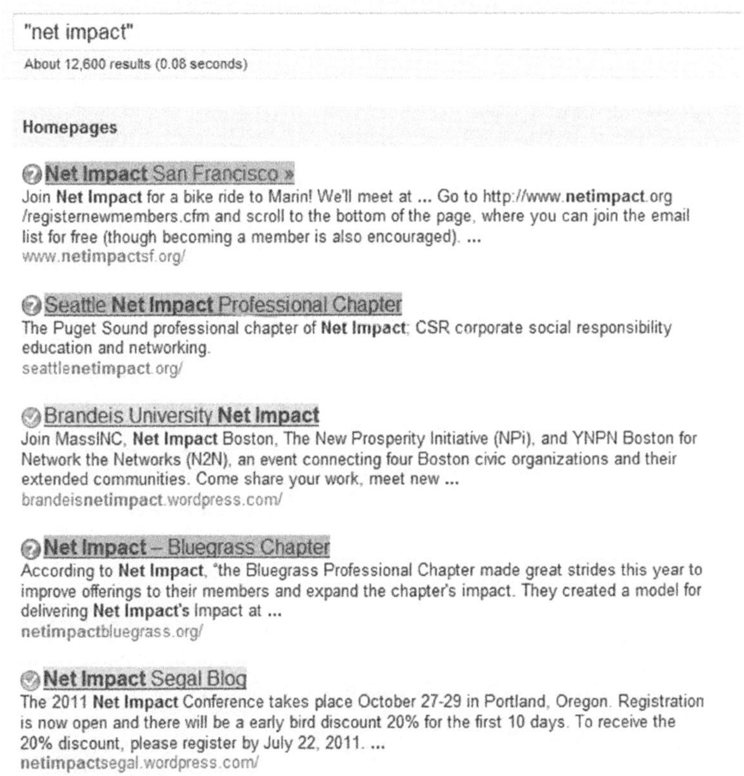

"net impact"

About 12,600 results (0.08 seconds)

Homepages

Net Impact San Francisco »
Join **Net Impact** for a bike ride to Marin! We'll meet at ... Go to http://www.**netimpact**.org
/registernewmembers.cfm and scroll to the bottom of the page, where you can join the email
list for free (though becoming a member is also encouraged). ...
www.netimpactsf.org/

Seattle **Net Impact** Professional Chapter
The Puget Sound professional chapter of **Net Impact**; CSR corporate social responsibility
education and networking.
seattlenetimpact.org/

Brandeis University **Net Impact**
Join MassINC, **Net Impact** Boston, The New Prosperity Initiative (NPi), and YNPN Boston for
Network the Networks (N2N), an event connecting four Boston civic organizations and their
extended communities. Come share your work, meet new ...
brandeisnetimpact.wordpress.com/

Net Impact – Bluegrass Chapter
According to **Net Impact**, "the Bluegrass Professional Chapter made great strides this year to
improve offerings to their members and expand the chapter's impact. They created a model for
delivering **Net Impact's** Impact at ...
netimpactbluegrass.org/

Net Impact Segal Blog
The 2011 **Net Impact** Conference takes place October 27-29 in Portland, Oregon. Registration
is now open and there will be a early bird discount 20% for the first 10 days. To receive the
20% discount, please register by July 22, 2011. ...
netimpactsegal.wordpress.com/

Figure 3.16   Blog search results for Net Impact

- help me understand where active chapters exist, and the reach of the parent organization
- help me understand what chapters are doing
- give me a way to track local activities of the organization
- point me to specific contacts in local areas (since many blogs include contact information).

Looking at the search results, I can find additional information about Net Impact's activities. For example, one of my search results points to Net Impact's Guide to Green MBA Programs (Figure 3.17). This annual report (now in its fifth year, as of August 2011) looks at the rise of corporate social responsibility themes in MBA curricula.

⊘ Business as UNusual: **Net Impact's** Guide to Green MBA Programs ... ⌕
www.greenbiz.com/feed/greenbiz
Aug 18, 2011 by admin - Block all www.greenbiz.com results
An annual guide offering extensive profiles of 106 MBA programs, focused on helping students
learn how to do well by doing good.
More results from GreenBiz.com Green and Sustainable Business News

⊘ MBA Programs | Business as Unusual: **Net Impact** 's Guide to Green ... ⌕
education.ance-information.net/
4 days ago by admin
Web Site: Download the free report here The fifth annual **Net Impact** offers extensive profiles of
106 MBA programs, developed with the collaboration of more than.

⊘ **Net Impact** Membership | Krannert MBA | Student Life Blog ⌕
www.krannertlife.com/
3 days ago by McCarty
Join more than 20000 members in nearly 280 chapters worldwide to make a **net impact** that
benefits not just the bottom line — but people and planet, too.
More results from Krannert Student Life Blog

⊘ August Newsletter is Available | **Net Impact** Seattle :: Professional ... ⌕
seattlenetimpact.org/
Aug 8, 2011 by admin
Check it out here. If you're not on the email list, sign up here so you don't miss the next one!
More results from Net Impact Seattle :: Professional Chapter

Figure 3.17 A selection of blog posting results for Net Impact. Note the first two results pointing to Net Impact's Guide to Green MBA Programs

Again, I could potentially find this information through the organization's website as well. Indeed, if I go to Net Impact's main site and look under "Publications," I do find the "Business as UNusual" report, which I also found through my blog search.

There are two advantages of conducting a blog search, in addition to checking an organization's website. First, a blog search potentially provides a broader perspective on the organization (more on this in a moment), and second, it can potentially help you find information from an organization that might not be findable (or easily findable) through the organization's site.

To expand further on the "broader perspective" point, another benefit of looking at who is blogging about an organization is that it gives me a better sense of the people tracking the organization, and the larger industry in which the organization plays. If I look at the bloggers who are blogging about this organization, I can likely find:

- additional organizations and companies that participate in the industry;

- more information and perspective on the industry from people who are knowledgeable about it;

- pointers to additional resources for information on the industry;

- the latest "buzz" in the industry and the companies which participate in the industry.

Example 3.4: Finding people and expertise

How would we use a blog search to find an expert? Let's take a look.

Let's say I'm looking for experts in the high-tech sector in the venture capital arena. If I do a search in Google Blog Search for "high-tech venture capital," I get results both for blogs and for blog entries (Figure 3.18).

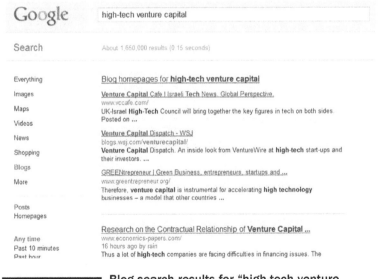

Figure 3.18 Blog search results for "high-tech venture capital"

If I click on the top link for "Blog homepages," I get a list of blogs around this topic (Figure 3.19).

The second link in this set of results takes me to the Wall Street Journal Venture Capital Dispatch blog – certainly one authoritative source on this topic. If we click into the blog page, we see an "About" section, which provides us not only information on the blog, but also contact information for the blog, and information on the experience of the bloggers (Figure 3.20).

Even with essentially no knowledge of this industry, by utilizing blog search, we've been able to locate an authoritative blog and connections to expertise in this area quite quickly.

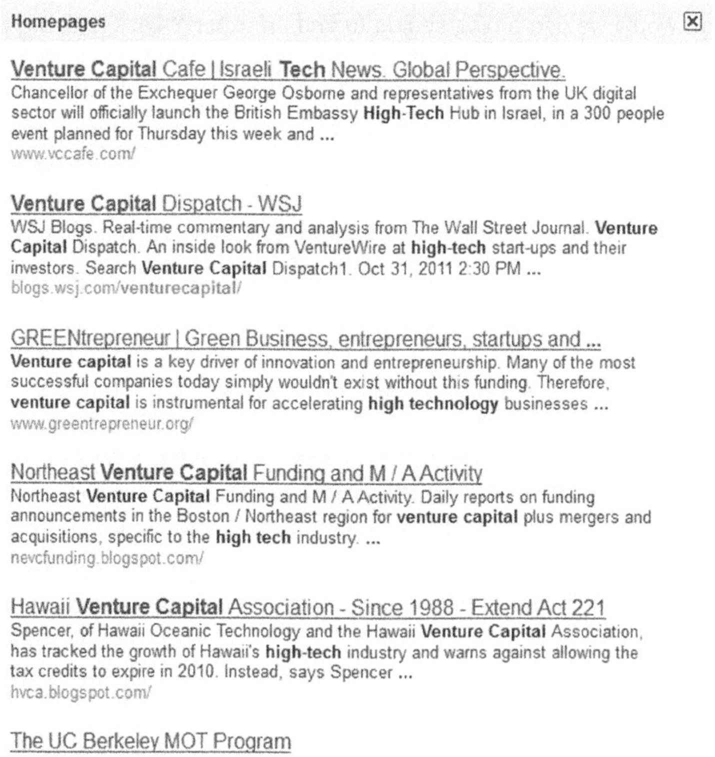

Homepages ☒

Venture Capital Cafe | Israeli **Tech** News. Global Perspective.
Chancellor of the Exchequer George Osborne and representatives from the UK digital sector will officially launch the British Embassy **High-Tech** Hub in Israel, in a 300 people event planned for Thursday this week and ...
www.vccafe.com/

Venture Capital Dispatch - WSJ
WSJ Blogs. Real-time commentary and analysis from The Wall Street Journal. **Venture Capital** Dispatch. An inside look from VentureWire at **high-tech** start-ups and their investors. Search **Venture Capital** Dispatch1. Oct 31, 2011 2:30 PM ...
blogs.wsj.com/venturecapital/

GREENtrepreneur | Green Business, entrepreneurs, startups and ...
Venture capital is a key driver of innovation and entrepreneurship. Many of the most successful companies today simply wouldn't exist without this funding. Therefore, **venture capital** is instrumental for accelerating **high technology** businesses ...
www.greentrepreneur.org/

Northeast **Venture Capital** Funding and M / A Activity
Northeast **Venture Capital** Funding and M / A Activity. Daily reports on funding announcements in the Boston / Northeast region for **venture capital** plus mergers and acquisitions, specific to the **high tech** industry. ...
nevcfunding.blogspot.com/

Hawaii **Venture Capital** Association - Since 1988 - Extend Act 221
Spencer, of Hawaii Oceanic Technology and the Hawaii **Venture Capital** Association, has tracked the growth of Hawaii's **high-tech** industry and warns against allowing the tax credits to expire in 2010. Instead, says Spencer ...
hvca.blogspot.com/

The UC Berkeley MOT Program

Figure 3.19 Blog homepages results for "high-tech venture capital"

About Venture Capital Dispatch

Produced by the editors of **Dow Jones VentureWire**, Venture Capital Dispatch tracks the fast-moving developments at the intersection of high-tech innovation and venture capital finance. Featuring lead editor Scott Austin and the VentureWire reporting team in the Silicon Valley, New York, Boston and Shanghai tech centers, Venture Capital Dispatch provides insight into the newest start-ups and latest trends in venture capital investing. Write us at **VCdispatch@dowjones.com**. For more information on Dow Jones products covering venture capital and other financial markets, go to **www.fis.dowjones.com**.

Follow Venture Capital Dispatch on Twitter

Like Venture Capital Dispatch on Facebook

Figure 3.20 Information on the Dow Jones Venture Capital Dispatch blog

Microblogs

What are they?

As stated earlier, microblogs function similarly to blogs, in that they allow you to post text, links, and images. The difference is that you typically have a character limit on the length of your post. In sharing content, you can think of microblogs as being similar to texting, with the ability to add links and images (or links to images). On the receiving end of content from microblogs, you can think of microblogs as being similar to RSS feeds. Following a microblog feed from an organization is similar to following an RSS feed from that organization. Following a microblog feed from an individual is like having an RSS feed about that individual's activities, thoughts, and interests.

Twitter is currently the most well-known microblogging platform, and so will be the tool on which we focus for our examples. The first "Tweet" (message posted on Twitter) was sent on March 21, 2006 by Jack Dorsey, who was working at Odeo at the time (Figure 3.21).

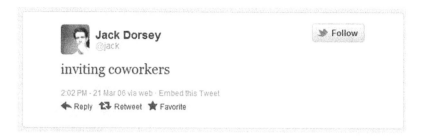

Jack Dorsey
@jack

Follow

inviting coworkers

2:02 PM - 21 Mar 06 via web · Embed this Tweet

← Reply ♺ Retweet ★ Favorite

Figure 3.21 The first tweet

Since then, Twitter has grown such that 1 billion tweets are sent every week. As of early 2012, Twitter had well over 500 million user accounts, and was on track to hit 600 million by mid-2012.

Today, "news breaks first on Twitter." During the 2011 earthquake in Japan, some people actually "tweeted" about the quake while it was occurring. Twitter has quickly become an instantaneous way to share news as it is happening, as evidenced by its usage, too, in social and political uprisings in Iran, Egypt, and other countries. On the business and industry side, individuals and organizations use Twitter as a way to share their "breaking news."

As mentioned earlier, Twitter is not the only microblogging platform, but it is the most well known. Yammer is a tool frequently used for an internal organizational microblog. Jaiku, another microblogging tool, was purchased by Google. We'll look at additional tools in this category at the end of this chapter.

Twitter glossary and basics

- **Handle**: A "handle" is a Twitter user name – for example, my personal Twitter handle is @scbrown5, and my business Twitter handle is @socialinfo. If you see just a Twitter handle, to find the actual URL for the Twitter feed you would put the handle into this URL structure: *http://twitter.com/[handle]*. Example: *http://twitter.com/socialinfo*.

- **Follow**: To subscribe to another Twitter user's Twitter feed. If you follow a person on Twitter, you will receive their Twitter updates.

- **Tweet (verb):** To write and send a Twitter message.

- **Tweet (noun):** A Twitter message.

- **Retweet or RT:** To re-send a Tweet from someone you follow to the people who are following you. Think of it as similar to forwarding an email.

- **Direct message or DM**: When you are following another Twitter user, and that user is following you, you can send direct, non-public messages back and forth.

Deciphering a tweet

To the new user of Twitter, some tweets seem almost indecipherable, due to the limited room for information and the various tools and "shorthand" being used within the tweet. Figure 3.22 is an example, and the following is some explanation.

In plainer English, this tweet is advertising the Oracle OpenWorld Conference that happened in October 2011. This tweet also uses a couple of "tags" or hashtags.

@ symbol: The @ symbol simply provides an active link to that Twitter account. In other words, there is another Twitter feed specifically called OracleOpenWorld, which (presumably) carries information about the conference. Putting in this kind of link allows anyone viewing the Twitter post to link through to that Twitter account. If you ever reply to someone's tweet, you will also see the @ symbol (and the handle of the person you're replying to) show up at the beginning of your post. So, for example, if I replied to this tweet, my tweet would start off with @Oracle. @Oracle would also get a notification that I mentioned its Twitter handle.

Oracle Oracle
Thirty days & counting to #Oracle OpenWorld! Follow
@OracleOpenWorld & bookmark blog for the latest show info:
bit.ly/rmYW07P #OOW11
2 Sep ☆ Favorite ↻ Retweet ↩ Reply

Figure 3.22 A sample tweet. What does it mean?

 # or hashtag: Twitter users use the # symbol to create either an on-the-fly or an "established" tag for Twitter posts. Using hashtags allows Twitter users to easily track a topic – whether that topic is a conference, an organization, a "keyword", or a concept. Simply typing in a hashtag symbol before a word automatically creates a tag. (We'll look more closely at hashtags for research use later in this chapter.)

If you were to click on #Oracle in this tweet, for example, you would pull up a list of all recent tweets using that hashtag. Alternatively, if you were to click on #OOW11 (the "established" hashtag for the Oracle OpenWorld 2011 Conference), you would pull up a list of all the recent tweets using that hashtag. This is another way to search for information via Twitter, as well as one way to track what's going on at any particular conference. Typically, you can pull up only the most recent tweets by using a hashtag, not a full archive.

Shortened URL: The shortened URL you see in the example starts with bit.ly – indicating that the true URL has been shortened using the bit.ly service, one of several free URL-shortening services available. You will find many shortened URLs being used in tweets, because URL shorteners allow users to shorten long URLs and so save space in their tweets. Several tools built upon Twitter, such as Hootsuite and Tweetdeck, have automatic URL-shortening features built into them as well.

More information on the basics of Twitter and deciphering tweets is available at The Twitter Glossary.[1]

What kind of business and competitive information can be found in microblogs?

As I've mentioned, microblogs, and Twitter in particular, essentially serve as RSS feeds for organizations and individuals. From a researcher's perspective, Twitter allows you an ongoing, "real-time" information stream. Just a few examples of the types of organizational and industry information you may find through a Twitter feed include:

- "breaking news" and news developments about an organization;
- "breaking news" and news developments in an industry;

- events: those sponsored by a company, those in which a company participates, and industry events;
- product information;
- sales and promotions;
- pointers to other company and industry Twitter feeds;
- "live" news feeds from conferences – to track buzz, latest trends, thought leaders and experts in the industry.

I think you'll be surprised by the amount of information such short messages can hold.

How do you get started using them?

Twitter has a very low "barrier to entry" – in other words, it's very easy to set up an account and get started using Twitter. Twitter is free to use.

Currently, you can search Twitter without signing up for an account, by using the advanced search option mentioned below. You can also sign up for an account. If you go to the Twitter site at *http://twitter.com*, you have an option to sign up for an account by providing your full name, email, and a password. The biggest challenge of getting your account set up is to choose a Twitter account name (or "handle"). Your "handle" needs to be a unique account name, and literally millions of account names have already been taken. That said, you usually can find an appropriate handle for your account after a few tries.

Twitter requires very little information in order for you to start following people and finding information. When setting up your Twitter account, consider how you might use it going forward. Are you using it just to follow Twitter feeds? Are you using it for your own personal goals? Are you using it professionally, or for your organization? The answer to these questions will determine how much and what kind of information you put into your Twitter account. Consider carefully how you will use your Twitter account, prior to starting your account.

Also, consider whether you might establish more than one Twitter account. For example, you might use one Twitter account just for your own personal use, and you might establish another for finding and sharing professional information. You might establish a third in order to track information.

If you are simply using your Twitter account to follow Twitter streams, you don't need to provide much information at all. In fact, you can be as anonymous as you like. This is a matter of personal preference.

If you do provide profile information, Twitter asks for very little: name, location, and biography (Figure 3.23). Much of this information can be left blank.

Once your account is set up, you can begin following other Twitter feeds. How do you find the relevant feeds to follow? While we'll cover more on this topic when we get into examples, some basic ways that you can find Twitter feeds are:

- **Search.** Twitter has a basic search box at the top of each page. If you conduct a search – on a topic, a keyword, a person, or an industry – you will get search results from tweets, as well as "people" search results (Figure 3.24).

  If you look at the "people" results, you will typically get a good basic list of accounts to follow for information on your topic.

- **Advanced search.** Twitter offers an advanced search feature at *http://twitter.com/search-advanced* which allows you to be a little more exact in your search – for example, you can search by exact phrase, language, and location (Figure 3.25).

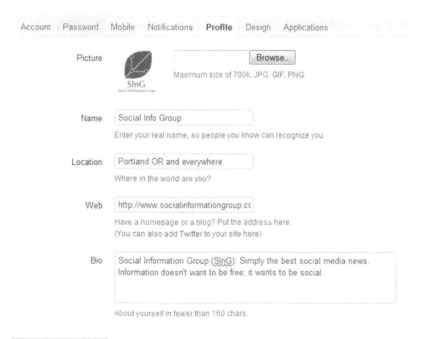

Figure 3.23 Profile information in Twitter

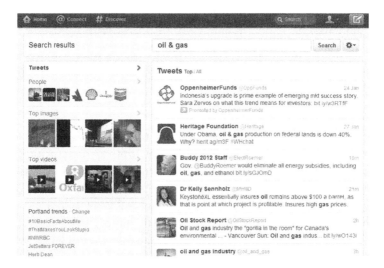

Figure 3.24 — Basic search results for "oil and gas" in Twitter. Search results from tweets are on the right; "people" results are on the left

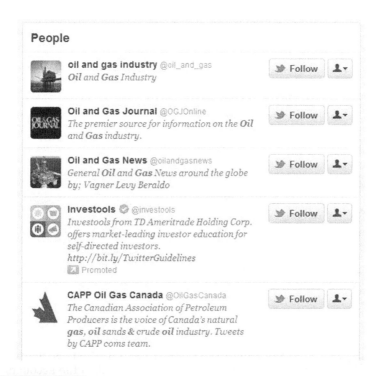

Figure 3.25 — List of Twitter accounts for oil and gas

- **Twitter account directories.** To discover some key Twitter topic feeds quickly, you can utilize Twitter feed directories such as:

  - Listorious
  - WeFollow
  - Twellow.

These directories allow Twitter users to list their Twitter accounts under one or more topic areas. These typically are "opt-in" directories, so are not necessarily complete listings of all relevant Twitter accounts available. Nonetheless, these directories provide an excellent source for the top Twitter accounts in a variety of subject areas and geographies.

When you start following accounts, you will immediately start receiving updates on your main Twitter account page, as shown in Figure 3.26.

Some initial tips for getting the most out of Twitter

Getting started on Twitter can be fun, and it can quickly become overwhelming. Once you start following more than, say, ten Twitter feeds – and especially if some of those feeds are very active, with multiple "tweets" a day – you start to realize that keeping up with information

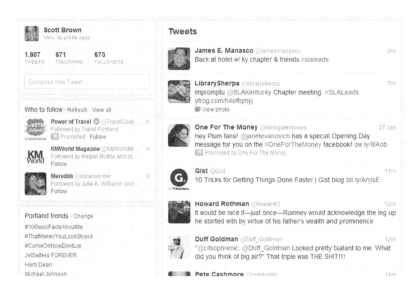

Figure 3.26 The main Twitter page when you've signed in (as of April 2012). Tweets from all of the accounts I follow feed in on the right

on Twitter can be a full-time job in itself! Many people start using Twitter, get overwhelmed, and then stop using it.

If you are interested in using Twitter long term, you may want to consider using a management tool like Tweetdeck (now a part of Twitter) or Hootsuite. With tools like these, you can categorize your incoming feeds into some streams, primarily by creating searches. If you are tracking particular businesses or industries, you can create your own custom searches for hashtags or keywords. Unfortunately, neither Tweetdeck nor Hootsuite has the ability to combine multiple Twitter streams into categories, which was one of the most useful features of Tweetdeck before it was purchased by Twitter.

Another way to manage incoming information is to make use of the "lists" feature on Twitter (Figure 3.27). This is simply another way to categorize your incoming Twitter feeds, as well as a resource for finding targeted Twitter topic lists. This may be the best work-around for the loss of the categorization features in Tweetdeck.

From your homepage, if you click on the "Lists" tab, you'll see that you can create lists, as well as see which lists your Twitter feed has been added to!

When you create a list, you can name it, provide a brief description of the list, and also indicate whether it is a public or a private list (Figure 3.28). For your competitive and business purposes, you may end up keeping your lists private.

Creating a list allows you to track particular companies, industries or topics more easily. Once you create your own list, you can easily view the aggregated tweets from those accounts in one place (Figure 3.29).

| Figure 3.27 | Example of a Twitter list I've created. I can create lists on a variety of topics, and add any Twitter user to my lists to track information |

Figure 3.28 Creating a Twitter list. I have the option to make it a public or private list

Figure 3.29 Just the tweets from my infojobs Twitter list

Unfortunately, within Twitter, there is no easy way to search for other people's lists. That's where the directories mentioned above – Listorious, Twellow, and WeFollow – come in handy. These directories can quickly provide you key Twitter feeds and lists on specific topics, as well as by geography. For example, if you're interested in Twitter feeds on healthcare in the UK, a quick search in Listorious for "healthcare UK" brings up not only individual Twitter feeds from the UK Department of Health, NHS Choices, and several other individual Twitter feeds, but also a couple of compiled lists of UK health Twitter feeds (Figure 3.30).

Still looking for people to follow? As you continue to follow other Twitter feeds, Twitter starts to do a pretty good job of suggesting other feeds for you to follow (Figure 3.31).

As of this writing, Twitter suggests new feeds for you to follow in a few ways.

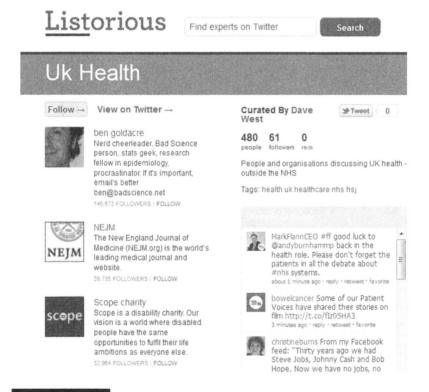

Figure 3.30   UK Health list of Twitter feeds on Listorious

- **Suggestions based on whom you already follow.** Twitter makes suggestions based upon whom you already follow – likely using an algorithm that looks at the feeds followed by the people you follow, among other things (Figure 3.32).

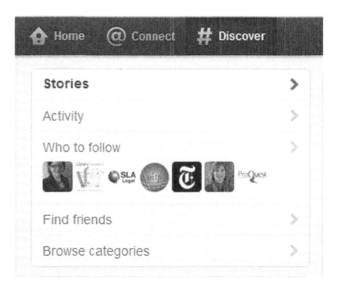

Figure 3.31 The Twitter "Discover" categories. Twitter offers a lot of different ways to find other Twitter feeds of interest to you

Figure 3.32 Suggestions on whom to follow

- **Feeds by interest area.** Twitter does offer categorized feeds by topic area, but these are typically very broad topic areas, such as government, fashion, books, music, and news (Figure 3.33).
- **Friends' Twitter feeds.** Twitter offers the ability to search for friends who are using Twitter based on your email accounts (Gmail, Yahoo!, and others), as well as based on your LinkedIn connections (Figure 3.34).
- **Search.** You can search for Twitter feeds by a person's name or by a topic keyword.

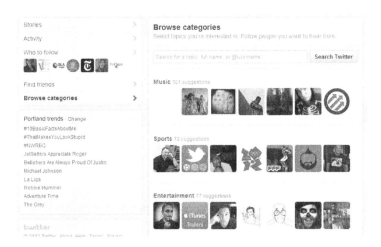

Figure 3.33   Categories and feeds that may be of interest to me

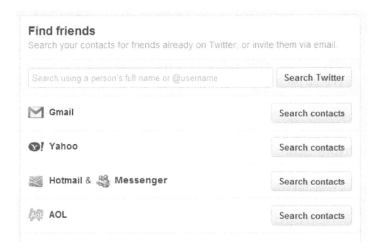

Figure 3.34   Friend finder options on Twitter

Similar to Pew Internet

 hrheingold Howard Rheingold · Follow
Independent thinker, online instigator, novice educator, expert learner, offline gardener.

 SunFoundation Sunlight Foundation · Follow
Working to change the relationship between citizens and their government with Internet technology.

Figure 3.35	Feed suggestions based on my recent content sharing in Twitter

One additional way Twitter suggests feeds is by looking at recent topics or keywords you have mentioned in your tweets. In Figure 3.35, Twitter is suggesting additional feeds to me based on the fact that I recently mentioned the Pew Research Center's Internet & American Life Project Twitter feed, @PewInternet.

Finally, before you get overwhelmed and quit Twitter altogether before you've even started, keep in mind that you can step in and out of the Twitter "stream." One of the positive and negative qualities of Twitter is its "always-on," real-time, 24-hour flood of information. I find it best to accept that I will never be able to capture and process *all* of the information available via Twitter. It's OK to "walk away" from it occasionally, and to come back to it. If you accept that you will never be able to keep up with all the information available in Twitter, you'll live a much more peaceful and productive life.

Example 3.5: Business example using Twitter

For our business example, let's take a look at a company in the oil and gas industry. Gulfsands Petroleum (*http://www.gulfsands.com*) is an independent oil and gas exploration and production company, based in London, with offices in Damascus and Houston. It has an

RSS feed available through its site, and it also happens to have a Twitter feed. To its credit, it makes its Twitter feed obvious on the main page of its website (Figure 3.36).

Let's take a look first at its Twitter feed at *http://twitter.com/ GulfsandsGPX* (Figure 3.37).

When we look at the information the company is sharing via the Twitter feed, it's pretty underwhelming (Figure 3.38). Primarily, the company is using the feed as simply another news channel. The tweets are almost exact copies of its news headlines. Its relatively small number of followers and tweets indicates a Twitter presence that is far from informative and dynamic.

In this example, do we simply accept this paucity of information, hang our heads in disappointment, and leave this Twitter feed?

WELCOME TO GULFSANDS

Gulfsands Petroleum Plc is an independent oil and gas exploration and production company, whose shares are traded on the London Stock Exchange (symbol: AIM:GPX). The Group's major focus is on the Middle East and North Africa where it has oil exploration and development projects in the Syrian Arab Republic, oil exploration projects in Tunisia, and upstream and midstream oil and gas business development activities in Iraq. Gulfsands also produces oil and gas from a portfolio of properties in the USA, offshore Gulf of Mexico.

Gulfsands' vision is to become one of the pre-eminent independent exploration and production companies in the Middle East and North Africa and as a preferred operator and partner. Gulfsands is focused on acquiring and developing significant interests in high impact projects in the Middle East and North Africa.

GULF OF MEXICO | TUNISIA | SYRIA | IRAQ

COMPANY NEWS

Aug 30, 2011
Tunisia: Commencement of Drilling Operations at Sidi Dhaher-1

Aug 26, 2011
Syria Operations Update

Aug 24, 2011
Syria Sanctions and Commercial Relationships with Makhlouf interests

Aug 24, 2011
Notice of General Meeting: Share Buy-Back Programme

SUBSCRIPTIONS

Get News through RSS FEED

Request more Info & News updates

Follow us on Twitter

Figure 3.36 Gulfsands' main web page. Note that it makes its social activities obvious on the page

Figure 3.37   Gulfsands' main Twitter page

GulfsandsGPX Gulfsands Petroleum
#Gulfsands Petroleum announces spudding of Sidi Dhaher-1 well in #Tunisia. 33 days to drill targeting both oil and gas. bit.ly/pWNxLi
30 Aug ☆ Favorite ⟲ Retweet ↰ Reply

GulfsandsGPX Gulfsands Petroleum
#Gulfsands #Petroleum Announces #Syria Operations Update. Aug. 26, 2011. #Oil Discovered at Yousefieh East. bit.ly/ovKCiB
25 Aug

GulfsandsGPX Gulfsands Petroleum
Gulfsands Petroleum announces #Syria #Sanctions and Commercial Relationships with #Maklouf Interests: Aug. 24, 2011. bit.ly/p9EedF
24 Aug

GulfsandsGPX Gulfsands Petroleum
Gulfsands Petroleum announces Share Buy-Back Programme: Aug. 24, 2011. bit.ly/qe5I74
24 Aug

GulfsandsGPX Gulfsands Petroleum
Gulfsands Petroleum announces Syria Operations Update: August 8, 2011. KHE-19H - 5516 bopd. bit.ly/o5NPpe
7 Aug

GulfsandsGPX Gulfsands Petroleum
Gulfsands Petroleum announces Syria Operations Update: July 11, 2011. bit.ly/ofBgn0
11 Jul

Figure 3.38   Some of Gulfsands' tweets

The answer is "No." In this case, we can take three approaches:

- conduct a search for Gulfsands in Twitter search;

- utilize the #Gulfsands hashtag that the company is using to see what other information we can find;

- look closely at the Twitter account to see what other information we can discover.

Let's start with the search. If we just do a simple search for "Gulfsands" in Twitter, we get the results shown in Figure 3.39.

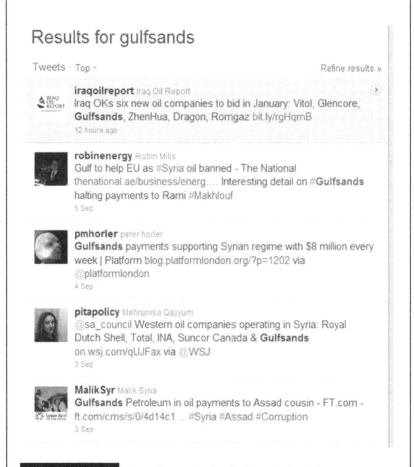

Results for gulfsands

Tweets · Top ⌄   Refine results »

iraqoilreport Iraq Oil Report
Iraq OKs six new oil companies to bid in January: Vitol, Glencore,
Gulfsands, ZhenHua, Dragon, Romgaz bit.ly/rgHqmB
12 hours ago

robinenergy Robin Mills
Gulf to help EU as #Syria oil banned - The National
thenational.ae/business/energ.... Interesting detail on #**Gulfsands**
halting payments to Rami #Makhlouf
5 Sep

pmhorler peter horler
Gulfsands payments supporting Syrian regime with $8 million every
week | Platform blog.platformlondon.org/?p=1202 via
@platformlondon
4 Sep

pitapolicy Mehrunisa Qayyum
@sa_council Western oil companies operating in Syria: Royal
Dutch Shell, Total, INA, Suncor Canada & **Gulfsands**
on.wsj.com/qUJFax via @WSJ
3 Sep

MalikSyr Malik Syria
Gulfsands Petroleum in oil payments to Assad cousin - FT.com -
ft.com/cms/s/0/4d14c1... #Syria #Assad #Corruption
3 Sep

Figure 3.39 Search results for Gulfsands in Twitter

Looking at this handful of results, there is some potential gold here. What did we find?

- **Gulfsands competitors**. The first tweet, from a stream called Iraq Oil Report, shows Iraq okaying six new oil company bids in January – including Gulfsands, as well as Vitol, Glencore, ZhenHua, Dragon Oil, and Romgaz. There is also a link to an article.

- **Inside information**. The second entry points to an article about a ban on Syrian oil. Only at the very end of the article is any mention of Gulfsands: "Gulfsands Petroleum, a British oil company, halted payments last month to a cousin of Mr. Al Assad and temporarily stripped him of voting rights. The cousin, Rami Maklouf, owns 5.75 per cent of the UK company."[2] This tiny bit of information has just given us some ownership information on this independent company, as well as a name to research, and some information on potential issues within the company. Quite a mini-goldmine!

- **Potential legal and operating issues.** The third tweet points to a blog entry about Gulfsands, with further information about the payments mentioned in the second tweet and article. The blog entry discusses issues that Gulfsands has had in ties with Syria, and provides a few links to news articles from Financial Times and Reuters, as well as Gulfsands news releases, for more information.

All this, based on a simple keyword search in Twitter!

Let's now follow the #Gulfsands hashtag. If we simply click on the hashtag, we will pull up search results for that hashtag (Figure 3.40).

As mentioned earlier, Twitter seems to limit the number of results on its hashtag searches. This example pulled up only what seem to be tweets with the #Gulfsands hashtag from the last week – one tweet. From the Gulfsands Twitter feed, we saw that Gulfsands has been using this hashtag – but none of its tweets show up in the hashtag search.

Results for #Gulfsands

Tweets · Top ⌄   Refine results »

robinenergy Robin Mills   ⟩
Gulf to help EU as #Syria oil banned - The National
thenational.ae/business/energ.... Interesting detail on #Gulfsands
halting payments to Rami #Makhlouf
5 Sep

Figure 3.40   **#Gulfsands hashtag search in Twitter**

So, in this example, our hashtag search was not particularly fruitful, since we had already found this one tweet from our Gulfsands search.

Before we leave our Twitter investigation, let's look more closely at Gulfsands' Twitter profile and feed. What can we learn from that?

If we look back at Gulfsands' main Twitter profile page (see Figure 3.37), we can gain some information about Gulfsands, its social media presence, and the oil and gas industry. We can learn information not only about the industry, but also about how the industry is using social media.

- If we scroll all the way down to the beginning of Gulfsands' tweeting (a luxury that we rarely have, simply because most accounts are much more active), we see that it started tweeting in May 2010. Back up at the top, we see that, as of this screenshot, it has tweeted only 51 times since May 2010. Additionally, as we've seen, its tweets are exclusively news and press releases re-purposed. What could we surmise from all of this?

  - Gulfsands was (and presumably is) interested in social media, and, in particular, Twitter as a way to build presence in the online world.

- Though it is using hashtags and URL shorteners, it's not really putting a lot of time and effort into Twitter – based on usage, frequency and type of tweets, low number of followers of Gulfsands (77), and low number of feeds that Gulfsands is following (35).

- Next, let's look at the Twitter feeds Gulfsands is following. Looking at the feeds that an organization is following gives you a sense of which companies, topics, and people the organization thinks are important. Looking at those feeds also points you to additional companies and industry resources that could be valuable to investigate further. In looking at the 35 feeds that Gulfsands is following, here are some things we might notice:

  - Gulfsands follows a lot of London-based sources. This is partly to be expected, since the Gulfsands headquarters is in the UK. It might also indicate a certain Euro-centricity of the organization.

  - There is an interesting mix of country Twitter feeds that Gulfsands is following: Iraq, Tunisia, Syria. While the company's website and news feeds may already have indicated these geographical focus areas for the company, it is worthwhile noting that the company is interested enough in these locations that it follows them on Twitter. Additionally, you, as a researcher, may be interested in looking at these feeds to see what information you can gather about these regions through their Twitter feeds.

  - Gulfsands is following some industry publications that will be worthwhile to look at more closely: *Upstream*, *World Oil Online*, *Oil & Gas Journal*, among others (Figure 3.41).

  - At the end of its follower lists, you can see that Gulfsands follows several global oil and gas company Twitter feeds, including Chevron, BP, and Shell, among others.

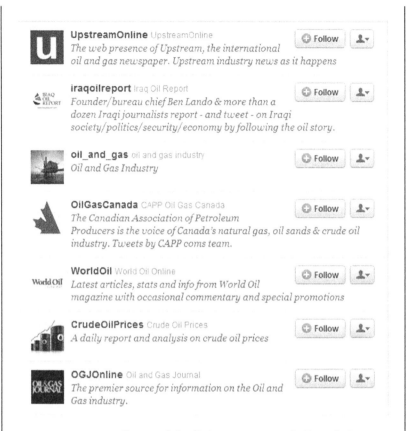

UpstreamOnline UpstreamOnline   ⊕ Follow   ⟁▾
The web presence of Upstream, the international oil and gas newspaper. Upstream industry news as it happens

iraqoilreport Iraq Oil Report   ⊕ Follow   ⟁▾
Founder/bureau chief Ben Lando & more than a dozen Iraqi journalists report - and tweet - on Iraqi society/politics/security/economy by following the oil story.

oil_and_gas oil and gas industry   ⊕ Follow   ⟁▾
Oil and Gas Industry

OilGasCanada CAPP Oil Gas Canada   ⊕ Follow   ⟁▾
The Canadian Association of Petroleum Producers is the voice of Canada's natural gas, oil sands & crude oil industry. Tweets by CAPP coms team.

WorldOil World Oil Online   ⊕ Follow   ⟁▾
Latest articles, stats and info from World Oil magazine with occasional commentary and special promotions

CrudeOilPrices Crude Oil Prices   ⊕ Follow   ⟁▾
A daily report and analysis on crude oil prices

OGJOnline Oil and Gas Journal   ⊕ Follow   ⟁▾
The premier source for information on the Oil and Gas industry.

Figure 3.41 Some of the Twitter accounts Gulfsands is following

- To add to our collection of relevant Twitter feeds in the oil and gas industry, let's look at who is following the Gulfsands feed (Figure 3.42).

  - From the screenshot in Figure 3.42, we find more pointers to other players in this market, whether they are direct competitors of Gulfsands or not. For example, we see Nordic Oil and Gas, another independent company based in Manitoba. We also see other related companies, such as NORSACO, a Norwegian development advisory company, as well as Mansfield Oil Company, a distribution company.

Figure 3.42   Followers of Gulfsands' Twitter account

– We also find EIN Shell News, an interesting resource specific to an individual company. If we scroll further down the list of Gulfsands' followers, we continue to find additional companies and news sources specific to Gulfsands and the oil and gas industry. We also find several followers who have no special relevance to our purposes.

Finally, let's look at the Twitter lists of which the Gulfsands Twitter feed is a member. On the Gulfsands profile, we see a link to the lists (Figure 3.43).

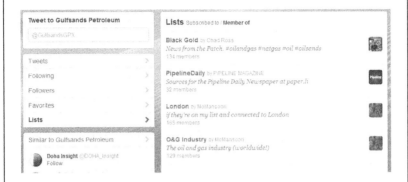

Figure 3.43   Twitter lists of which Gulfsands is a member

- Of the four lists, two may be of interest to us. The last list, O&G Industry, will likely give us additional industry and expert Twitter feeds. If we take a look at this list, we see it is following 130 Twitter accounts in the oil and gas industry. If we click on the "Following" tab, we see a mix of industry sources: individuals tweeting about the industry, companies, and job boards (which may be another valuable resource, depending on what information we're seeking) (Figure 3.44). It's always worthwhile to also take a look at the person who has put together the list – is that person a particular expert or contact for the industry?

- The other list of interest, PipelineDaily, is very interesting indeed. This list was put together by @PIPELINEtweets, for the purpose of creating a paper.li resource. (More about paper.li in just a bit.) Just like the O&G Industry list, we can take a look at the "Following" tab for this list (Figure 3.45). Again, we see many rich sources for information on the oil and gas industry: Saudi Aramco, OPEC News, Platts Gas, and EIA Gov, which provides statistics from the US government on the energy industry. For any researcher tracking this industry, these feeds will provide real-time information and "buzz" on trends, companies, and events.

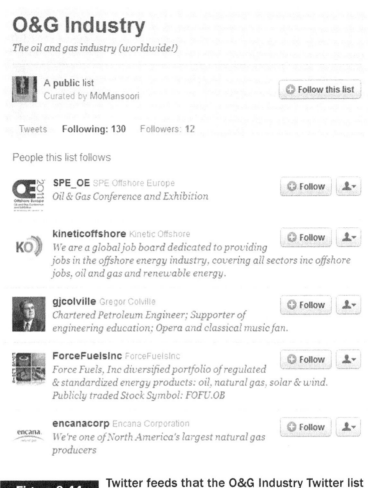

O&G Industry

The oil and gas industry (worldwide!)

A public list
Curated by MoMansoori

⊕ Follow this list

Tweets   **Following: 130**   Followers: 12

People this list follows

SPE_OE SPE Offshore Europe
Oil & Gas Conference and Exhibition

⊕ Follow ♦▾

kineticoffshore Kinetic Offshore
We are a global job board dedicated to providing jobs in the offshore energy industry, covering all sectors inc offshore jobs, oil and gas and renewable energy.

⊕ Follow ♦▾

gjcolville Gregor Colville
Chartered Petroleum Engineer; Supporter of engineering education; Opera and classical music fan.

⊕ Follow ♦▾

ForceFuelsInc ForceFuelsInc
Force Fuels, Inc diversified portfolio of regulated & standardized energy products: oil, natural gas, solar & wind. Publicly traded Stock Symbol: FOFU.OB

⊕ Follow ♦▾

encanacorp Encana Corporation
We're one of North America's largest natural gas producers

⊕ Follow ♦▾

Figure 3.44   Twitter feeds that the O&G Industry Twitter list is following

– What is paper.li? Paper.li (*http://paper.li*) is a free online utility that allows anyone to create a "real-time" online newspaper from any Twitter feed (Figure 3.46).

   The advantage of using Twitter lists is that you can create a Twitter list on a topic area (as we have seen), and then feed that into paper.li to create very specific and focused "gazette-style" online newspapers.

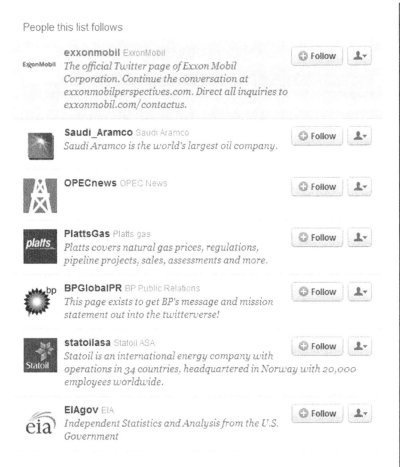

People this list follows

exxonmobil ExxonMobil   Follow
The official Twitter page of Exxon Mobil Corporation. Continue the conversation at exxonmobilperspectives.com. Direct all inquiries to exxonmobil.com/contactus.

Saudi_Aramco Saudi Aramco   Follow
Saudi Aramco is the world's largest oil company.

OPECnews OPEC News   Follow

PlattsGas Platts gas   Follow
Platts covers natural gas prices, regulations, pipeline projects, sales, assessments and more.

BPGlobalPR BP Public Relations   Follow
This page exists to get BP's message and mission statement out into the twitterverse!

statoilasa Statoil ASA   Follow
Statoil is an international energy company with operations in 34 countries, headquartered in Norway with 20,000 employees worldwide.

EIAgov EIA   Follow
Independent Statistics and Analysis from the U.S. Government

Figure 3.45   Twitter feeds that the PipelineDaily Twitter list is following

So what have we found from our example with Gulfsands? Are we disappointed because Gulfsands hasn't done much with its Twitter feed? We found:

- competitor information;

- some leads on inside information;

- some leads on potential legal and ethical entanglements;

- some insight into Gulfsands' efforts in and commitment to social media;

Figure 3.46   Example of a paper.li on the Alaskan oil and gas industry

- some insight into geographic areas where Gulfsands operates, or intends to operate;

- some terrific company, industry, and publication Twitter feeds that will continue to give us further information and buzz about the oil and gas industry.

All this from a Twitter feed that isn't very active or impressive! (Sorry, Gulfsands.)

Example 3.6: Non-profit organization

For our non-profit example, let's look at the Twitter feed (@the1010project) for The 1010 Project (*http://www.the1010 project.org*), a non-profit organization focused on breaking the cycle of poverty (Figure 3.47).

The 1010 Project is definitely an active Twitter user: as of this screenshot, 1632 tweets, 3446 followers, and on a multitude of lists!

Figure 3.47 The 1010 Project on Twitter

(Unfortunately, the new Twitter interface doesn't allow you to see a rolled-up number of lists that include a particular Twitter account.) The 1010 Project account is also following over 2000 other Twitter accounts. If we look at the organization's website (by following the link in the Twitter bio), we see that the organization is using a few different social media tools in addition to Twitter, including Facebook and YouTube. This all indicates to us that The 1010 Project actively uses social media as a part of its marketing and awareness strategy.

We can use all the techniques we used with our business example for our non-profit example. Let's start by looking at a sample of tweets. In reviewing some recent tweets, we see that the organization uses its Twitter feed to promote its events and causes, and to share news about its areas of focus and global charity (Figure 3.48). This is all relatively typical, and to be expected. Let's see what information we can find that is unique to this organization.

In reviewing this small selection of tweets, we get a bit more insight about The 1010 Project. In the first tweet, we see that it indicates that the organization Ecta International shares office space with The 1010 Project. This bit of information tells us two

the1010project The 1010 Project
Our ECTA friends share office space with us! RT @ECTAendeavors: New Blog! Check out what ECTA's got coming up. bit.ly/oAt2Ut
4 Oct

the1010project The 1010 Project
Still time to buy your discounted tickets to Rapids vs. FC Dallas game and support @the1010project this Saturday: bit.ly/mYH2J3
29 Sep

the1010project The 1010 Project
Shop for a Cause Holiday Gift Market returns - Get all your info here: bit.ly/nFF7pC
29 Sep

the1010project The 1010 Project
Wangari Maathai, founder of the Green Belt Movement and Nobel Peace Prize winner, has died: nyti.ms/pSAVMl
26 Sep

the1010project The 1010 Project
@GivingFirst Thanks for the RT, GivingFirst. Your platform is a great addition to our fundraising!
26 Sep

Figure 3.48 A selection of tweets from The 1010 Project

things: one, we have a lead for finding out the location of the offices, and who else might be in the building; and two, we potentially have some insight into what other partnerships or connections The 1010 Project may have with other non-profit organizations.

In the next two tweets, we get some information on events and promotions that The 1010 Project is sponsoring.

In the last tweet, which is a response to another organization, Giving First, we have a lead to another possible partner organization, as well as some information as to how that organization might work with The 1010 Project ("Your platform is a great addition to our fundraising!").

In just this short selection of tweets, we are able to get some leads and insight into connections that might not otherwise be obvious.

As of this writing, The 1010 Project Twitter account follows 2182 other accounts. Based on 3446 followers, the account follows about two-thirds of the accounts that follow it. While The 1010 Project is observing good Twitter etiquette by following back a lot of its followers, this is not necessarily good for us in finding leads. It would take some time and dedication to go through all 2182 accounts to find the relevant leads! If we take a look at just a few accounts that it follows, we immediately see only one account that stands out: ECTAendeavors, which is the same organization mentioned in a recent tweet (Figure 3.49).

Let's take a step back and look at both the individuals that The 1010 Project follows, and the list of accounts following The 1010 Project. If we look at these lists from the point of view of a non-profit organization similar to The 1010 Project, we essentially have access to a very good "leads" list – people and Twitter accounts

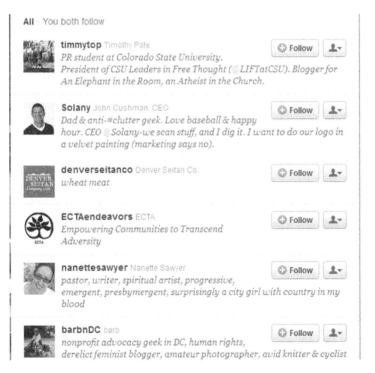

All · You both follow

timmytop Timothy Pate
PR student at Colorado State University.
President of CSU Leaders in Free Thought (@LIFTatCSU). Blogger for
An Elephant in the Room, an Atheist in the Church.

Solany John Cushman, CEO
Dad & anti-#clutter geek. Love baseball & happy
hour. CEO @Solany-we scan stuff, and I dig it. I want to do our logo in
a velvet painting (marketing says no).

denverseitanco Denver Seitan Co.
wheat meat

ECTAendeavors ECTA
Empowering Communities to Transcend
Adversity

nanettesawyer Nanette Sawyer
pastor, writer, spiritual artist, progressive,
emergent, presbymergent, surprisingly a city girl with country in my
blood

barbnDC barb
nonprofit advocacy geek in DC, human rights,
derelict feminist blogger, amateur photographer, avid knitter & cyclist

Figure 3.49 Some of the Twitter accounts The 1010 Project follows. ECTAendeavors is fourth down the list

that are interested in initiatives like The 1010 Project. If I were part of a non-profit organization and were interested in building followers of my Twitter feed, I would be very interested in following both the accounts following The 1010 Project and the accounts The 1010 Project follows. (The same would hold true for any organization – for-profit organizations, educational institutions, etc.)

Before we wrap up this example, let's look at the lists on which The 1010 Project is listed. As of this writing, the Twitter account is listed on 268 lists! Again, that is a large number of lists to scan – but what can we find?

In looking at just a small selection of these lists, we see that people are generally categorizing The 1010 Project feed with non-profits, charities, and NGOs (non-governmental organizations), and also with other organizations located in the Denver/Boulder/Colorado area (Figure 3.50).

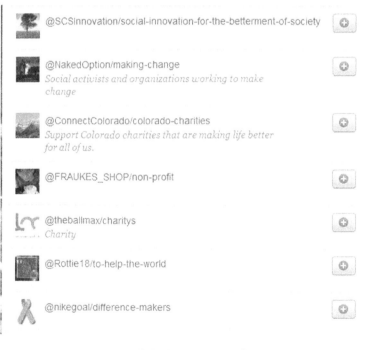

Figure 3.50   **Some of the Twitter lists of which The 1010 Project is a member**

For any list topic, you'll likely find a pretty good list of other Twitter accounts to follow. While some of the examples here are likely too broad for our purposes, one example we see listed here is a list called Colorado Charities, put together or "curated" by an account called ConnectColorado. When we click on the list and go to the "Following" tab to see the accounts included in the list, we get an impressive list of Colorado-based charities with Twitter feeds – as of this writing, close to 500 feeds! (Figure 3.51)

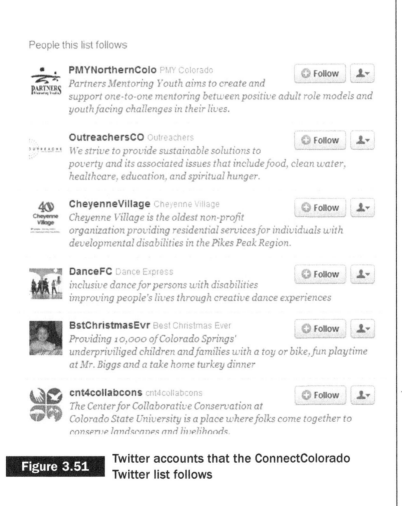

People this list follows

PMYNorthernColo PMY Colorado   ⊕ Follow ↴
Partners Mentoring Youth aims to create and support one-to-one mentoring between positive adult role models and youth facing challenges in their lives.

OutreachersCO Outreachers   ⊕ Follow ↴
We strive to provide sustainable solutions to poverty and its associated issues that include food, clean water, healthcare, education, and spiritual hunger.

CheyenneVillage Cheyenne Village   ⊕ Follow ↴
Cheyenne Village is the oldest non-profit organization providing residential services for individuals with developmental disabilities in the Pikes Peak Region.

DanceFC Dance Express   ⊕ Follow ↴
inclusive dance for persons with disabilities improving people's lives through creative dance experiences

BstChristmasEvr Best Christmas Ever   ⊕ Follow ↴
Providing 10,000 of Colorado Springs' underpriviliged children and families with a toy or bike, fun playtime at Mr. Biggs and a take home turkey dinner

cnt4collabcons cnt4collabcons   ⊕ Follow ↴
The Center for Collaborative Conservation at Colorado State University is a place where folks come together to conserve landscapes and livelihoods.

Figure 3.51   Twitter accounts that the ConnectColorado Twitter list follows

A good general rule in reviewing lists on Twitter is to look for two things:

- **Lists that have specific topic names**. A list of "Colorado businesses," for example, is likely not going to be very helpful – and probably will provide so much information that you'll quickly get overwhelmed. A more targeted list, such as the Colorado Charities list we found, is going to be more helpful and (hopefully) less overwhelming.

- **Lists curated by organizations**, if you can find them. This is not to say that lists curated by individuals are not valuable – in fact, excellent lists are put together by many individuals. However, organization lists will often list other organization feeds, which will help you quickly build your information "pipeline."

A final tip on looking at lists: if you scroll *all* the way down to the end of the list of 268 lists on which The 1010 Project is listed, you'll see the first accounts that included The 1010 Project feed on their lists. Why would you want to do this? While it's a bit of a far-reaching strategy, often the first people who put a Twitter account on a list are going to be people very close to or involved with that organization. This is, admittedly, an oblique strategy, but it may provide you additional clues to the organization, its founding, and its connections.

So what did we find in looking at The 1010 Project's Twitter feed? At a quick glance, we found:

- events and promotions in which The 1010 Project is involved;

- information on potential partners of the organization;

- some terrific organization and industry Twitter feeds that will continue to give us further information and buzz in this area.

In this example of The 1010 Project, we reviewed only a small sample of its tweets. If you are seriously tracking an organization, you will want to review a much larger selection of tweets to look for trends.

Why would we "stalk" a non-profit organization in this way? In other words, why would we take a competitive view of a non-profit organization? Shouldn't we be nicer to charitable organizations?

Part of what I hope to illustrate is that we certainly can approach any organization – non-profit or otherwise – from a competitive standpoint. Every organization has to have some consideration about keeping its doors open – in other words, making at least enough money to keep operations going. Because of this, every organization has at least some competitive drive. The type of information we're uncovering can help with understanding the competition and the market.

Another way to approach this research is in the interest of understanding the competitors and the market with the goal of improving one's own practices – seeing and understanding what other "players" in the industry are doing with social tools, and potentially leveraging those practices in the promotion of the organization. If a strictly competitive approach seems distasteful – especially in the realm of non-profits or other altruistic endeavors – think of this research approach as a way to find best practices in social marketing. And, of course, there is no reason why the two approaches can't be undertaken at the same time.

Additional Twitter tools

In addition to simply going through the tweets in a feed, there are tools that can help you to more quickly identify high-level trends and discussions in Twitter. Because Twitter has an open API – meaning that software developers can build tools to interface with Twitter and the information in Twitter – there are a multitude of tools that aggregate the tweets from any particular Twitter feed in different ways. While I don't have the space to discuss them all here (and they are constantly emerging, changing, and going away), we'll look at some broad categories of Twitter tools and some of the current tools in those categories.

Graphical representations

These tools typically take the content from a Twitter feed and represent it graphically. A few examples are given in Table 3.1.

As you can see, there are a lot of interesting Twitter tools out there. Word clouds in particular are one interesting way to quickly get a sense of a Twitter feed's topics. (This tip thanks to Marcia Rodney of RSL Research.)

Table 3.1   Graphical Twitter tools

Name	Unique feature(s)
Tweet Topic Explorer	Displays keywords of a Twitter feed, with larger circles for words used more often, and color coding to locate those words in the Twitter stream.
Trendsmap	Trendsmap is a mash-up of Twitter feeds and a world map, so that you can search for any keyword or hashtag and see real-time tweets superimposed on a map. (Figure 3.52)
Mirror.me	By entering a user's Twitter handle, you can quickly and easily get a word cloud of that user's feed. A quick and easy way to see the topics from a Twitter feed. (Figure 3.53)
Wordle	Wordle is similar to Mirror.me, but not specific to Twitter. You can paste in blocks of text or submit an RSS feed, and Wordle will create a word cloud based on that content.
NearbyTweets	Similar to Trendsmap, NearbyTweets allows you to find keywords and hashtags in tweets specific to a location. However, NearbyTweets does not provide the map function of Trendsmap. (Figure 3.54)

Figure 3.52   Trendsmap. This example illustrates a search for #occupy, the hashtag associated with the Occupy Wall Street movement. The size of the hashtags on the map indicates the amount of activity coming from that area. By clicking down into those hashtags, you can view the specific tweets coming from those locations

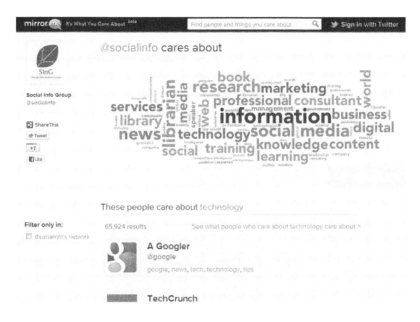

Figure 3.53
Mirror.me example, using @socialinfo. Not only can you quickly and easily see the topics in the feed; you can also click on any of the terms to bring up other Twitter accounts that use that term frequently. In this example, I clicked on "technology"

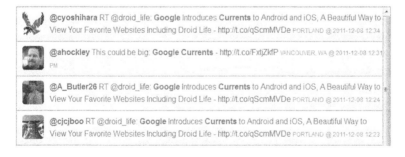

Figure 3.54
NearbyTweets. In this example, I use Portland, Oregon as the location and Google Currents as the topic. Real-time updates scroll in

Twitter feed analyzers

In general, these tools look at the content from tweets and provide some kind of aggregated view and/or analysis of the content. There are many Twitter feed analyzers, as well as many that have come and gone, and more that will emerge well after this writing. Table 3.2 shows a few of the best as of April 2012.

Table 3.2   Twitter feed analyzers

Name	Unique feature(s)
Twtrland	Twtrland provides concise analysis on frequency and content of tweets, top followers for a Twitter account, and aggregates recent images shared on the account. (Figure 3.55)
TweetReach	Search for a URL, Twitter handle, keyword or hashtag, and TweetReach finds tweets that match your search and reports back on the reach and exposure for those tweets. (Figure 3.56)
Tweetgrid	Tweetgrid allows you to compare up to nine Twitter searches (hashtag, keyword, user) in real time. (Figure 3.57).

Figure 3.55   Twtrland. In this example, you see an analysis of the New York Times Twitter feed, @nytimes. You can see information on top followers, most retweeted tweets, types of tweets, etc.

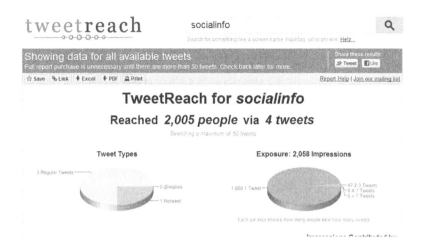

TweetReach example using socialinfo. With TweetReach, you can get a sense of how followers of a Twitter account interact with that account: Do they retweet it a lot? Does it get a lot of activity and attention?

Figure 3.56

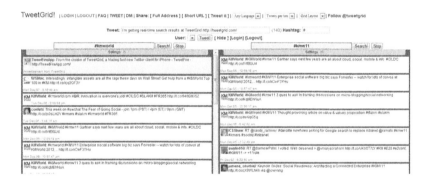

Tweetgrid. This example compares the two hashtags #kmworld and #km11. Tweetgrid may be helpful if you are tracking two or more breaking stories on Twitter

Figure 3.57

Caveats

As with all social media, you never know how much or how little you'll find. Also, be sure to cross-check your information if possible.

Some more specific caveats for blogs and for microblogs are given below.

Blogs

- **Check into the credentials and qualifications of bloggers.** While, in general, blogs are more reliable and "transparent" sources than microblogs – simply by the nature of their setup and the amount of content shared via blogs – it is critical that you follow up on the credentials of any blog that you rely on for information. Responsible bloggers will provide information about themselves and their background and credentials plainly on their blogs. Even blogs produced by groups will provide information and links to the authors. If you find blogger information difficult to find or non-existent, be wary (Figure 3.58).

For example, if we look at the IBM Research blog in Figure 3.58, it certainly looks official. The design is clean, the IBM Research Facebook page is linked on the site, and IBM Twitter feeds are fed into the blog. However, if we look for authorship information, there is no "about" link, and no easy way to find who is responsible for the blog. Granted, this could be due to poor practices on the part of IBM Research – however, these clues alert us that we should investigate this blog more deeply before accepting it as an "official" IBM Research blog.

Figure 3.58   Example IBM Research blog. Is this the "real" IBM Research blog?

Another clue is the URL: *http://ibmresearchnews.blogspot.com/*. It would be unusual for a top global company to utilize a URL with "blogspot" in it.

One way to investigate the ownership of a site is to utilize WhoIs (*http://whois.net*). WhoIs can help you find the owner behind URL domains. However, it may not work with blog links, such as BlogSpot.

Another way to approach this is to look for "vetted" lists of official company blogs. In our example of IBM, we can find lists on the IBM. com site of syndicated feeds, at *http://www.ibm.com/blogs/zz/en/*. In reviewing this list, I was unable to find the IBM Research blog. In the interest of confirming the authenticity of an organizational blog, it would be worthwhile to examine an organization site carefully to identify the "official" blogs of the organization.

Finally, I conducted a search for "IBM Research blogs". I was finally led to the IBM Research Almaden page at *http://www.almaden. ibm.com/*, which had a link on the left to several IBM Research social properties – including the IBM Research blog, which is indeed listed as *http://ibmresearchnews.blogspot.com/* (Figure 3.59).

While I have to admit that a thread of skepticism remains on my part, it seems that we have confirmed that this is an official IBM Research

Figure 3.59 IBM Research – Almaden web page. See IBM Research blog link in lower left corner. This does indeed link to the IBM Research blog at *http://ibmresearchnews. blogspot.com*

blog, and you've seen a bit of the process of verifying a blog. However, I will state again that I am surprised that the IBM Research blog does not provide a more transparent and well-documented blog.

Due to the fact that anyone can create a blog and, potentially, make their blog look "official," it's important to be sure you aren't relying on information posing as "official" that is actually being produced by another source.

Microblogs

- **Look for "verified" Twitter accounts.** Because so many "spoof" and unofficial accounts were being created – for example, see the Fake Steve Jobs Twitter feed at *https://twitter.com/#!/FSJ* – Twitter recently began verifying accounts, and making this information more obvious on the site. When you see the blue-checked "Verified" account, you can be relatively sure you are looking at the official account of that entity (although as of this writing, an account "verified" by Twitter was actually revealed to not be a verified account) (Figure 3.60).

| **Figure 3.60** | Example search for Microsoft accounts in Twitter. The blue checks indicate "verified" accounts. You can see verified accounts for Microsoft, Windows, and Microsoft News in this screenshot |

- **Verify your information closely.** I re-emphasize this because Twitter is increasingly becoming a place for the circulation of rumors and misinformation – especially in breaking-news and disaster situations. Often times, false or doctored photos also circulate via Twitter – many of which are later proved to be fake. For example, during the riots in London in late 2011, a photo of the London Eye burning as a result of the riots was circulating via Twitter – when actually no such thing happened. What's interesting is that many news agencies are stepping into the role of verifying and correcting misinformation circulating via Twitter.

  In the case of breaking news, then, verifying the information gathered via Twitter against reliable news-reporting sources can help you make sure that you have the correct information.

Protecting your information

Obviously, if you are simply looking at blogs and Twitter feeds without creating a blog or Twitter account yourself, you don't need to worry too much about protecting your information. If you are utilizing these types of tools yourself, both blogs and microblogs typically request less "profile" information than do tools such as LinkedIn and Facebook. You have more control over the amount of information you share via these tools. However, there are a few best practices in utilizing these tools yourself.

Blogs

- **Decide how you want to accept comments.** Do you want to allow "anonymous" comments? Do you want comments at all? Do you want to approve them prior to their being posted? Do you want to "lock them down" after a few months? Typically, with any blog platform, you can fine-tune how you handle comments.

  There are no "hard and fast" or general rules around accepting comments. There are good reasons why you might allow anonymous comments – for example, if you are posting and starting conversations on sensitive topics where people might be discouraged from engaging in the conversation if they were identified. For general discussion around topics that aren't highly sensitive, I would recommend not allowing anonymous posts, and choosing the option of reviewing all comments before allowing them to be posted.

Microblogs

- **To protect your tweets or not?** When setting up a Twitter account, you do have the option to "protect" your tweets. This means that people cannot start following your account without your approving them to do so, and that your tweets don't appear "publicly." In other words, people cannot see your tweets unless they are connected to you – and you get to decide who is connected to you.

  There are legitimate reasons to protect your tweets – especially since we've been exploring ways to mine others' tweets for information! Depending upon your use of Twitter, you may not want others seeing your tweets, your followers, and who you are following. If you are using Twitter to give yourself more visibility as an expert yourself, then you probably don't want to protect your tweets. You always have the option to create more than one Twitter account, and to use them for different purposes. It's up to you to make a decision about whether or not you protect your tweets.

  Do keep in mind that, once a person is connected with you, they can not only see your tweets; they can also see whom you follow and who is following you.

- **Profile information.** You can put as much or as little information in your profile as you like. Again, depending upon your usage of Twitter, you may choose to put identifying information and links in your profile, or you may choose to put no information in your profile. For example, if I'm utilizing a Twitter account simply to follow some Twitter feeds, I may not put any information in my profile, because I don't care whether people follow me or not. However, if I'm using it as a way to participate in the conversations on Twitter, and to connect with other people, then it's in my interest to at least put some identifying information in my Twitter profile.

Other tools in this category

Blog platforms will continue to change and evolve as online publishing tools, and so blogs will continue to be rich sources of business and industry information. New tools for searching and finding blogs will continue to emerge as well.

Many blog-listing sites these days are "opt-in" sites – in other words, you would need to add a blog to the site in order for it to show up, unlike a search engine, which actively searches for blogs on the open web. While the opt-in nature of blog-listing sites can be limiting in finding a complete list of blogs for a particular topic or keyword, the opt-in model can sometimes be helpful in finding blogs in a more orderly fashion – even though you may not find *all* the blogs you're seeking.

For example, Bloglines Local allows you to find local blogs in the United States. Suppose you are investigating bloggers in a particular city in the United States. Bloglines Local can help you find blogs down to a specific city in a specific state (Figure 3.61).

What's the advantage of a tool like this? For a traveler, Bloglines Local is a great way to get a sense of a city in the US prior to visiting. From a business or industry perspective, local blogs can often give a sense of the people, culture, business, and events of a city. In the screenshot for Indianapolis, Indiana (Figure 3.62), we not only see general blogs about Indianapolis, but also blogs about Indianapolis real estate, news, and arts.

Blogging and microblogging features continue to be embedded in other online tools. For example, Facebook and LinkedIn updates are very similar in function to microblogging: you can post links, photos, and short updates easily. Blogging platforms such as WordPress have evolved well beyond just being blogging tools, and now provide content

Top Cities Listing

Albuquerque, NM	Milwaukee, WI
Anchorage, AK	Minneapolis, MN
Atlanta, GA	Nashville, TN
Austin, TX	New York, NY
Birmingham, AL	Oklahoma City, OK
Boston, MA	Omaha, NE
Boise, ID	Orlando, FL
Brooklyn, NY	Philadelphia, PA
Charlotte, NC	Phoenix, AZ
Cleveland, OH	Pittsburgh, PA
Chicago, IL	Portland, OR
Cincinnati, OH	Raleigh, NC
Colorado Springs, CO	Rochester, NY
Columbus, OH	Sacramento, CA
Dallas, TX	San Antonio, TX
Denver, CO	San Francisco, CA
Fort Lauderdale, FL	San Jose, CA
Houston, TX	Saint Louis, MO
Indianapolis, IN	Saint Paul, MN
Jacksonville, FL	Salt Lake City, UT
Kansas City, MO	San Diego, CA
Los Angeles, CA	Scottsdale, AZ
Las Vegas, NV	Seattle, WA
Louisville, KY	Spokane, WA
Memphis, TN	Tampa, FL
Mesa, AZ	Tucson, AZ
Miami, FL	Tulsa, OK

All States

AL, AK, AZ, AR, CA, CO, CT, DE, DC, FL, GA, HI, ID, IL, IN, IA, KS, KY, LA, MA, MD, ME, MI, MN, MO, MS, MT, NC, ND, NE, NH, NJ, NM, NV, NY, OH, OK, OR, PA, RI, SC, SD, TN, TX, UT, VA, VT, WA, WI, WV, WY

Figure 3.61   Bloglines listing of blogs by US city and state

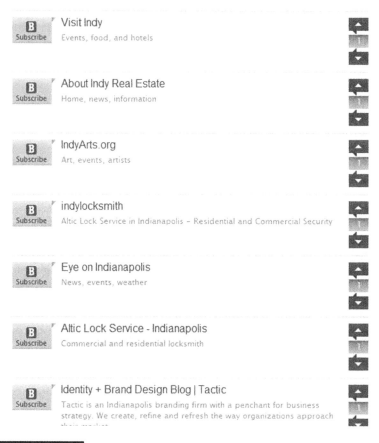

Figure 3.62   Indianapolis blog listings in Bloglines

management functionality. Entire websites, with shopping-cart functionality, are built upon the WordPress platform.

That said, standalone blogging and microblogging tools continue to evolve and change as well. A few examples:

- **Tumblr**: Tumblr is probably best described as a cross somewhere between a blog and a microblog. Tumblr positions itself as a platform to "effortlessly" share text, photos, links, videos, and other content from anywhere – a browser, a phone, via email, etc. And indeed, Tumblr is very easy to use once you get set up, and usually visually striking. It's very easy to share content from other Tumblr users' blogs, but the drawback is that there is no easy way to leave comments on others' Tumblr blogs.

- **Yammer:** Yammer is a free, "private" social microblogging tool. The idea is that you sign up with your official work email (for example, scott. brown@mycompany.com), and, as long as your official work email is verified, you are then able to communicate via Yammer with any other person using that same work email domain. In my example, I'd be able to communicate with anyone else signed in to Yammer from mycompany.com. While many companies are adopting internal microblogging tools, Yammer has served this purpose (albeit outside of the company firewall) for quite a few years. Yammer claims to be utilized by companies such as Ford, Pitney Bowes, Thomson Reuters, and LG.

- **Sharetronix:** Sharetronix bills itself as "the world's favorite open source microblogging platform," and is available in free and paid personal and business versions. Although it is based on the concept of microblogging, it has additional features not found on Twitter, such as dashboards, the ability to create groups, and the ability to create and share online "business cards."

Microblogging functionality is increasingly being integrated into social collaboration platforms. In fact, the "update" function in both Facebook and LinkedIn is essentially an integration of microblogging capabilities. I think stand-alone, generic microblogging tools like Twitter and Yammer may phase out relatively quickly in favor of social collaboration platforms that provide microblogging as just one piece of a collaboration tool. I also think you'll likely start to see more specialized microblogging platforms, focusing, for example, on specific topic areas, or on specific purposes, such as connecting investors.

Review

As we wrap up this chapter, let's review the types of information we found.

For blogs, we can find information on:

- an organization's corporate culture
- how that organization is addressing corporate social responsibility: what it is doing to be more responsible to its customers, communities and environment
- strategy, approach, and philosophy
- an "inside" view to the organization

- breaking news
- executive perspective and personality
- product news
- breaking news of a different kind from bloggers outside of the company
- product issues
- customer, partner, and stakeholder sentiment
- location information
- additional organizations and companies that participate in the industry
- perspective on the industry from people who are knowledgeable about it
- pointers to additional resources for information on the industry
- the latest "buzz" on the industry and the companies which participate in the industry

For microblogs, we can find:

- "breaking news" and news developments about an organization
- "breaking news" and news developments in an industry
- events: those sponsored by an organization, those in which an organization participates, and industry events
- product information
- sales and promotions
- pointers to other organization and industry Twitter feeds
- "live" news feeds from conferences
- competitors
- inside information
- potential legal and ethical entanglements
- some insight into the organization's efforts in and commitment to social media
- location information
- additional organization, industry, and publication Twitter feeds
- events and promotions

Because blogs and microblogs share a similar history, we've seen that we can get similar information in both tools. Each also provides its own unique information and underlying dynamics.

In the next chapter, we move from the written word to the audio and visual realm – and find more unique information there!

Notes

1. Twitter (2012) The Twitter glossary. *Twitter*. Available from: *http://support. twitter.com/entries/166337-the-twitter-glossary* [Accessed 25 April 2012].
2. A. Yee, (2011) Gulf to help EU as Syrian oil banned. *The National* (4 September). Available from: *http://www.thenational.ae/business/energy/gulf-to-help-eu-as-syrian-oil-banned* [Accessed 25 April 2012].

4

Video, audio and images

Abstract: This chapter looks specifically at finding information using video, audio, and image resources, such as YouTube, Blinkx, iTunes, Flickr, and others. Common characteristics of video, audio, and image resources are explored. For YouTube, iTunes, and Flickr, the chapter outlines the different kinds of information that can be found in these tools, and provides search examples for each tool to illustrate search techniques and results. Tips for searching each tool are provided. The chapter also explores ways to protect your personal information, and cautions on using each tool. The chapter concludes with a list of additional sources, and a review of the content covered in the chapter.

Key words: Images, photos, Flickr, Picasa, video, YouTube, Blinkx, iTunes, podcasts, online video.

What are they?

Some readers may remember the days of "green screens" – "dumb" terminals that connected to a main computer. All you ever saw on a computer screen were green lines of text; that was the extent of computer connection and experience. Some readers may also remember when fax machines were the cutting edge of technology. It seemed amazing – at the time – that I could send a picture to you using a phone line, at a relatively inexpensive price. Sure, the picture was in black and white, and never very clear, but the technology still had the ability to impress the world.

Most students entering college today have always had access to video, audio, and images via the Internet. As computing power has increased each year, the clarity and quality of image files and video streaming have steadily improved, to the point where the average person can enjoy high-quality, high-definition streaming movies over his or her computer, television, or mobile device.

These days, the popularity of video sites such as YouTube and image sites such as Flickr means that information sleuths have access to a *lot* of information. Yes, you can watch the latest Lady Gaga, Beyoncé, or U2 video on YouTube. You can post your holiday photos to share with your friends on Flickr (and on a variety of other sites, such as Facebook). However, more and more businesses, organizations, and associations are posting video, audio, and pictures as well. Businesses may post interviews with executives. Interns at companies may post video about their internship experiences. Associations may post photos of their latest service projects. These are just a few examples of the types of information you can find via video, audio, and image content.

How do they work?

Video-, audio-, and image-sharing sites primarily allow users to (relatively easily) upload this type of content for sharing, and for others to find that content. Some common features across all of these tools include:

- **Content identification, description, and tagging.** Typically, when you post content into any of these sites, you have the ability to provide a short descriptive text, as well as the ability to tag your content to make it more findable.

- **Content categorization and collections.** In YouTube, you can create "playlists" in order to categorize videos. In Flickr, you can create "galleries" to organize images and make them accessible by topic, time-frame, geography, or in any other way you wish.

- **Ease of sharing and/or embedding content.** Once you've uploaded your content, most sites then allow you to notify others about your content via social networks or other sharing mechanisms. This ability to share content extends to sharing others' content as well. For example, on YouTube, you can not only link to a video; you can also embed a video (in a blog entry, for instance), email a link to the video, or share the video via Facebook, Twitter, Google+, or a variety of other ways (Figure 4.1).

- **"Liking" or "favoriting" content.** In the YouTube screenshot in Figure 4.1, you also see the ability to give a "Like" or "Dislike" to any particular content. In many services, you can create a "favorites" list.

- **Profiles.** As in many social tools we've looked at so far, you often have the ability to provide some profile information. The type and amount you can provide will vary, depending on the service.

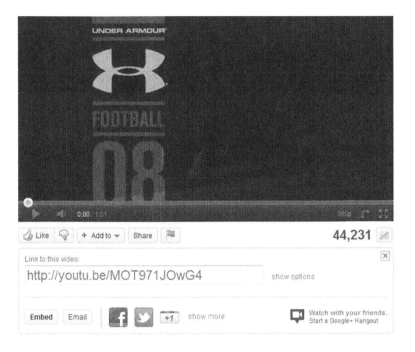

Figure 4.1   Sharing options on a YouTube video

- **User commentary.** In addition to "liking" or "favoriting" content, users often have the ability to add comments to content.
- **Search capabilities.** Content-sharing sites will have varying abilities to search for content. Some are more sophisticated than others, but most provide a basic search, and the ability to browse or search via tags.

Examples of these sites

Video

There are many video sources available. Some of the top video sites – and some of the best for relevant organization and industry content – currently include:

- **YouTube:** Probably the most well-known video site, currently. YouTube was purchased by Google in 2006.

- **Vimeo**: A growing video site that was created by film and video creators who wanted to share their work. While the site is still dominated by filmmaking content, organizations are increasingly using Vimeo as a platform for their videos.

- **Blinkx**: Essentially a video search engine. As of April 2012, Blinkx claims to provide access to over 35 million hours of video and draw from over 720 media partnership sources.

- **DailyMotion**: As of April 2012, DailyMotion boasts over 114 million unique monthly visitors, and is available in 32 localized versions.

Some video services, such as Vimeo and DailyMotion, are distinguishing themselves from YouTube in the realm of "protected content" and cracking down on copyright infringement. While YouTube seems to universally have the broadest reach, keep an eye on "smaller" services that focus on copyright and protected content. My guess is that you'll continue to see good content move into these types of services.

Audio (generally meaning podcasts)

- **iTunes**: While you can get a lot of entertainment content on iTunes, you can also access millions of podcasts.

- **Podcast Alley**: Another great source for podcasts. You can search for podcasts, or browse by topic.

Images

- **Flickr**: Currently, Flickr is one of the most popular photo-sharing sites, and it is a source we will be using for our example searches.

- **Picasa** (*http://picasaweb.google.com*): As the URL indicates, Picasa is a part of Google's offerings. Picasa (*http://picasa.google.com*) is photo-editing software offered by Google, and users can share their photos via Picasa Web Albums. One of the interesting things about Picasa is the ability to search for "Faces only" – allowing you to find pictures with people in them. Similar to Flickr, you can also search for only Creative Commons photos.

- **SmugMug**: SmugMug was developed out of a love for fine photography, and has been dedicated to helping photographers market and sell their photos. As of April 2012, SmugMug claims to be host to billions of photos. I never would have thought of SmugMug as a place to search for company or organization photos, but I've found good results in searching SmugMug along with other image sources.

We'll look at video, audio, and image sources separately as we explore the types of information available and go through our examples.

Video resource: YouTube

What is it?

YouTube promotes itself as "a forum for people to connect, inform, and inspire others across the globe and acts as a distribution platform for original content creators and advertisers large and small." It is basically a platform for people to share video clips. Some statistics from YouTube's site, as of April 2012:

- 60 hours of video are uploaded every minute; this means an hour of video is uploaded onto YouTube *every second*.
- Over 4 billion videos are viewed every day.
- 70 per cent of YouTube traffic comes from outside of the United States; the site is localized in 39 countries across 54 languages.

YouTube was acquired by Google in 2006. As of this writing, in January 2012, video shared within Google Plus is being integrated into the YouTube front page, if you are signed into your account and have a Google Plus account.

Individuals, organizations, associations, and many other entities use YouTube to share video that they have created or produced. Yes, you can also find video that likely has been uploaded illegally or in violation of copyright. YouTube regularly removes content that violates copyright.

What kind of business and competitive information can be found there?

YouTube and other video sources are good supplemental sources for business and competitive information. In many ways, they provide information that "paints a richer picture" of an organization. Some approaches and applications include:

- Searching for video of company executives. A company might post interviews or speeches by the CEO on a video site, or you might find a news clip of an executive being interviewed. Through these, you can get a sense of the CEO, his or her strategic focus, and his or her style and manner. Is he friendly? Is he irritable? Is he brusque? What topics does she come back to regularly?

- Depending upon the size and activity of the organization, you might also find product release videos, commercials, "behind the scenes" footage, and/or video of experts in the organization discussing products, technologies, or services informally. Often, you can get an "insider" view of an organization from this type of video.

- Some organizations also post video from events – organization events, trade shows and conferences, and meetings. From these types of videos, you can get a sense of what events the organization attends and/or sponsors, what they present at those events, and the organization's presence at the event (Do they have a big booth? Are they new to the event? What kind of people talk with them?).

- Increasingly, interns for organizations are posting video, discussing their desires and aspirations in working for an organization, and/or discussing their experience in their internship at an organization. This type of video is very helpful both for the potential intern who is interested in working for an organization, and for the organization in its recruitment of interns. Interns can get a sense of the experience of working for an organization from a peer who has gone through the experience. Intern videos – ideally, positive ones – help the organization recruit interns, essentially through peer marketing.

- Again, depending upon the size of the organization, you may also find "external" video from those outside of the organization talking about the organization's products or services – including product "fails." Usually if someone external is talking about it, it's negative – but that's potentially good information if you're looking for company and competitive information.

    For example, one of the things you will see posted in YouTube is product "fails." Product "fails" are examples of a product that is not working as it should, and often times, failing catastrophically. For an example, search for "laptop fire" on YouTube, and you'll see some pretty dramatic instances (Figure 4.2).

These are just a few examples of the type of information you might find via YouTube.

Figure 4.2 Laptop fire video on YouTube

How do you get started using it?

The beauty of a tool like YouTube, in contrast with social networks, is that you don't have to sign up or create a profile to start using it. You simply go to *http://www.youtube.com* and begin searching.

You do have the option to sign up for a free account and profile, so that you can upload your own videos. We'll talk a little bit about protecting your profile information later in the chapter.

Some initial tips for getting the most out of YouTube

As with any social tool, always be sure to search thoroughly. Utilize all of your methods of finding information. In a source like YouTube, you can do a keyword search, and you can also browse by channels.

To illustrate this point, let's conduct a quick search for Safeway (*http://www.safeway.com*), a large grocery chain in the United States and Canada. If we do a keyword search on Safeway, we get a list of videos related to Safeway. If we scroll down our results list, we also see that Safeway has a channel, called Safeway Inc. (Figure 4.3).

In addition to the video search results, I always find it helpful to look at an organizational channel if it is available. Not only will you find additional videos that likely wouldn't turn up in your search results, but you also get a more comprehensive sense of how the organization uses video to promote itself, and the organization's areas of focus. An organization might post commercials, video about events, or content helpful to customers. In the example in Figure 4.4, from the fall of 2010, Safeway is promoting videos that can help its customers with their Thanksgiving meal.

If you are searching specifically for interviews or news clips, here is a tip that will help you narrow down your search. For this example, we'll conduct a search in YouTube for Steve Jobs. When we get our results, we can click on the "Filter and explore" link dropdown (Figure 4.5).

Depending upon your topic search, you may see, under the "Explore" options on the right, some news channels: ABCNews, CBSNewsOnline, and CNETTV, among others. If you hover your mouse just to the right

Frugal TV - Safeway 101
In this episode Nathan travels to Washington DC to shop at Safeway! Have you ever wondered if Safeway doubles or even if they accept coupons? This ...
by frugaltv · 7 months ago · **7,885 views**
HD

Safeway Opening Special
One of the opening specials at the new Safeway at Doncaster shoppingtown was half price toilet paper. It was so funny to watch the customers fight ...
by famous55 · 3 years ago · **15,617 views**

Safeway
Safeway Inc. is one of the largest food and drug retailers in North Amer...
⊕ Larree Renda Safeway Foundation Message
by Safewayinc · **46 videos** · 157 subscribers
CHANNEL

Tucson Safeway Reopens, Memories Linger
The Safeway supermarket in Tucson, Ariz. has reopened for business, one week after the shooting rampage which claimed the lives of six people ...
by CBS · 10 months ago · **390 views**

Figure 4.3 · Search results for Safeway on YouTube. You'll see the Safeway channel in the third result

Figure 4.4 The Safeway channel on YouTube

Figure 4.5 Filter options on YouTube results

of those channel names, a red plus sign will pop up, which will allow you to search for your terms within that channel (Figure 4.6).

Here's where it gets interesting! Take a look at the search string in the search box after we get our results for Steve Jobs in CBSNewsOnline (Figure 4.7).

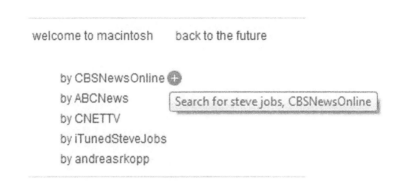

welcome to macintosh   back to the future

by CBSNewsOnline ⊕

by ABCNews

by CNETTV

by iTunedSteveJobs

by andreasrkopp

Search for steve jobs, CBSNewsOnline

Figure 4.6 Narrowing results by source. Note that, in this example, if you hover your mouse over the + sign, you see what you will actually be searching

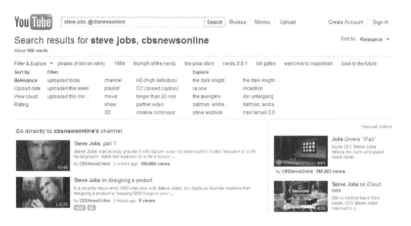

Figure 4.7 Search results for Steve Jobs in the CBSNewsOnline channel in YouTube

The search string comes up as "steve jobs, @cbsnewsonline." Going forward, if we want to search a specific channel, we can simply use this search string. So, for example, say we wanted to search for Occupy Wall Street in the CBSNewsOnline Channel. We can then create our own search string of "occupy wall street, @cbsnewsonline" (Figure 4.8).

This search requires an extra step or two, but can be very effective in locating relevant video clips. Again, you will have various levels of success with this search strategy on topics not broadly covered by major news outlets.

Figure 4.8	Search results for Occupy Wall Street in the CBSNewsOnline channel in YouTube. Note that this search utilizes a typed search in the search box

Example 4.1:   Business and competitive use

For our business and competitive example, let's use the TopShop retail stores. TopShop (*http://www.topshop.com*) is a UK-based trendy retail outlet focused on youth fashion, and is part of the Arcadia Group brand portfolio. TopShop claims 300 stores in the UK and over 100 international stores.

As we've discussed earlier, in conducting our research, it's a good idea to start with "traditional" tools to establish a base of information about a company. In a quick search of Hoover's (*http://www.hoovers.com*), we discover that the CEO of Arcadia Group is Ian Grabiner, and that Arcadia Group is owned by billionaire Sir Philip Green. Let's keep this information in mind as we conduct our search on YouTube.

TopShop is a good example to use for YouTube for a variety of reasons. To start, let's do a simple search for TopShop (Figure 4.9).

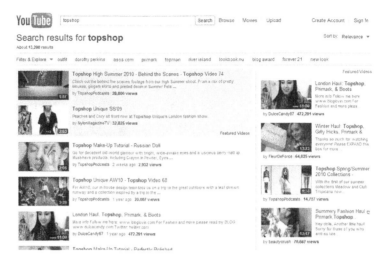

Figure 4.9 **Search results for TopShop in YouTube. Note "haul" results toward the bottom of the screenshot**

Because TopShop's business is fashion, we expect to see lots of videos related to fashion, and we get exactly that. TopShop video is heavy on fashion and make-up tips, which is certainly appropriate for the company's target customer.

However, let's take a look at another aspect of our results. Several of the results in the screenshot in Figure 4.9 have the word "haul" in the title. What's going on here?

A phenomenon happening in YouTube is "haul" videos. Typically, young shoppers create videos to talk about the bargains they discovered at various retail shops. You might think that these kinds of videos are frivolous, and certainly, in many ways, they are. It does take a special kind of patience to be able to sit through hours of video of young people discussing their purchases. But consider this from a competitive standpoint. By searching for "haul" videos on YouTube, you could gain insight into what kinds of products are being discounted and sold at various retailers – especially unadvertised discounts and sales. I have known colleagues who have effectively used "haul" videos to keep track of their competitors' sales and discount strategies. So the presence of "haul" videos in our TopShop results is actually a good thing, especially if we're looking for that competitive information.

Let's go back to our results. We see that there is a channel called "TopshopPodcasts". If we click through to this channel, we find that this seems to be the main channel for TopShop on YouTube (Figure 4.10).

Again, many of the videos in the TopShop channel are geared toward fashion and make-up tips. Other videos include clips from the London Fashion Week event in September 2011. From these clips, you get a sense of the types of events in which TopShop participates, as well as the type of clientele and partners to which TopShop caters (Figure 4.11).

Additional videos feature Kate Moss, and also share "behind the scenes" clips from events. Again, all of these clips paint a much richer picture of the company. Watching these videos, it's striking

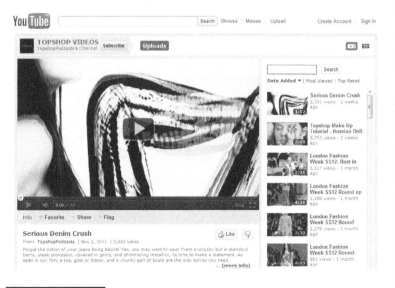

Figure 4.10   The TopShop channel on YouTube

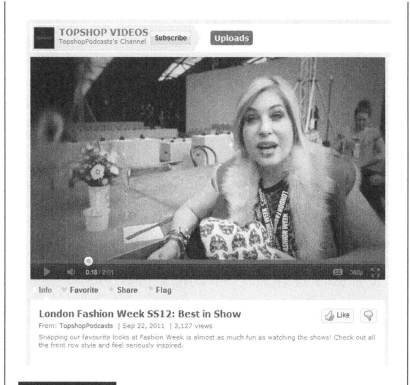

TOPSHOP VIDEOS
TopshopPodcasts's Channel   Subscribe   **Uploads**

0:18 / 2:01   CC   360p

Info   ▼ Favorite   ⁺ Share   ⁼ Flag

London Fashion Week SS12: Best in Show   👍 Like   🖓
From: TopshopPodcasts | Sep 22, 2011 | 3,127 views
Snapping our favourite looks at Fashion Week is almost as much fun as watching the shows! Check out all
the front row style and feel seriously inspired.

Figure 4.11   A video clip in the TopShop channel

how quickly one can get a sense of the company and the clientele
(Figures 4.12 and 4.13).

Before we leave this search example, let's conduct a search for
our Arcadia Group owner, Sir Philip Green. If we conduct a search
on "Sir Philip Green" and then use the "Filter" option to sort by
upload date, we get some relevant results (Figure 4.14).

Thankfully, Sir Philip Green is a visible figure. In our results, we
get an interview with him from Crain's Midday Report, and several
other interview clips. In viewing these clips, again, it's striking how
one gets a sense of Sir Philip Green – from his speech patterns
and usage, his gestures, his approach, and several other verbal
and non-verbal cues. Interviews and clips of executives can provide
a very interesting perspective.

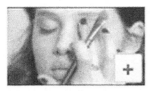 Topshop Make-Up
Tutorial - Russian Doll
3,052 views - 2 weeks
ago

 London Fashion
Week SS12: Best in
3,127 views - 1 month
ago

 London Fashion
Week SS12 Round up
1,286 views - 1 month
ago

 London Fashion
Week SS12 Round
1,279 views - 1 month
ago

 London Fashion
Week SS12 Round-
881 views - 1 month
ago

 London Fashion
Week SS12 Daily

Figure 4.12 List of videos on the TopShop channel

Kate Moss Topshop Autumn / Winter 2010
40,158 views - 1 year ago

Kate Moss Topshop - Behind the Scenes -
34,471 views - 4 years ago

Spring Summer 11 Trends Film -
34,471 views - 9 months ago

Topshop Make Up Tutorial - Statement
31,519 views - 1 year ago

Mark Fast, Mary Katrantzou, Danielle
30,240 views - 2 years ago

Topshop & Elle SS08 Collections - Topshop
30,209 views - 3 years ago

Figure 4.13 Further videos on the TopShop channel. Note the variety of topics and focus areas

Figure 4.14   YouTube search for Sir Philip Green

Lastly, if you view any video, be sure to take a look at the video "suggestions" that come up on the right side of the screen. Often times, you can find additional relevant video by browsing through these suggestions. In this example, we see clips that give an alternative perspective, such as "The Billionaire Philip Green in Action," and "Cambridge TopShop Protest" (Figure 4.15).

Figure 4.15   Video clip featuring Sir Philip Green

Example 4.2: Government agency

You can typically find similar content for non-profit, government, and other organizations as you would for for-profit organizations via YouTube: commercial and informational clips. Of course, these other organizations will use YouTube and video-sharing sites for additional reasons as well: for example, to post public-awareness information, and to share other important information.

Let's take a look at a US government organization on YouTube: the Centers for Disease Control and Prevention (CDC) (*http://www.cdc.gov*). CDC is part of the US Department of Health and Human Services, and seeks to "collaborate to create the expertise, information, and tools that people and communities need to protect their health – through health promotion, prevention of disease, injury and disability, and preparedness for new health threats." From the CDC website, we can find that Thomas R. Friedan is currently the director of CDC. (We'll hold on to this information for later investigation.)

If we do an initial search in YouTube on Centers for Disease Control (in this case, it's going to be worthwhile to also search for CDC), we get an interesting mix of results. We can quickly find the CDC YouTube channel, which is CDCStreamingHealth (Figure 4.16).

In addition to CDC channel results, we also get some interesting further items: a satirical release from the CDC on the zombie apocalypse, for example. However, we also get a video posted by the US Embassy in Tokyo in which Jana Telfer of the CDC is presenting on the effects of radiation (due to the Japanese earthquake in March 2011) in April 2011 (Figure 4.17).

This one video gives us both a view into the type of presentation that CDC staff give, as well as a lead for further searching. We might search for more videos from Ms Telfer, or search for "CDC embassy", "CDC radiation", or other combinations of search terms to see what else we can find related to this particular topic.

Figure 4.16 YouTube search for Centers for Disease Control (CDC). Note that the CDC channel, CDCStreamingHealth, shows up on several of our search results

Figure 4.17 Video of a presentation by a CDC staff member

We'll come back to a related search. For now, let's look at the CDC channel in YouTube (Figure 4.18).

If we simply scroll through the videos available on the right side, we start to see some of the areas that the CDC addresses. Two categories of interest to us are Global Health and CDC en Español (Figure 4.19).

The CDC en Español channel is of interest, if only to know that the CDC is creating content in languages other than English. To get a full picture of the organization, it would be worthwhile to continue to search for Spanish-language content from CDC.

In the Global Health category, we see a video on field training programs from the CDC (Figure 4.20). This video in itself tells us a bit about how the CDC works with other countries' ministries of health to build response capacity globally.

If we look at the Global Health category videos, we also are able to access video on CDC's response to various health issues in the world (Figure 4.21).

Figure 4.18   The main CDC channel on YouTube

Global Health (10)

Field Training Programs Save Lives
CDCStream... - 210 views

CDC Global Disease Detectives: Answers
CDCStream... - 290 views

CDC Global Disease Detectives: Clues and
CDCStream... - 359 views

see all

CDC en Español (12)

Hablemos de la Influenza
CDCStream... - 526 views

Influenza (:30)
CDCStream... - 298 views

Influenza (:60)
CDCStream... - 383 views

Figure 4.19   Some of the CDC video categories on YouTube

Figure 4.20   CDC video on YouTube

As we've seen from this example, video can quickly tell us a lot about the areas of focus for an organization like the CDC. Yes, much of this content is likely available from the CDC site and other sources as well, with a little digging. However, from the main page of the CDC site, it would not be immediately obvious to us to look for CDC content in YouTube – the CDC does not explicitly link to its YouTube channel, although it does link to its Facebook and Twitter accounts (Figure 4.22).

Before we leave the CDC channel, let's go back to its main YouTube channel page, and look at the channels to which CDC subscribes (Figure 4.23). Similar to Facebook "likes," the other YouTube accounts to which CDC subscribes give us a broader sense

« Back to Playlists
Global Health

More Info

CDCStream... - 252 views

CDC Responds to
Cholera in Haiti
CDCStream... - 260 views

CDC Responds to
Earthquake in Haiti
CDCStream... - 264 views

CDC Responds to
Meningitis in Burkina
CDCStream... - 223 views

CDC Responds to
Nodding Disease in
CDCStream... - 1,541 views

Global Disease
Detectives in Kibera
CDCStream... - 505 views

Global Disease
Detectives
CDCStream... - 1,380 views

Figure 4.21   CDC's Global Health category videos on YouTube

Figure 4.22 — CDC's main website. Note that CDC links to its Facebook and Twitter accounts from its site, but not to its YouTube channel

Figure 4.23 — A sample of the other YouTube accounts to which the CDC channel on YouTube subscribes

of various related agencies and organizations on YouTube. Some of the channels include the National Institutes of Health, the Environmental Protection Agency, the US Food and Drug Administration, AIDS.gov, and a variety of other agencies. If we are interested in health agencies in the United States in general, we can find quite a treasure trove of video information simply by being alerted to other video channels available in YouTube.

As we wrap up this example, let's go back and do a search for the CDC Director, Thomas R. Friedan. If we conduct a search for "CDC Thomas Friedan", we get a strong set of results (Figure 4.24).

In addition to several videos of Mr Friedan speaking at a variety of venues, we also get a few news clips (from CSPAN and CBS News), and results from other US government channels, such as the US Health and Human Services channel (USGOVHHS). Similar to our earlier search, if we were looking specifically for news clips, we could create a search string of "CDC Thomas Friedan, @CSPAN", and get results specifically from the CSPAN channel (Figure 4.25).

Figure 4.24 Search results for "CDC Thomas Friedan" on YouTube

Figure 4.25 Search for "CDC Thomas Friedan" on the CSPAN channel in YouTube

In reviewing our two examples, what types of information did we find?

- news clip interviews with executives;
- a sense of those executives' styles;
- for retail organizations, some information on the types of discounts and specials they offer;
- a view of the focus areas of the organizations;
- the types of events in which the organizations participate;
- a richer sense of the style, focus, and "personality" of the organizations.

Finally, you can use YouTube subscriptions to keep up on any channel within YouTube. You must create your own YouTube account to subscribe to channels (Figure 4.26). When you subscribe to a channel, the updates will appear on your home YouTube page. You also have the option to receive email updates when new videos are uploaded to the channel(s) to which you subscribe.

Caveats

The main caveat in searching for video, no matter what your source, is that you never know how much or how little content you will find. You might search for video for an organization and come up completely empty handed. You might search and come up with a wealth of information. No matter what your search results, I think it's always worthwhile to conduct a search for any organization, and organization executives, in video sources. I am almost always pleasantly surprised by what I find.

| Figure 4.26 | Subscribing to the CDCStreamingHealth channel on YouTube. You can subscribe to any channel on YouTube to be alerted to newly posted videos |

Protecting your information

As mentioned previously, you don't need to have an account to search YouTube, so you typically don't need to worry much about protecting your information. However, if you do register on YouTube and have an account, you can take a few steps to protect yourself and your information.

- **Sign out of your account before searching, or after using YouTube.** This not only makes you more anonymous, but also, as a minor point, potentially keeps others from inadvertently influencing your recommendations. For example, my daughter, who is very interested in anime, often searches on YouTube for anime clips – and I've often forgotten to sign out of my account. As a result, my "recommended" clips and channels are *not* reflective of my tastes and interests (Figure 4.27).

- **Clear your history, both to "hide your tracks" and to potentially get better results.** Currently, you can clear your "history" on YouTube by clicking on the "down" arrow next to your sign-in name at the top of the YouTube page (Figure 4.28).

  If you click on History, you will get a full list of your history, and you have the option to clear it (Figure 4.29).

- **Watch your subscriptions and favorites.** As you've seen, we've been able to find great information by looking at organizations' channel

| Figure 4.27 | My recommendations on YouTube. I'm not a big anime fan, but my daughter is. I should have signed out of my YouTube account. D'oh! |

Figure 4.28 View of my activity on YouTube. Using the down arrow next to my account name will allow me an option to clear my history

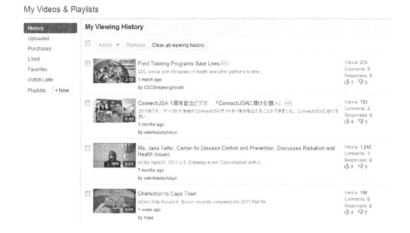

Figure 4.29 Listing of my recent viewing history on YouTube

subscriptions. Potentially, other YouTube users can also see *your* subscriptions. This isn't necessarily a bad thing, but, if you're tracking channels in areas that are "sensitive," think carefully before you subscribe to a channel. For example, if I work for a pharmaceutical company, I might think twice about subscribing to channels in new areas that my company is researching. You can remove public visibility to your subscriptions, but your subscriptions will still be visible to your friends on YouTube. An alternative is, of course, not to have any friends on YouTube.

- **Manage your profile and privacy settings.** One of the nice things about YouTube is that you don't have to provide much information at all in your profile. Mine is almost empty. Also, be sure to review your privacy settings regularly. Currently, you can limit the "findability" of your channel, and also change the public visibility of your favorites, subscriptions, friends, and Google profile (Figure 4.30). Again, this

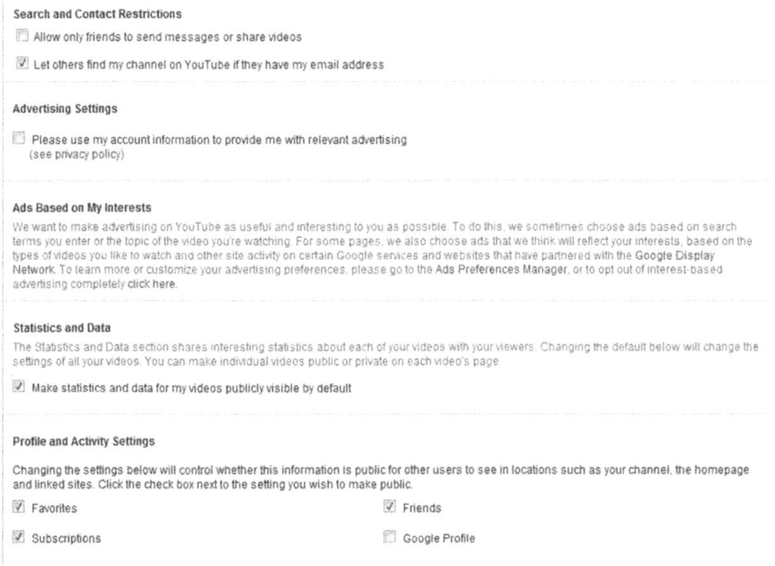

Search and Contact Restrictions

☐ Allow only friends to send messages or share videos

☑ Let others find my channel on YouTube if they have my email address

Advertising Settings

☐ Please use my account information to provide me with relevant advertising
   (see privacy policy)

Ads Based on My Interests

We want to make advertising on YouTube as useful and interesting to you as possible. To do this, we sometimes choose ads based on search terms you enter or the topic of the video you're watching. For some pages, we also choose ads that we think will reflect your interests, based on the types of videos you like to watch and other site activity on certain Google services and websites that have partnered with the Google Display Network. To learn more or customize your advertising preferences, please go to the Ads Preferences Manager, or to opt out of interest-based advertising completely click here.

Statistics and Data

The Statistics and Data section shares interesting statistics about each of your videos with your viewers. Changing the default below will change the settings of all your videos. You can make individual videos public or private on each video's page.

☑ Make statistics and data for my videos publicly visible by default

Profile and Activity Settings

Changing the settings below will control whether this information is public for other users to see in locations such as your channel, the homepage and linked sites. Click the check box next to the setting you wish to make public.

☑ Favorites   ☑ Friends

☑ Subscriptions   ☐ Google Profile

Figure 4.30   Some of the privacy options on YouTube

will affect the visibility of this to the "public" – those not signed in to YouTube – but your friends in YouTube may still be able to see this information. If your work is sensitive, err on the conservative side.

Other tools in this category

Though I've mentioned a few of these tools in the introduction of this section, a short list of additional tools in this category includes:

- Vimeo
- Blinkx
- DailyMotion
- Yahoo! Video
- Bing Video.

More "live streaming" video sites are emerging these days, and more video sites are offering live streaming video. These types of sources provide live online-streaming video across a variety of topics, and often provide archived streams as well. If you are doing in-depth research utilizing video sources, be sure to investigate streaming sources such as the following:

- UStream.tv
- Justin.tv: Justin.tv seems to be focused on more popular content, but it may be worthwhile browsing through some of the categories available. A positive feature of the site is the availability of an interface in a multitude of languages besides English.

Other popular video sites include:

- VEVO, which focuses on music videos;
- Hulu, focusing on television and movies.

Related tools

The related tools in this category are tools that provide access to documents, such as presentations, PDFs, and other formats. I'm including these with video-related tools because these tools often provide similar business, competitive, and industry information as you would find in video sources.

- **Slideshare:** Slideshare is a growing online resource into which people primarily post slide presentations, in PDF or Microsoft PowerPoint formats (Figure 4.31). In addition to presentations, users can upload documents, videos, and webinar recordings onto the site. As of April 2012, Slideshare claims 60 million monthly visitors, and ranks among the most-visited 200 websites globally.

  I include Slideshare as a source because it is increasingly becoming a very useful source to find presentations that can be valuable in a variety of ways:

  - Many organizations – large and small – maintain channels within Slideshare as a way to post and share presentations. These channels, similar to YouTube channels, allow you to easily locate information posted by a particular organization or business entity.
  - In addition to "official" organization channels, you can find presentations from employees of an organization, including executives, which can give you valuable information about the organizational strategy, products, and direction.
  - You can find conference presentations, which can give you great industry information, as well as views into what organizations are doing internally. Often, employees will present at conferences

Figure 4.31 Slideshare

about their practices and experiences. These can be a great resource for researchers.

- You can find "outsider" views of organizations – in other words, presentations posted by people talking about an organization.

It is worth your while to confirm the reliability of the presenters for any slide set, especially presentations by "outsiders," as it could be relatively easy to post false or erroneous information about an organization. That said, you will likely find some valuable information in Slideshare.

- **Scribd**: Scribd (pronounced "skribbed") positions itself as "the world's largest social reading and publishing company," focusing on the ability to share any kind of written content (Figure 4.32). In this respect, it's a complementary counterpart to video sources and Slideshare, in that it focuses on text-based documents. That said, quite a few presentations are posted into Scribd. In mid-2011, Scribd also launched a new service called Float, which allows users to access Scribd and other publisher content via a variety of devices.

  Similar to Slideshare, you can find a variety of information:

  - Organizations can create channels within Scribd to share information. It's worthwhile taking a look at these channels, because, since Scribd focuses on text documents, you can find presentations, documentation, and workflow documents, among other things. If you are interested in finding *product or process documentation*, Scribd might be an excellent place to look.

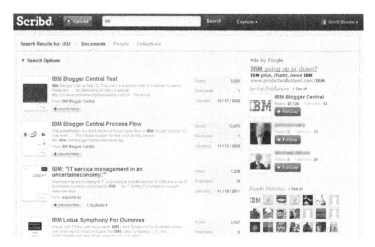

Scribd search for "IBM". In this example, we find not only presentations, but also process diagrams, white papers, and documentation

- Again, in addition to "official" organization channels, you can find presentations and documentation from employees of an organization, which might give you a more operational view of an organization.

Review

Whenever I utilize video sources – no matter how much I've used them previously – I almost always come away surprised at the amount of information I find. To review, some of the information we found or could find includes:

- video of organization executives, including interviews, presentations, and speeches;
- product videos, including product release videos, commercials, "behind the scenes" footage, video of experts in the organization discussing products or technologies, and product "fails";
- organizational events, trade shows and conferences, and meetings;
- "outside" perspective on the organization, including video from organization interns, employees, and customers.

Because video is a different medium than text, we can gain a different kind of knowledge of the organization – a visual, non-verbal, and, in some senses, more "human" view of the organization and its people.

Audio tools

What are they?

For the purposes of this book, audio tools include any kind of source that will allow you to discover and access audio files that might be useful in business and industry research. Generally, this means accessing podcasts.

Podcasts can come in either audio or video versions (sometimes referred to as a "vodcast"), and are basically a digital audio or video file that can be downloaded or streamed via a browser or a device such as a mobile phone. For our purposes, since we've already covered video sources, this section will focus exclusively on audio podcasts.

Some tools that fall into this category include:

- **iTunes**: Apple's directory and resource for "hundreds of thousands" of podcasts. The big advantage of iTunes is that it is a podcast outlet for major media outlets, such as ABC World News, the BBC, BusinessWeek, CNN, National Public Radio (NPR), and TED, among others.
- **Podcast Alley**: As of April 2012, Podcast Alley contained over 90 000 podcasts and 6 million episodes.
- **Podfeed.net**: In comparison, as of April 2012, Podfeed.net featured 19 000 podcasts and over 2.5 million episodes.

An important thing to remember about these kinds of sources is that they are opt-in sources. In other words, they don't go out and actively find podcasts; podcast producers (and other people) need to actively list their podcasts in these sources in order for the podcasts to be found through these sources. This means that these sources, while helpful, will not list *every* podcast available.

In our exploration of audio sources, we'll look at iTunes as our example source, since iTunes has a large amount of podcasts, active participation by the major media outlets, and relatively good categorization.

iTunes

What is it?

The iTunes application itself is a free, stand-alone product you can download from Apple, Inc. It is not browser based; the functionality of iTunes works on a desktop, and also via mobile applications on iOS products (Apple devices such as iPad, iPhone, and Touch). iTunes serves as a way to purchase, download, and play digital music, videos, podcasts, and books, among other things. Although it is an Apple product, it is available to download on both Apple products and PC platforms.

While you can certainly download music, movies, and digital books, our focus for iTunes here will be on podcasts. All of the podcasts (at least the ones of interest to us) are available for free via iTunes. iTunes offers access to thousands of podcast series, and hundreds of thousands of episodes.

What kind of business and competitive information can be found there?

Similar to video, podcasts can give you some valuable information about organizations.

- Interviews with executives, product experts, or other key individuals within an organization. Because of the "radio show" format of audio podcasts, you can often find in-depth interviews with key people in an organization. Podcasts can often provide more in-depth information and interviews than videos, simply because of the longer format and listener expectations of podcasts. While video clips are typically short – under five minutes – many podcast formats are longer, anywhere from 15 minutes to over an hour. Many podcast listeners download podcasts for listening on their commutes. As a result, podcast creators typically have more time to fill and more opportunity to share information.

- "Broadcasts" from organization events, trade shows and conferences. Again, because of the "radio show" format, many podcasters will produce "live" episodes while attending organizational events, product launches, or conferences.

- Depending upon the size and visibility of the organization, you may also find podcasts talking about the organization's products or services. These might take the form of product reviews from third parties, for example.

How do you get started using it?

To get started, simply go to the Apple iTunes download page. You can either search for "Apple iTunes" to find it, or go to the Apple iTunes site (currently at *http://www.apple.com/itunes/*). Once you download iTunes, launch it. You don't need to set up an account or sign in in order to search iTunes for podcasts. In fact, you don't need to have an account to subscribe to and download podcasts.

From the main iTunes Store, you will find a tab along the top for Podcasts (Figure 4.33).

| Figure 4.33 | Main page of iTunes. See Podcasts category along the top |

Along the side, or from the drop-down menu along the top, you can see the broad categories of podcasts available via iTunes. These include Business, Education, Government & Organizations, and Technology, among others (Figure 4.34).

You can, of course, also search for podcasts by using the search box on the main iTunes interface. When you conduct a keyword search, you get results from all content areas available on iTunes, including music, video, podcasts, and apps. We'll take a look at an actual search in our example so you can see how to navigate this.

Some initial tips for getting the most out of iTunes

As with all the tools we've covered so far, iTunes has a basic search box. Searching for any keyword or phrase will pull results from across iTunes formats: apps, podcasts, music, video, and ebooks. You can then narrow down your search just to podcasts – which, in iTunes, also includes video podcasts.

While keyword searching will likely get you to what you're seeking, if you're researching an industry, be sure to browse the podcast categories as well. Although the categories are broad, browsing by category can give you an idea of some of the top sources in that category (including "What's Hot," "New and Noteworthy," and "Top of the Charts" – the most popular podcasts).

Also, when you select a category, be sure to scroll all the way down iTunes to find "More [in the category you've selected]." This somewhat hidden section will provide you with further sub-categories of podcasts in most categories. In the example in Figure 4.35, I was browsing the Government & Organizations category, and found sub-categories in Local, National, Non-Profit, and Regional.

Figure 4.34 Podcast categories in iTunes

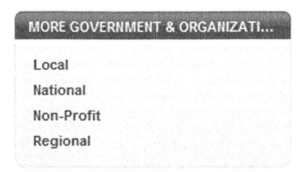

Figure 4.35 Sub-categories for the Government & Organizations
podcast category in iTunes

Example 4.3: Business search

Let's take a look and see what kind of information we can find for Vodafone (*http://www.vodafone.com*), one of the leading telecommunications companies in the world, headquartered in England and with offices globally.

If we do a simple keyword search in iTunes, we get some interesting results across several different formats in addition to podcasts.

For example, we see apps produced by Vodafone (Figure 4.36), as well as some results in the iTunes U and Books categories (Figure 4.37).

Figure 4.36   iPhone apps results for Vodafone in iTunes

Figure 4.37   iTunes U and Books results for Vodafone in iTunes

We'll come back to the apps results later in this section. In this search example, it's worthwhile taking a look at the iTunes U and Books results before we dive into the podcast results. In iTunes U, we see one piece from the UC Berkeley Hass School of Business series, which provides an interview with former Vodafone CEO Arun Sarin from 2009. This almost hour-long interview would likely provide some interesting insight into a top executive of the company. The Books results include a few pieces from some newswire services, available via iTunes. While we might not choose to subscribe to these services (in contrast to podcasts, these services involve a charge), there may be some information to glean from these results.

Let's turn now to our podcast results specifically. We can narrow down our results to just podcasts by either clicking on the "See All" arrow next to the podcasts results, or clicking on the Podcasts category in the "Filter by Media Type" section at the top of our results. Note that each option brings up a different look at the results. Clicking on the "See All" arrow simply gives us a laundry list of podcast results (Figure 4.38).

While this may be valuable, the results from the Podcasts category are typically going to give us results that are more organized and relevant. (Note, too, that there is a "Power Search" option – this only gives us the option to search for our keywords in the title field or the artist field.)

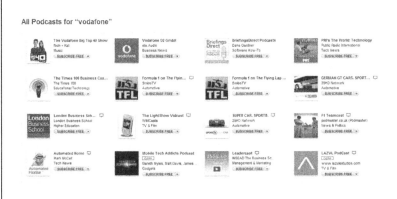

Figure 4.38 Full podcast results for Vodafone in iTunes

In our "Filter by Media Type" results (Figure 4.39), we see, first, two podcasts with Vodafone in the title. One is "The Vodafone Big Top 40 Show," which features music, and "Vodafone D2 GmbH," a German-language podcast on the telecommunications industry. In looking at the episodes, we see a lot of activity in 2008, and then only a few postings since then (although there is a post on December 15, 2011). Depending upon the organization, you may find quite a few podcasts being produced, or none.

Let's look at our episode results (Figure 4.40). In this example, this is where the gold is. One of our results is from BriefingsDirect Podcasts – an HP case study on how Vodafone Ireland is using HP solutions for its business service delivery. This half-hour episode provides insight on how Vodafone is using the solution, as well as the types of services Vodafone Ireland provides. So, from this podcast, we can find an example of how Vodafone operates, and get a sense of the types of services delivered out of its Ireland offices.

Note that we can sort our episode results by release date, so we can get a better sense of the oldest and the newest episodes (Figure 4.40). What's striking from this example is that we get results going back to 2006. This example shows that iTunes can not only serve as a source of recent information about an organization; it can also provide historical information.

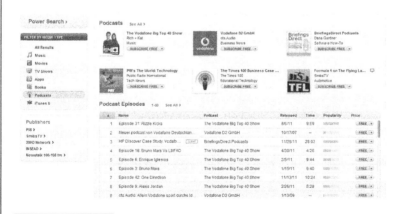

Figure 4.39   Podcasts category results for Vodafone in iTunes

Podcast Episodes 1-50   See All >

	Name	Podcast	Released ▲	Time	Popularity	Price
26	November Films on Vodafone	The LightShow Vidcast	11/9/05	--		FREE
48	"Vodafone Radio": Alle CeBIT-Neuheiten v...	Vodafone D2 GmbH	3/13/07	--		FREE
46	Vodafone-Podcast "Happy Birthday Hand...	Vodafone D2 GmbH	6/13/07	--		FREE
50	Die Vodafone Jugendschutz-Initiative: Geg...	Vodafone D2 GmbH	8/16/07	--		FREE
2	Neuer podcast von Vodafone Deutschlan...	Vodafone D2 GmbH	10/17/07	--		FREE
49	Surfen im Internet, Herunterladen von Mus...	Vodafone D2 GmbH	10/23/07	--		FREE
47	Vodafone-Podcast mit allen Infos rund um ...	Vodafone D2 GmbH	11/21/07	--		FREE
36	AH0002 - Vodafone USB Stick 3G Mo...	Automated Home	2/10/08	0:58		FREE
34	Vodafone livel-Podcast mit Top-Trends de...	Vodafone D2 GmbH	3/4/08	--		FREE
12	Ich + Ich im Interview: Was bewegt Adel T...	Vodafone D2 GmbH	7/14/08	--		FREE

Figure 4.40 Podcast episode results for Vodafone. Note that we have results all the way back to 2006!

If we re-sort by most recent episodes, we again find some gold among the Top 40 episodes. From the London Business School, we get two recent profiles of Vodafone executives. We see a profile of Vittorio Colao, Chief Executive at Vodafone, as well as a profile of Warren Finegold, Chief Executive of Global Business Development at Vodafone, who also happens to be an alumnus of the London Business School. Similar to videos, through these types of interview podcasts, we can get a sense of the executives at a particular organization – as well as some potential insight into the organization and its strategy.

While results from a podcast search will vary, the types of information you can potentially find in podcasts include:

■ interviews with top executives

■ industry perspective from the organization

■ information on internal operations and/or products

■ historical information on the organization and its executives.

This is just a short list of the information we located in this example.

Mobile apps via iTunes

In Chapter 6, we'll look briefly at mobile apps and how these might figure into the future of social information. However, I want to take a moment here to talk about apps search results.

What can we infer from apps results in iTunes? Let's take a quick look at our apps search results from Vodafone by clicking on the "See All" link next to our apps results (Figure 4.41).

There are a couple of approaches here that may provide some further insight. First, does the organization produce its own apps? Many organizations are developing and offering their own apps to access their content via mobile devices. Usually, they will make these apps available via their websites, but it's always worthwhile to search on a source like iTunes or Android Market as well. The "official" apps offered by the company will give you a sense of a couple of things:

- How are their customers using their apps? Are they using their apps to access services from the organization? If so, which services? This will give you a sense of customer usage and demand.

All iPhone Apps for "vodafone"

Figure 4.41   **All apps results for Vodafone in iTunes**

- What are the growing services and areas of focus for the organization? An app usually provides access to "leading edge" and popular products and services of an organization. In this way, apps point to focus areas, as well as strategic growth areas – or areas where the organization is *hoping* it will have growth.

What if an organization doesn't offer "official" apps? There might be a few explanations for this. One might simply be that the company is in the process of developing an app or apps. Another might be that its services may not lend themselves to an app (though increasingly, apps are being offered from almost every type of organization). Another might be that the company is *intentionally* not offering an app.

Whether or not an organization offers "official" apps, you can get a good sense of customer access points and growing areas of focus simply by looking at available apps for any organization.

Caveats

As with all social tools, you never know how much or how little information you may find in searching for podcasts.

- With any podcast source, be sure to check the date of the podcast. As we've seen, there is some potential historical value in older podcasts. However, it's easy to get excited about a lot of results from a search, only to look at the dates and see they're all older than is useful for your purposes!

- Podcasts take time to listen to – so take this into consideration if you have limited time to gather information. Yes, you may find great information via podcasts, but be sure to allow yourself the time to get through the podcast(s).

Protecting your information

The nice thing about iTunes – and most other podcast sources – is that you don't need to register in order to search for and download podcasts.

Because of this, you don't really need to worry much about sharing information you'd rather not share. Additionally, even if you have an iTunes account, your account is relatively private. The average person Googling or using iTunes will not be able to tell if you have an iTunes account, and will not be able to see what you've downloaded.

However, be aware of the various "sharing" features on iTunes. In Preferences, you can choose to share your library locally (or not). The Ping, Genius, and iTunes Match features potentially share your library selections, so if you are sensitive about the podcasts you are downloading, you may want to be sure these features are turned off, so that others do not have visibility of the content you're downloading.

Additional tools in this category

As mentioned earlier, video podcasts can provide similar information as audio podcasts. The primary difference between video podcasts and video that you find on a source like YouTube is that typically, video podcasts are produced in a similar "episode"-style format as audio podcasts.

A couple of video podcast sources are:

- Videopodcasts.tv
- Podfreaks.

As with audio podcasts, it would be worthwhile to do a search in these types of sources as well, as you may find interviews with top executives and thought leaders, industry perspective and, in some instances, breaking news.

Review

As we wrap up this section, let's review the types of information we can find in podcasts:

- interviews with executives, product experts, or other key individuals within an organization, and with thought leaders in the industry;
- case studies;
- "broadcasts" from organization events, trade shows and conferences;
- in-depth discussions of an organization's products or services.

Finally, let's take a look at image tools.

Image tools

What are they?

You may or may not remember the days before broadband Internet access. In those days, sharing images – in fact, simply downloading a single image – was an exercise in patience. Even relatively small images took what seemed like an eternity to download. If you were trying to download anything larger than 1MB, you could expect to wait a long time.

These days, billions of images are uploaded, shared, and viewed, with barely any wait time. Sites like SmugMug allow amateur and professional photographers to share their high-quality, high-resolution images quickly and easily. Travelers – and everyone else – seem to be taking more pictures than ever, and upload hundreds of images at a time to sites like Flickr. And more and more sites and mobile apps allow the easy uploading of photos and video, no matter where you are.

In this section, in contrast to video and audio, we focus primarily on still images and the type of information that can be found by searching for those images. We will not be covering stock photo sources such as iStockPhoto and Fotolia, although those are obviously image sources as well. We will look at sources where individual users can upload their images to a site.

Examples of these types of sites include:

- Flickr
- Picasa – a Google property
- SmugMug.

Another perhaps surprising source for images is Facebook, though, as of this writing, there is no way to specifically search for photos in Facebook. We'll come back to this later in this section.

Flickr

What is it?

Flickr is an immense online source of images and video uploaded by its users. You'll find both individual and organizational accounts on Flickr. Users can tag and organize their photos, set their photos' visibility to public or private, and put their photos into sets and categories (with a paid account). To clarify the terminology used on Flickr, a set contains one or more photos. A collection can contain one or more sets or collections.

Because of the ability to tag and organize photos, Flickr positions itself as "almost certainly the best online photo management and sharing application in the world." While this claim may or may not be true, the advantage to you as a researcher is Flickr's dedication to functionality that helps users manage and organize images and video. Granted, the quality of the organization of photos relies on the organizational skills of the users themselves, resulting in a wide spectrum of "findability." We'll look at this issue more closely in our example searches.

In August 2011, Flickr announced that it had hit 6 billion uploaded images. While this seems like a big number – it is, and it's the reason we're taking a look at Flickr – in comparison, Facebook claims that its users upload 250 million photos *a day*. Pixable (*http://www.pixable.com*), a company that developed an app that works with Facebook photos, reports that Facebook reached 60 billion photos at the end of 2010.

While Facebook is obviously an immense source of images, it does not have (and does not aim to have) the same accessibility and findability that Flickr provides. This may change in the future, but as of now, we do not have the ability to mine images in Facebook.

What kind of business and competitive information can be found there?

Similar to video and audio sources we've explored so far, image sources like Flickr can provide some "three-dimensional" information on an organization. The types of information you might find include:

- product release photos, and/or multiple views of a particular product;
- photos from events: organization events, trade shows and conferences, and organizational meetings, for example;
- photos of employees and customers: these might be in the form of photos of organization events, which can include executive photos, as well as attendees at trade shows.

What can we learn from this type of information?

- **Additional product information.** Potentially, you could find images of different product versions, beta versions, and products released in different parts of the world. You might also find photos uploaded by users – which might provide the negative aspects of a product. (See the "laptop fire" video example earlier in this chapter.)

- **Location and site information.** In a retail example like Sports Authority, we can find several retail store photographs. For someone working in competitive analysis in retail, being able to gather some site information and photographs via a tool like Flickr saves having to travel extensively to competitive sites.

- **Event intelligence of a different kind.** Who attends the events? Who attends, say, a talk on medical devices? Who are the speakers at these events, and what do they look like? How many people were there? Was the room packed or was it mostly empty?

- **Organizational culture.** What goes on at employee events? Are they casual and fun, or are they formal? Where do they go, and what do they do? What does that say about the organization and how it spends money? Do the employees look like they're having fun? Do they do volunteer work? How many participate?

This is just a short list of the types of information you can potentially glean from a Flickr search.

How do you get started using it?

The nice thing about Flickr is you don't have to sign up for an account to start finding images. You can simply go to *http://flickr.com* and start searching (Figure 4.42).

| Figure 4.42 | Main Flickr page as of April 2012. Note search box in upper right corner |

As we've seen with many social tools, the initial search box is not terribly useful as far as crafting a search. However, this doesn't mean there aren't some effective ways for getting at images within Flickr.

Some initial tips for getting the most out of Flickr

There are a few ways to start your exploration of Flickr – some of which are not very intuitive.

Typically, you'll start off with a basic search using the initial search box. This is a good way to get a sense of the types and amount of images you'll find in Flickr.

- **Click the "Explore" link at the top of the initial Flickr page.** While the Explore page overall isn't terrific, there are a few parts of this page that can be helpful.
  - **Select photos by month** – if you're looking for only the most current photos (Figure 4.43). This will, of course, give you *all* photos for that month.
  - **Search by location** – especially if you're doing site searching for a specific location, this feature could be quite useful (Figure 4.44).
  - **Explore tags** – while this gives only a small selection of the tags available in Flickr, you can get a sense of the use of tags (Figure 4.45).
- **Click the "Search" link next to the basic search box.** If you don't put a search term in the search box, and just click on "Search," you'll go to a "next level" search page that allows you to construct a bit more complex search. This interface allows you to search for your terms in photos, groups, or people (users), as well as to search either in "full text" (including descriptions) or just in tags.
- **Advanced search.** The other option you'll see in the "next level" search as described immediately above is an "Advanced Search" link. In Flickr's current advanced search, you can choose to search all words, any word, or exact phrase; you can also exclude words, limit results by content type (photos/videos, screenshots/screencasts, and illustration/animation) and by date. (Unfortunately, location search is not a function in advanced search as of this writing.)

In our example search, we'll take a look at different ways to use these features.

Explore interesting photos on Flickr by
choosing a point in time...

Select a month

Figure 4.43   Selecting photos by month in Flickr

Where'd you take that?

Explore millions of geotagged photos and videos!

Location search: [   ] GO

Figure 4.44	Location search in Flickr

Explore Flickr through tags

art beach blue bw california canada canon china christmas city concert england europe family festival film flower flowers food france friends germany green instagramapp iphoneography italy japan live london music nature new newyork night nikon nyc paris park party people photography portrait red sky snow square squareformat street summer sunset travel trip uk usa vacation water wedding white winter

Figure 4.45	Tag cloud in Flickr

Example 4.4: Business search

The organization I'm going to use for our Flickr search example – though I'll probably regret it – is the Coca-Cola Company (*http://www.thecoca-colacompany.com* – the company page, as opposed to the product page at *http://www.coca-cola.com*), one of the most recognizable brands internationally.

Why do I say I'll regret it? First, Coca-Cola produces an extensive list of drink products, from water to soft drinks to energy drinks to sports drinks to tea and coffee. Second, because Coca-Cola (or Coke) is so well known and has such a long organizational history, there are massive amounts of images and information available about the company and its products.

However, the reason I am going to get past my regret is to illustrate ways you might consider narrowing your searches in order to target the information you are truly seeking.

In this instance, let's assume I want to see what information is available on Coca-Cola's events, and any type of "corporate" information I can find on the company.

Let's start off with a basic search for just "Coke" (the shorter, and typically more commonly used term for the product and company), for comparison (Figure 4.46).

While our search retrieves Coke product images (and thankfully we didn't come up with any pictures of illegal white substances), obviously a basic search on "Coke" doesn't get us much. However, if we look on the right, we see some suggested groups – including "Coca-Cola," which has over 6000 members and over 20 000 photos (Figure 4.47).

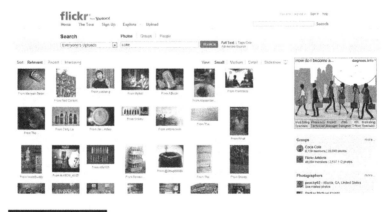

Figure 4.46 Search for Coke in Flickr

If we click into this group, serendipitously we find several pictures of Coca-Cola trucks. Interestingly, we also see a few photos from the "Coca-Cola Christmas Truck" in London in late December 2011 (Figure 4.48).

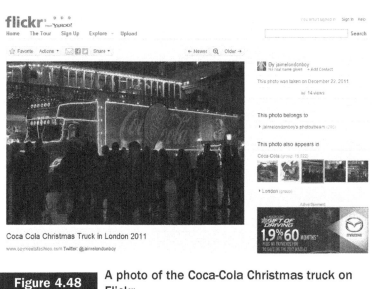

Figure 4.48   A photo of the Coca-Cola Christmas truck on Flickr

Immediately, we've started to pick up on the type of images and information that might be available via Flickr: how Coca-Cola transports its product, and some of the latest events and promotions by the company, including locations. (If you search further for the Coca-Cola Christmas Truck, you will find pictures of the trucks in several locations around London.)

Let's scroll down the main Group page, where we find a bit about the group itself (Figure 4.49).

Note that part of the group's scope is to include advertising pictures. Whenever you look at a Group within Flickr, be sure to take a look at the description of the group to find out what kind of images you can expect to find there. This will help you to save time and target those groups that will be most fruitful to your search.

Another thing to note is that, below the set of initial images, you have a search box that will search *only within that group*. A next step for me here might be to conduct a search for "advert" or "advertising" within this group. If I do conduct a search for "advert," I can pull up decades' worth of Coca-Cola advertisements (Figure 4.50). This is not surprising for Coca-Cola, which has turned its older advertisements into a cottage art industry.

Let's click back to our first set of results, and try a different approach. You'll see that our basic search was a "full text" search.

About Coca-Cola

Photos of anything related to Coca-Cola: cans, bottles, adverts, trucks!

Please add as many coca cola related photos as you can!... get it?... CAN!.. nevermind.

||| ONE MAIN RULE |||
Please make sure that the Coca Cola object is the main focus of the photo. No off-topic photos that just happen to have Coca Cola somewhere in the image :-)
http://www.flickr.com/groups/colastuff/

Figure 4.49   Description of the Coca-Cola group on Flickr

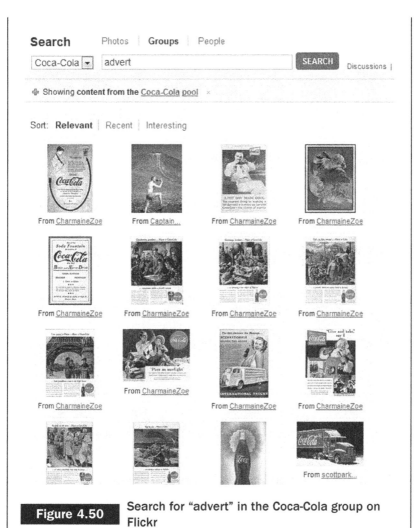

| Figure 4.50 | Search for "advert" in the Coca-Cola group on Flickr |

If we click on the "Tags Only" option, we get a different set of results (Figure 4.51).

What's striking is that we not only get a different set of image results; we also get a different set of groups! We now have the original Coca-Cola group that we found, and we also have The Coca-Cola Company group as well (Figure 4.52).

We will come back to the search features in a bit. Before we do, let's explore The Coca-Cola Company group.

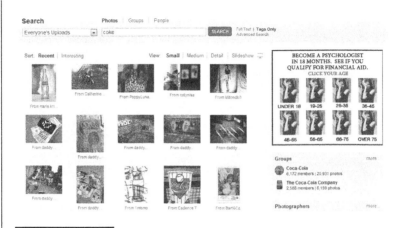

Figure 4.51   "Tags Only" search for Coke in Flickr

Figure 4.52   The Coca-Cola Company group on Flickr

As it turns out, this is the "official" Coca-Cola company group in Flickr. How do we confirm that this is indeed "official?"

Organizational groups in Flickr don't always provide direct links back to official websites. Also, a lot of "unofficial" groups on social tools will post organizational logos, making the task of determining authority quite difficult sometimes. In this example, there is a statement that the group is sponsored by Coca-Cola, with a link back to the Coca-Cola Company page (which is quite different than the product page at *http://www.coca-cola.com*). To be honest, when I first followed the Coca-Cola Company link, I confirmed that *http://www.thecoca-colacompany.com* was linked from the Coca-Cola product site – because the Coca-Cola Company site didn't look quite "official" to me!

Finally, if we scroll down to the "About" section on the group, we see a bit more about the focus of the group. Indeed, it is sponsored by Coca-Cola, and the company provides guidelines about the group and the driving philosophy of it:

> We at The Coca-Cola Company are continually inspired by the creativity that lives among fans and lovers of our brands. The purpose of our Flickr Group is to enable you to use this creativity to **find and share moments of happiness through photographs**.[1]

In a way, this brief description of the purpose of the group illuminates some of the power of Coca-Cola's brand, and its focus on images to convey its brand and its message. We also understand that this is a group primarily driven by other Flickr users – so we likely won't find a lot of images submitted officially by Coca-Cola.

Though we've gotten some clues about Coca-Cola – how it approaches image in its brand, some recent events, and the importance of advertising – let's go back to our search.

Just for fun, let's try a search for "new Coke," using Advanced Search. (As a very brief history of "new Coke," Coca-Cola released it as a re-formulation of its "Classic" Coke in the mid-1980s, setting off a huge public backlash. Coca-Cola eventually stopped making "new Coke.")

If we go up to the basic search box, let's click on the "Search" link, which takes us to the Advanced Search screen (Figure 4.53).

Though the Advanced Search options aren't very advanced, we can conduct a slightly more targeted search. In this example, we'll search for the phrase "new Coke" in tags.

Advanced Search

Search for	The exact phrase ▾	new coke
Tip: Use these options to look for an exact phrase or to exclude words or tags from your search. For example, search for photos tagged with "apple" but not "pie".		○ Full text ● Tags only
	None of these words:	

Search by content type

Tip: Check the boxes next to content you'd like to see come up in searches

- ☑ Photos / Videos
- ☐ Screenshots / Screencasts
- ☐ Illustration/Art / Animation/CGI

Search by media type

Tip: Filter to only display either photos or videos in your search results.

- ● Photos & Videos
- ○ Only Photos
- ○ Only Videos

☐ HD videos only

Figure 4.53 Advanced search in Flickr

Our initial results are quite interesting! (Figure 4.54) Not only do we get images of the "new Coke" can, but we also get some images of "new Coke" ads, and images of some memos from an exhibit at the World of Coca-Cola on "Project Kansas" – Coca-Cola's code name for "new Coke."

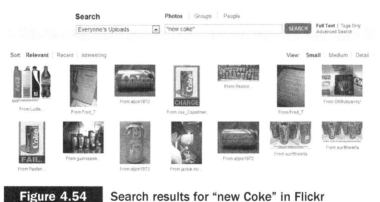

Figure 4.54 Search results for "new Coke" in Flickr

Again, this example is more for fun. Could we find information on Project Kansas and "new Coke" elsewhere? Yes, certainly we could find the information. The images, however, bring a different level of "information" and richness to our search. Having access to the images of the advertising, the packaging, and the documents not only gives us a different kind of "information" about it – it also provides unique information. Especially for searches for marketing and branding, Flickr can provide information – in the form of images – that is very unique.

Example 4.5: Quick industry and location searches in Picasa

The functionality of Picasa is very similar to Flickr, though there are some unique features. With Picasa, you have the option to limit your search results to images containing faces – or to those without faces. So, for example, if you were conducting a search for an executive, you could limit your results to just photos with faces to more quickly narrow down on pictures of the executive (Figure 4.55).

| Figure 4.55 | Example of using the "Faces only" filter on Picasa. In this instance, only pictures of IBM executive Sam Palmisano are shown |

As mentioned previously, Picasa is increasingly being integrated with Google Plus, and so the availability, searchability and functionality of Picasa will likely evolve and change very quickly. However, I wanted to share it as a resource here, and to provide a quick example search.

In this example, let's say I'm interested in finding images related to an industry – the coffee industry in Rwanda. As background, the US Agency for International Development (USAID) has put $12 million toward developing the coffee industry in Rwanda since 2000. What does this project look like in action, and what does the coffee industry look like in Rwanda?

If we conduct a simple search of "coffee Rwanda" in Picasa, we immediately get some images of the farms, production, and people of the coffee industry in Rwanda (Figure 4.56).

To illustrate the geographic capabilities of image search, let's conduct a very specific search for a building in a specific location. In this next example, I'll conduct a search for the Longmont Public Library in Longmont, Colorado (Figure 4.57).

If we click on the first image, we see a picture of the Longmont Public Library (Figure 4.58). Also, to the right, we see that this image is part of an album called "Longmont".

Figure 4.56   Search for "coffee Rwanda" in Picasa

Figure 4.57 Search for "Longmont Public Library Colorado" in Picasa

Figure 4.58 Photo search result for "Longmont Public Library Colorado" in Picasa. Note on the right that this is part of an album called "Longmont"

If we click into that album, we see a whole portfolio of pictures of the city of Longmont – giving us a relatively good view of what the city looks like (Figure 4.59). (Google realized the value of having images of a location long ago, by providing its "Street View" feature in Google Maps.)

If we go back to our original search results and click on one of the drumming photos from Longmont Public Library, we see that those images are part of an album called "Drumming Story Longmont Library" (Figure 4.60).

And again, if we click into that album, we see a whole series of photos taken at this drumming event at the Longmont Public Library – giving us not only various views of the library, but also a view into the kinds of events held there and the type of people that attend these events (Figure 4.61).

Figure 4.59   The album "Longmont" on Picasa

Figure 4.60   Photo of an event at the Longmont Public Library. Note, on the right, that this is part of an album called "Drumming Story Longmont Library"

Figure 4.61   Drumming Story Longmont Library album on Picasa

Through this example, we can see three additional uses of image sources. The first is to use these sources to provide images to supplement and add visual value to our research and analysis. If a picture is indeed worth a thousand words, then sources like Flickr and Picasa provide us billions of descriptive words. The second is to utilize these sources for location images. You can conduct very specific place searches within these sources to pull up images that provide a whole additional dimension to your information.

The third is the usefulness of these types of tools to do community research. Since many people utilize image sources like Flickr and Picasa to upload personal photos, these sources are becoming interesting and useful resources for investigating the nature and make-up of local communities. I believe these tools have the potential of becoming an important and interesting source in civic and governmental research, as well as in site research.

Again, we can never be guaranteed the depth or quality of the images we may find. However, I think it's always worthwhile to take a look and see what kind of images might come up for almost any search.

Caveats

As with all social media, be sure to double-check your information. Since images can be so easily downloaded, repurposed, and openly altered using image manipulation software (as we discovered in discussing Twitter), it becomes increasingly important to confirm the reality of the images you find.

If you think you are looking at an official organization page, do some checking to confirm that. Does the official organization's web page link to the page or group on Flickr, for example?

Especially when finding images such as the Project Kansas/new Coke memos, be sure to see if you can find similar images from more reliable sources (such as organization websites).

If you are unable to confirm a source, be sure both to note that when sharing the information with anyone, and to weigh the verification of the unconfirmed information into your decision making.

Protecting your information

As of this writing, you don't need to have an account to search Flickr or Picasa, so you typically don't need to worry much about protecting your information. However, if you do register on Flickr or Picasa and have an account, you should take a few steps to protect yourself and your information. Especially with Picasa, which is increasingly being integrated into Google Plus, you can't be too sure that your searches and "interests" won't be reflected unexpectedly in your Google Plus activity. (After all, Google Plus is very Facebook-like, and Facebook is notorious for sharing your activity with your connections.)

If you are sensitive about your image searches, here are some tips:

- **Sign out of your account before searching.** If you sign out of your Google account, it *looks* like you can't search Picasa without signing in again. This is actually not true; it just takes a little poking around to get back into the search interface.

- **Use an alternative email and profile for searching.** If you find that you can't access features in an image source without signing in, create a dummy email account with no identifying information, and register using that email (and utilize non-identifying information for your profile).

- **Manage your profile and privacy settings.** Especially in a tool like Google Plus, managing your profile, information, and privacy settings is going to be increasingly complex, simply because information is shared and accessible across more tools. For example, I wouldn't be surprised if photos shared in Google Plus will start to show up in Picasa if they are not identified as "private." This may not be an issue for you, but if you are using image tools for sensitive or competitive research, you may want to search without signing in, and/or create an anonymous account.

Additional tools in this category

As mentioned earlier in this chapter, SmugMug is another image source to investigate. I never would have thought of SmugMug as a place to search for company or organization photos, but I've found good results in searching SmugMug in certain cases.

Photobucket is another source worth investigating. Although I don't think it has quite the organizational and industry richness that sources like Flickr and Picasa have, it does combine image and video searching (as other sources do), and may be useful in particular for product searches.

As of this writing, Pinterest has become a very popular image-sharing tool. Pinterest positions itself as an "online pinboard" – a way to share and organize images. It provides several categories and ways to share images. Users can create their own collections of images as well. Already, it has become a great tool to use to find images from organizations and industries, similar to Flickr.

However, it has also become a touchstone in the ongoing, larger controversy of users' sharing of copyrighted material. Issues such as the ownership of content shared on social tools and copyright infringement will continue to plague tools like Pinterest. How the company resolves these issues successfully will determine whether the tool remains useful. Watch Pinterest as it grows – it will be interesting to see if this becomes another rich source of organization and industry information. I believe images are already being heavily integrated into social tools, and will continue to be. Will Facebook photos become more searchable in the future? We'll see. But images will continue to be an important resource for researchers in any field.

Review

As we wrap up this section on image search, let's review the types of information we can potentially find in image sources.

- product photos;
- photos from company events, meetings and conferences;
- photos of company employees and customers;
- advertising images;
- location and site images;
- unique marketing, historical, and "artifact" images. By this, I'm referring to the photos of the Project Kansas/new Coke documentation in our search example. A lot of organizations are putting their "historical" information online as a way to not only preserve the information but also make it available to others.

Review of the chapter

Were you as pleasantly surprised as I was by the information we found in this chapter's examples? As we discussed at the beginning of the chapter, video, audio, and images are becoming more and more common and accessible online. While a lot of fun and entertaining video, audio, and images are available online, we've seen that we can find some relevant and unique information on organizations and industries via these "alternative" sources.

I think researchers often tend to overlook the visual and audio information that is available via these tools. If we can train ourselves to think about these sources from a slightly different perspective, we can bring a lot of relevant information and impact to our work and to our knowledge base.

Note

1. Coca-Cola Company (2012) The Coca-Cola Company. *YouTube*. Available from: *http://www.flickr.com/groups/thecoca-colaco/* [Accessed 25 April 2012].

5

Social search engines

Abstract: This chapter looks specifically at finding information using social search engines, such as Samepoint, SocialMention, and Addictomatic. Common characteristics of social search engines are explored. The topic of "sentiment," the ability of social search engines to determine the positive or negative "tone" of a post, is discussed. For Samepoint and SocialMention, the chapter outlines the kinds of information that can be found in these tools, and provides search examples for each tool to illustrate search techniques and results. Tips for searching each tool are provided. The chapter also explores ways to protect your personal information, and cautions on using each tool. The chapter concludes with a list of other tools in this category, including search engines for information about individuals (such as ZabaSearch and Pipl), and a review of the content covered in the chapter.

Key words: Social search, social search engines, sentiment, Samepoint, SocialMention, people search.

What are they?

Social search engines are tools that conduct any kind of keyword search over several different social properties. They often integrate "non-social" search results as well – for example, a social search engine might pull in search results from news sources, as well as from LinkedIn, Twitter, and other social sources.

How do they work?

Social search engines work very similarly to "regular" search engines, but they focus on retrieving search results from social sources, such as Twitter, Facebook, and LinkedIn. Like "regular" search engines, social search engines will search across a variety of sources, and will utilize some type of algorithm to rank your search results by relevance and/or date.

Some common features of social search engines include:

- **Searching publicly available information from social sites**, as well as utilizing any APIs (application programming interfaces) that are available for social tools. For example, Twitter makes its API available to developers via its developer site (*https://dev.twitter.com/*). The API makes some of the raw information in Twitter available for other uses – including apps and social search engine results.

- **Tying in results from non-social tools.** Often, in addition to results from blogs, microblogs, and forums, you will also get website results and news results.

- **Providing search capabilities and search results broken out by type of social property.** Many social search engines allow you to break out your search results by category, such as forums, blogs, and microblogs.

- **Providing analysis of "sentiment,"** increasingly a feature in social search engines – for example, determining if what is being said about a company or a product is positive, negative, or neutral. Currently, this sentiment analysis, at least in available free tools, is not particularly accurate. We will look more closely at sentiment later in this chapter.

What kind of business and competitive information can be found there?

Because social search engines search across a multitude of social properties, the type of information you find is broad in nature.

- **Social search engines provide a broad view of the "buzz" at the moment.** You can quickly see your search term across many different social sources, and see the latest topics being discussed.

- **They can give you clues as to where to search more deeply.** An organization search, for example, will quickly show where that organization is active – YouTube, Twitter, Facebook, or any other tool covered by the search engine. Once you see where the organization is active, go to those individual tools and search more deeply. Social search engines only really "skim off the top" – social search engine results from YouTube, for example, will not give you the same depth of results as a direct search within YouTube.

- **They can alert you to tools you may not know about, or may have forgotten about.** Some tools, like Addictomatic, cover a broad range of well-known and lesser-known sources. By using a tool like Addictomatic for a search, I've often rediscovered sources that provided good additional information about an organization.

Examples of these tools

A few examples of social search engines include:

- **Samepoint**: Samepoint searches across a variety of social sources, as well as web news. Samepoint also looks at "social tone" or sentiment. We'll cover Samepoint more in our example search.

- **SocialMention**: SocialMention is similar to Samepoint, though it searches some sources not covered by Samepoint – specifically, comments from sources like BoardReader, and "answers" sites like Yahoo! Answers. SocialMention is also one of the few search engines that provide the ability to create an RSS feed or email alerts from a search (though, at the time of this writing, those features are a bit unstable). Similar to Samepoint, SocialMention also looks at sentiment, and allows you to filter by positive, negative, or neutral search results. It also breaks out results by top keywords. SocialMention also attempts to quantify "strength" (likelihood that your search term is being discussed), "sentiment" (positive to negative mentions), "passion" (repeat mention of your search term), and "reach" (range of influence).

- **Addictomatic**: Addictomatic searches a broad variety of social properties, and displays results in a more web-based layout (rather than a list of results) (Figure 5.1). As mentioned earlier, Addictomatic also allows you to choose from a variety of sources.

- **Topsy**: Topsy is notable because it does allow you to create email alerts, and it has integrated Google Plus search results. You can also sort results by language.

- **WhosTalkin** (the URL of which looks appropriately like "who stalkin"): WhosTalking is worth checking out because of its search across multiple image tools and bookmarking services.

Figure 5.1 Addictomatic. Note all of the different social properties Addictomatic can search

- **Yauba**: Yauba is a terrific social search tool – one of my favorites, because it also provides document search results (PDF, Microsoft Word and PowerPoint) all in one search. Yauba also calls itself an "anonymous" search engine, in that you can view your results without identifying your IP address. However, in the past year Yauba has disappeared on and off. As of April 2012, the Yauba site indicates that the search engine will return, but it is currently not available – unfortunately.

While many social search engines search the same social properties, for each of the tools and examples, we'll look at some of the unique features and content of that tool.

Samepoint

What is it?

The Samepoint site states, "Since 2008, Samepoint has been providing Social Media Search Results on an international level." Up until 2012, Samepoint branded itself as a "reputation management search engine," produced by Darren Culbreath (*http://www.darrenculbreath.com*). In the first half of 2012, the Samepoint interface and access changed, and users are now required to sign in, either by registering on the Samepoint site or by signing in via Twitter or another online property.

Samepoint in its current iteration offers three functional pieces: social search, a "real time" dashboard, and a "top topics/brand search." The social search allows users to search across social properties as well as conduct domain searches. The "real-time" dashboard provides search results as well as some analysis around sentiment and influencers. The "top topics/brand" search has some pre-determined brand searches set up, and offers a search box as well. We'll take a look at all three of these functions in our example.

Samepoint is also an example of a social search tool that provides "sentiment" tracking – the ability to track the tone of online comments and conversation – hence, the tagline of being a "reputation management" search engine. Theoretically, organizations can track the tone of conversations happening online, so that they can then take action to manage those conversations, or react in an appropriate manner. I'll discuss sentiment more in the section "Some initial tips for getting the most out of Samepoint."

Like all social search engines, Samepoint searches across many different social platforms. Samepoint relies on web search results from Bing, the Microsoft search engine. Though the interface will likely continue to change, the current categories of sources for social search include:

- **Social media sites**: Returns results from a variety of social media properties, including blogs like WordPress and Tumblr, as well as Facebook, Yelp, and LinkedIn.

- **LinkedIn**: Returns search results from LinkedIn Groups, Answers, and Companies. An interesting way to zero in on information specifically being shared in LinkedIn.

- **Government sites**: This essentially allows you to perform a ".gov" domain search, similar to what you could do in Google Advanced Search. A ".gov" domain search primarily returns US government site results.

- **Education sites**: Similar to the Government search, this performs a ".edu" domain search, similar to what you could do in Google Advanced Search. This will return results from any ".edu" domain.

- **Organizations**: Similar to the Government and Education searches, this performs a ".org" domain search, again similar to what you could do in Google Advanced Search. This will return results from any ".org" domain, theoretically non-profit organizations (though this is not always the case).

- **Military**: This function used to return results from social tools used by US military agencies, including the Navy, Air Force, Marines, Army, and Coast Guard. However, as of April 2012, the results from a military search seem to perform only a general web search. This does not seem to be working as of this writing.

- **Negative:** In theory, this capability allows you to quickly identify negative comments, a key functionality in responding to online conversations. We'll come back to this feature in our discussion of sentiment.

- **Reviews:** Searches across reviews from sources like Amazon, Citysearch, Tripadvisor, and Yelp. With these sources, Samepoint might be particularly useful in finding reviews across a variety of organizations, products, and services, including restaurants and hotels.

In conducting a search, Samepoint pulls back results across all of these sources. It seems to sort results by relevance, which means that, typically, an organization's top social properties become readily apparent after conducting an overall search.

In previous iterations of Samepoint, results could be further segmented by individual sources, such as individual social sources. However, the version of Samepoint in April 2012 unfortunately does not support this. This is an unfortunate example of a social tool's losing valuable functionality.

What kind of business and competitive information can be found there?

We've already touched on some of these points, but what are the advantages of Samepoint in searching for business and competitive information?

- It can provide a broad and current view of the "buzz" on an organization, product, or service.

- It can give you clues as to where to search further.

- It can alert you to sources you may not know about, or may have forgotten about.

- It can provide a search mechanism for tools that don't have a "built-in" search mechanism, such as Tumblr. In Chapter 2, on social networks, we looked at how you can work around searching for Ning networks using Google Advanced Search. This is workable, but the advantage of a tool like Samepoint is that it can help search social properties that don't have a search engine on the site.

- Samepoint has a focus on particular US government entities, making it a great starting-point for topics in this area.

- Samepoint's sentiment ranking is a bit more transparent than that of other social search engines. This means that you can determine Samepoint's sentiment ranking reliability a bit more easily than you can that of other social search engines. We'll look at the sentiment indicators in our search results.

How do you get started using it?

To use Samepoint, go to *http://www.samepoint.com* and either register for an account, or sign in using Twitter, Facebook, or another access mechanism as listed on the site. Once you are logged in to the site, you can choose Social Search/Social Mentions, Real-Time/Dashboard, or Top Topics/Brand Search.

Some initial tips for getting the most out of Samepoint

As we'll see, each social search engine has its own strengths and weaknesses. One of Samepoint's strengths is that it searches some unique US sources. That said, my philosophy is that it's worthwhile trying out many different search engines if you are searching a company, industry, or topic in any depth. You never know what you might find.

Conversely, if you conduct a search in Samepoint for a particular organization or topic and don't find much information, don't spend too much more time trying to mine it further. If you find some leads – for example, that an organization seems to be active in posting videos on YouTube – then go and search YouTube more, rather than try to mine more deeply on social search engines.

A word about sentiment

Mining social tools for sentiment is an extremely tricky thing. Sentiment tools cannot track sarcasm, for example. Free sentiment tools, in particular, don't seem to be very good at all at accurately tracking sentiment. Some of the paid and subscription tools for sentiment tracking and "reputation management" – tools such as Radian6, that allow the user not only to closely track information

---

in a variety of social tools, but also to respond via integrated workflow tools – definitely do a better job of highlighting negative sentiment. We won't go into those tools here, other than to emphasize again that free social sentiment tools like Samepoint (and some of the others we'll look at) currently are not very good at identifying positive or negative sentiment. You, as a researcher, should carefully check and verify any determination of sentiment made by these tools before accepting any verdict on "sentiment."

Let's take a quick look at an example from Samepoint.

Example 5.1: Government entity search

For this example, let's do a quick search for the US Federal Reserve Banks (*http://www.federalreserveeducation.org/about-the-fed/structure-and-functions/districts/*). To provide a brief background, each of the 12 US Federal Reserve districts has a bank. The Federal Reserve Banks are the operating arms of the central bank of the United States, and serve banks and the US Treasury. The Federal Reserve Banks also provide information and services to the public.

So let's jump into a search for Federal Reserve Bank on Samepoint. We'll start off by just doing a straight search for "Federal Reserve Bank" (with quotes).

Using Samepoint, it's important to note a few things in our initial search results (Figure 5.2). All search results come up with a sentiment ranking, identified as "Social Tone." We've touched on the questionable nature of sentiment ranking, especially within free tools, but let's use this as a specific example. One result, titled "End the Fed Network! Sound Money for America," indicates the words that Samepoint has identified as positive or negative. On the negative side: "inflation" and "distortion." On the positive side: "supply," "free," "responsible," and "for." Overall, the color scale indicates that this post is more positive than negative.

1 day ago   The Federal Reserve Cartel: Part I: The Eight Families « LEFT ...
BIS is owned by the Federal Reserve, Bank of England, Bank of Italy, Bank of Canada,
Swiss National Bank, Nederlandsche Bank, Bundesbank and Bank of France. Posted: 1
day ago

Tweet   **Source:** http://deanhenderson.wordpress.com/2011/06/01/the-federal-reserve-cartel-part-i-the-eight-families/
Social Tone:
Negatives Words: (None found in this post)
Positive Words: (None found in this post)

2 days, 14 hours ago   End The Fed Network - Sound Money for America! Audit the Fed ...
The Federal Reserve Bank, through its inflation of the money supply and the distortion of
free markets resulting from its intervention, is responsible for the current ... Posted: 2
days, 14 hours ago

Tweet   **Source:** http://endthefedusa.ning.com/
Social Tone:
Negatives Words: inflation, distortion
Positive Words: supply, free, responsible, for

3 days, 20 hours ago   Federal Reserve Bank of San Francisco - Government Organization ...
To connect with Federal Reserve Bank of San Francisco, sign up for Facebook today.
Posted: 3 days, 20 hours ago
Source: http://www.facebook.com/SFFedReserve

Figure 5.2   **Samepoint social media site search results for Federal Reserve Bank**

While, admittedly, the words "inflation" and "distortion" often have negative connotations, words like "supply," "responsible," and "for" – especially "for" – are much less geared toward any kind of sentiment at all. Indeed, the link of this search result leads to a Ning network called "End the Fed" (*http://endthefedusa.ning.com/*) which calls for the repeal of the US Federal Reserve Act – a decidedly unfavorable approach to the Federal Reserve Bank. Lesson: Cast a very critical eye on any kind of sentiment ranking from any tool.

Searching for Federal Reserve Bank (or any topic) in social media sites can help to quickly identify which social media tools an organization uses, or which social media tools are most active for a particular topic. If we scroll further down the page, we see that several of the Federal Reserve Banks have their own LinkedIn and Facebook pages (Figure 5.3).

In addition to the Federal Reserve Bank (FRB) sites, we also find some other properties focused on the FRB. These include the Ning group mentioned above, mention of the Atlanta FRB on Yelp, and the San Francisco FRB site on Facebook.

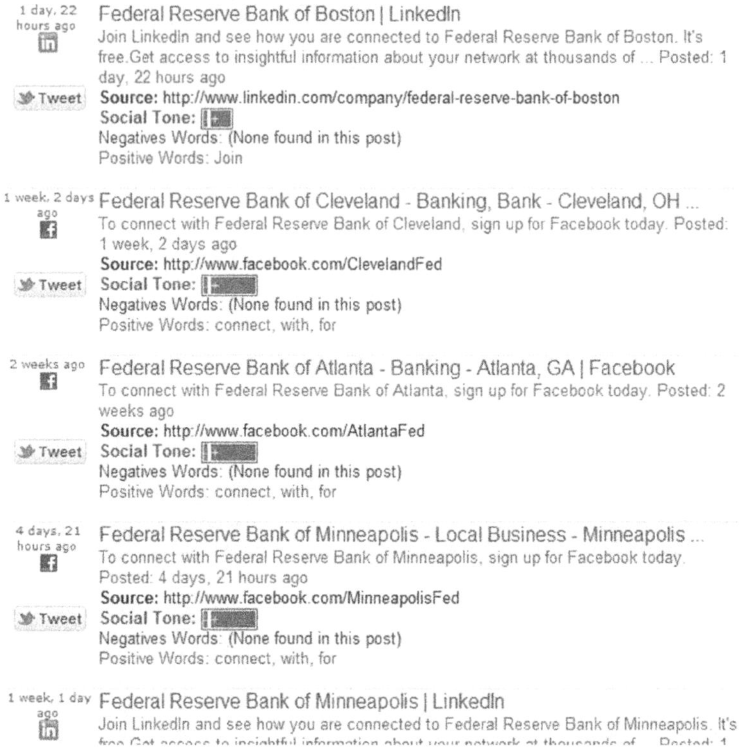

1 day, 22 hours ago

Federal Reserve Bank of Boston | LinkedIn
Join LinkedIn and see how you are connected to Federal Reserve Bank of Boston. It's free.Get access to insightful information about your network at thousands of ... Posted: 1 day, 22 hours ago

Tweet **Source:** http://www.linkedin.com/company/federal-reserve-bank-of-boston
Social Tone:
Negatives Words: (None found in this post)
Positive Words: Join

1 week, 2 days ago

Federal Reserve Bank of Cleveland - Banking, Bank - Cleveland, OH ...
To connect with Federal Reserve Bank of Cleveland, sign up for Facebook today. Posted: 1 week, 2 days ago
Source: http://www.facebook.com/ClevelandFed

Tweet **Social Tone:**
Negatives Words: (None found in this post)
Positive Words: connect, with, for

2 weeks ago

Federal Reserve Bank of Atlanta - Banking - Atlanta, GA | Facebook
To connect with Federal Reserve Bank of Atlanta, sign up for Facebook today. Posted: 2 weeks ago
Source: http://www.facebook.com/AtlantaFed

Tweet **Social Tone:**
Negatives Words: (None found in this post)
Positive Words: connect, with, for

4 days, 21 hours ago

Federal Reserve Bank of Minneapolis - Local Business - Minneapolis ...
To connect with Federal Reserve Bank of Minneapolis, sign up for Facebook today. Posted: 4 days, 21 hours ago
Source: http://www.facebook.com/MinneapolisFed

Tweet **Social Tone:**
Negatives Words: (None found in this post)
Positive Words: connect, with, for

1 week, 1 day ago

Federal Reserve Bank of Minneapolis | LinkedIn
Join LinkedIn and see how you are connected to Federal Reserve Bank of Minneapolis. It's free.Get access to insightful information about your network at thousands of ... Posted: 1

Figure 5.3   Some results for Federal Reserve Bank in Samepoint. Note that we've located several Facebook pages for branches of the Federal Reserve Bank

One of the powerful applications of a social search engine is that, in doing this 30-second search on Samepoint, we've very quickly identified some of the top social properties where we might conduct further research. This initial set of search results also allows us to quickly review recent activity on social networks.

With a tool like Samepoint, it can be worthwhile conducting results in each category to see what comes up. For the rest of our example, I'll highlight some of the unique information located by Samepoint.

Negative comments: The results here are both useful and confusing. The useful part is that some of the results themselves actually are generally negative in tone, which may be very useful for any search. The confusing pieces are 1) some results identified here as "negative" make absolutely no sense at all, and 2) the sentiment ranking doesn't correspond with what are supposed to be negative comments. In Figure 5.4, you'll see what has been determined to be a negative posting, yet the "sentiment bar" ranks it quite positively.

6 days, 21 hours ago
Obama Tries To Fire Up Frustrated Supporters Ahead Of 2012 - Digg
Obama Tries To Fire Up Frustrated Supporters Ahead Of 2012. huffingtonpost.com ... Replace the Federal Reserve Bank with a credit union that actually pays down our debt and ... Posted: 6 days, 21 hours ago
Tweet Source:
http://digg.com/news/politics/obama_tries_to_fire_up_frustrated_supporters_ahead_of_2012
Social Tone:
Negatives Words: Fire, Frustrated, down
Positive Words: with, credit

1 week, 3 days ago
profiles | LinkedIn
Sr. Analyst at Federal Reserve Bank of Dallas, Bank Admin Manager at Federal Reserve Bank of Dallas, Houston Branch, Sr. Analyst at Federal Reserve Bank Posted: 1 week, 3 days ago
Tweet Source: http://www.linkedin.com/pub/dir/jason/ritchie
Social Tone:
Negatives Words: (None found in this post)
Positive Words: (None found in this post)

2 days, 19 hours ago
m | Facebook
is on Facebook. Join Facebook to connect with and others you may know. Facebook gives people the power to share and makes the world more ... Posted: 2 days, 19 hours ago
Tweet Source: http://www.facebook.com/jazmine.breeding
Social Tone:
Negatives Words: (None found in this post)
Positive Words: Join, connect, with, know, power, share, more

6 months, 1 week ago
Something Happening Here: So the American People Are "Waking Up ...
"Hate your next door neighbor, but don't forget to say grace." In fact ... be LOANED into existence: the US Treasury gets a "loan" from the Federal Reserve Bank ... Posted: 6 months, 1 week ago
Tweet Source: http://itsafluffy.blogspot.com/2011/10/so-american-people-are-waking-up-fine.html
Social Tone:
Negatives Words: (None found in this post)

Figure 5.4 Some "negative" search results from Samepoint. Note the Facebook result in particular. While it comes up as negative, its "Social Tone" is decidedly positive. And why would a senior analyst profile for someone at the Federal Reserve Bank at Dallas come up as negative?

Government sites: This tab is quite useful if you are looking for any kind of US government information for your search term(s). Again, this search seems to look for .gov domain sites and information (Figure 5.5). While you can conduct this type of search using Google Advanced Search – and probably get better results using a tool like USA.gov – it's worthwhile seeing what the comparable search capabilities are, as well as looking for .gov domain results for a topic you might not typically search in government sites.

One of the biggest drawbacks with current iterations of most social search engines is that the individual results, as we have seen, can be very scattered and irrelevant. The time needed to sort through the sheer number of results may simply not be worth the effort. That's one of the reasons I recommend using these tools in a very quick and cursory manner. Find out in which tools the conversations are happening, and then go search those tools individually.

| Figure 5.5 | Federal Reserve Bank search in government sites in Samepoint Note the different set of results: Board listings, manuals, forms |

Before we leave Samepoint, let's look at the Real-Time and Brand functions. If we do our same search for "Federal Reserve Bank" in Real-Time, we don't get a lot of information back. Samepoint tells us that "overall comments are positive" – but this is an aggregated view of the tone of the results, and we've already seen that the sentiment determination is not very good. Depending on the topic, Samepoint can come back with some aggregated information on top conversation points (topics related to the search), top influencers and sources, and "social media ecosystem," which indicates on which social media properties our search is most active (Figure 5.6). However, the functionality is not reliable as of this writing.

Finally, the Topic/Brand search has some pre-determined searches for some top brands, such as Coca-Cola, IBM, McDonald's, and China Mobile. A search here brings up results from across a variety of sources, including Twitter. However, the mix of sources seems a bit scattered – social media properties are included, as

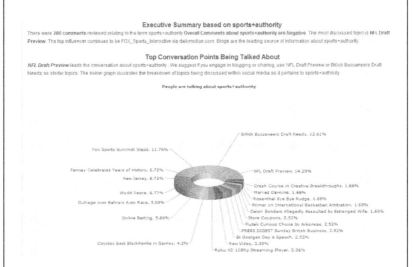

Executive Summary based on sports+authority

There were 200 comments reviewed relating to the term sports+authority. Overall Comments about sports+authority are Negative. The most discussed topic is NFL Draft Preview. The top influencer continues to be FOX_Sports_Interactive via dailymotion.com. Blogs are the leading source of information about sports+authority.

Top Conversation Points Being Talked About

NFL Draft Preview leads the conversation about sports+authority. We suggest if you engage in blogging or sharing, use NFL Draft Preview or Billick Buccaneers Draft Needs as starter topics. The below graph illustrates the breakdown of topics being discussed within social media as it pertains to sports+authority.

People are talking about sports+authority

Figure 5.6	"Real-Time" results using sports + authority as an example on Samepoint. Note that Real-Time can identify topics associated with my search

well as web news. The benefit here is to see what sites are most active in our search, as well as to see who the "influencers" are – who are those people mentioning Federal Reserve Bank the most (Figure 5.7)?

So what were we able to find relevant to the Federal Reserve Bank in Samepoint?

- Very quickly, we were able to locate the social platforms that we should search further. Especially if an organization doesn't list its social platforms on its website, a tool like Samepoint can quickly point us to some starting-points for further search. This is one of the main advantages of social search engines.

- We identified some other social sites that might be worth investigating – for example, the "End the Fed" Ning site. Social search engines can quickly identify not only the "official" platforms for an organization, but also, potentially, the top "alternative" platforms for a different perspective on an organization.

Figure 5.7   Topic/Brand search for Federal Reserve Bank in Samepoint. Top sites and influencers related to my search results are shown on the left

- Similarly, we were able to identify some "influencers" that might be worth investigating or following. Whether the influencers identified are "for" or "against" the topic we're researching, it may be valuable to be aware of their perspectives.

- Negative sentiment (outside of the "Social Tone" feature). If you're looking for current "dirt" on an organization, the negative sentiment feature allows you to quickly identify this, and the platforms on which to search further for negative comments.

SocialMention

What is it?

SocialMention is another social search engine that searches across over 100 social media properties. As of early 2012, SocialMention is offering a couple of useful added features. One, it allows you to search across a spectrum of social media properties, and it also allows you to pick and choose the ones you want to search (similar to Addictomatic) (Figure 5.8).

You also have the option to search across categories of social platforms, such as blogs, comments, images, etc. – similar to Samepoint (Figure 5.9).

The best thing is that SocialMention seems to be offering the ability to set up ongoing alerts. However, as of April 2012, the alerts feature is not working (and claims to be back up within a week). The ability to set up alerts or RSS feeds from social search engines is critical, and something that will be a strong advantage in any social search engine that is able to offer this effectively and reliably.

What kind of business and competitive information can be found there?

The same type of information you can find in Samepoint applies to SocialMention.

- It can provide a broad and current view of the "buzz" on an organization, product, or service.

- It can give you clues as to where to search further.

socialmention*

Real-time social media search and analysis:

| | in | All | Search |

or select social media sources

☐ ask	☐ backtype	☐ bbc	☐ bebo	☐ bing
☐ bleeper	☐ blinkx	☐ blip	☐ blogcatalog	☐ blogdigger
☐ bloggy	☐ bloglines	☐ blogmarks	☐ blogpulse	☐ boardreader
☐ boardtracker	☐ break	☐ clipmarks	☐ clipta	☐ cocomment
☐ dailymotion	☐ delicious	☐ deviantart	☐ digg	☐ diigo
☐ facebook	☐ faves	☐ flickr	☐ fotki	☐ friendfeed
☐ friendster	☐ google blog	☐ google buzz	☐ google news	☐ google video
☐ highfive	☐ identica	☐ iterend	☐ jumptags	☐ kvitre
☐ lareta	☐ linkedin	☐ metacafe	☐ msn social	☐ msn video
☐ mybloglog	☐ myspace	☐ myspace blog	☐ myspace photo	☐ myspace video
☐ netvibes	☐ newsvine	☐ ning	☐ omgili	☐ panoramio
☐ photobucket	☐ picasaweb	☐ pixsy	☐ plurk	☐ prweb
☐ reddit	☐ samepoint	☐ slideshare	☐ smugmug	☐ spnbabble
☐ stumbleupon	☐ techmeme	☐ tweetphoto	☐ twine	☐ twitarmy
☐ twitpic	☐ twitter	☐ twitxr	☐ webshots	☐ wikio
☐ wordpress	☐ yahoo	☐ yahoo news	☐ youare	☐ youtube
☐ zooomr				

Figure 5.8 SocialMention, and the variety of social sources it can search

socialmention*

Real-time social media search and analysis:

| | in | All | Search |

or select social media sources

				All
☐ ask	☐ backtype	☐ bbc	☐ bebo	Blogs
☐ bleeper	☐ blinkx	☐ blip	☐ blogcatal	Microblogs
☐ bloggy	☐ bloglines	☐ blogmarks	☐ blogpulse	Networks
☐ boardtracker	☐ break	☐ clipmarks	☐ clipta	Bookmarks
☐ dailymotion	☐ delicious	☐ deviantart	☐ digg	Comments
☐ facebook	☐ faves	☐ flickr	☐ fotki	
☐ friendster	☐ google blog	☐ google buzz	☐ google ne	Events
☐ highfive	☐ identica	☐ iterend	☐ jumptags	Images
☐ lareta	☐ linkedin	☐ metacafe	☐ msn soci	News
☐ mybloglog	☐ myspace	☐ myspace blog	☐ myspace	Videos
☐ netvibes	☐ newsvine	☐ ning	☐ omgili	Audio
☐ photobucket	☐ picasaweb	☐ pixsy	☐ plurk	
☐ reddit	☐ samepoint	☐ slideshare	☐ smugmu	Questions
☐ stumbleupon	☐ techmeme	☐ tweetphoto	☐ twine	☐ twitarmy

Figure 5.9 Example of the categories SocialMention can search – blogs, microblogs, etc.

■ It can alert you to tools you may not know about – or may have forgotten about.

SocialMention offers a few unique search features as well:

■ The ability to view results grouped by keyword, user, hashtag, and source. This feature is helpful in several ways:
  – You can quickly identify the top keywords associated with any search. For an organization, you can quickly identify what people typically talk about when they post about that organization.
  – You can quickly identify people (users) who write about your search terms. This will allow you to investigate those people further.
  – Identifying the hashtags associated with a keyword is amazingly valuable, especially in going back and searching Twitter further. If you are searching for an organization, you can identify the hashtags most associated with that organization within Twitter, whether those hashtags are topics or events. If you're searching for an industry, you can potentially find the top events associated with that industry.
  – Finally, the sources function allows you a quick view of where to search in more depth.

■ The ability to filter posts identified as negative, neutral, and positive. Narrowing on negative posts is similar to the "Negative comments" category in Samepoint, but with SocialMention, you can also focus on positive comments as well.

■ In addition to attempting to analyze sentiment, SocialMention also attempts to quantify strength (likelihood that your search term is being discussed), sentiment (positive to negative mentions), passion (repeat mention of your search term), and reach (range of influence). While these measures individually may not mean much, they provide us a way to compare, for example, different company searches to see relative discussion activity for organizations – or any comparable entities.

  For example, let's use two politicians. If we search for Mitt Romney (one of the US Republican candidates in early 2012), we see strength at 38%, sentiment 5:1, passion at 32%, and reach at 37% (Figure 5.10).

  If we compare that with a search for Barack Obama, President of the United States in early 2012, we see strength at 32%, sentiment 4:1, passion at 29%, and reach at 37% (Figure 5.11).

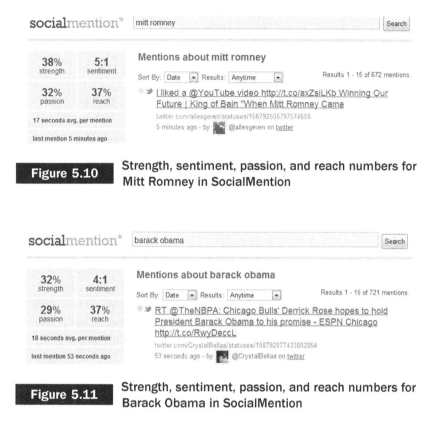

Figure 5.10 Strength, sentiment, passion, and reach numbers for Mitt Romney in SocialMention

Figure 5.11 Strength, sentiment, passion, and reach numbers for Barack Obama in SocialMention

Again, while these numbers don't mean much on their own, it lets us know that currently, more discussion is happening around Mitt Romney, and generally the sentiment of that discussion is more positive than the discussion around Barack Obama. The numbers provide a rough ability to compare discussions.

How do you get started using it?

With SocialMention, all one does is go to *http://www.socialmention. com*, and start searching.

One of the drawbacks I repeatedly see with SocialMention is that the search can sometimes be *incredibly* slow – to the point of having to abandon the search. The search speed has improved over time, but

I continue to run into occasions where, especially if my Internet connection is not fast enough, I never get search results returned.

Some initial tips for getting the most out of SocialMention

As I've discussed, each social search engine has its own unique features. I've mentioned some of the unique features of SocialMention already. If you are searching a company, industry, or topic in social tools in any depth, it's worthwhile searching each tool.

Especially for comparative purposes, as we saw in the political entity search above, SocialMention can give you at least a crude comparison point.

As I mentioned with Samepoint, if you conduct a search for a particular topic and don't find much information, I recommend not spending much more time trying to mine it further.

Example 5.2: Comparative search

Rather than conduct a search using another set of keywords, I'd like to illustrate a search using the same example, Federal Reserve Bank, so you can see some of the unique features of SocialMention in action.

We'll start with a basic search. Keep in mind, again, that you can do a more targeted search either by selecting specific sources, or by using the drop-down menu to select a specific social "category" (such as blogs, videos, etc.).

Also, keep in mind that you may see the screen shown in Figure 5.12 for a while!

Searching content from across the universe...

Figure 5.12 SocialMention search "wait" screen

Be patient. SocialMention's search speed seems to be improving, but on a slow Internet connection, you may need to wait quite a while, or give up your search until later.

When you get your search results, a few things to notice quickly:

- **Look for the RSS and email alert options** (Figure 5.13). Again, as of April 2012, the email alert option is not working. The RSS feed can be used in a reader as of this writing. The results are a bit unfiltered and messy, but this can be very helpful to keep up on results from your search.

  Note too on the screenshot in Figure 5.13 that you can download a CSV (comma separated values) file containing your search results. Downloading the full file, to me, is even messier than the RSS feed, but it may be helpful, depending on your search. For example, you could quickly download a table containing the titles and links of all of your search results.

  A more useful related tip, however, is that you have the option to download separate CSV files for sentiment, keyword, user, and hashtag (Figure 5.14). If you are looking for Twitter hashtags on a particular topic, conducting a search on that topic via SocialMention and then downloading the CSV of the hashtags will pretty quickly and easily get you the hashtags related to that topic.

Figure 5.13 RSS feed and other options for capturing SocialMention search results

CSV Data

- a] Sentiment
- a] Top Keywords
- a] Top Users
- a] Top Hashtags

Figure 5.14 Options for downloading CSV data from a SocialMention search

- **Look at the sentiment ratio for a quick gauge of the conversation** (Figure 5.15). In this search example, sentiment is 2:1 – which means positive mentions are relatively low compared to negative mentions. This quickly gives you a rough "feel" for the overall sentiment of recent discussion. As I continue to emphasize, don't take sentiment at face value. (In just a moment we'll look at the individual items labeled "positive," "neutral," and "negative" to see how accurate it is.) That said, the sentiment "ratio" that SocialMention provides does at least give you some sense of the conversation. Be sure to investigate further.

19% strength **2:1** sentiment

26% passion **33%** reach

Figure 5.15 Strength, sentiment, passion, and reach indicators in SocialMention

- **Look at the other numbers** (Figure 5.15). A "strength" of 19% indicates that our current search terms are not a particularly hot topic at the moment. I don't know that the "passion" percentage tells us much in this instance. A "reach" of 33% indicates that this topic is somewhat broadly discussed, but this number would likely have more meaning in a comparative search, as we discussed earlier.

Next, let's dig into the sentiment, keywords, users, and sources breakouts.

Sentiment

In the example in Figure 5.16, most mentions are identified as "neutral." Let's first take a look at the positive mentions by clicking on "positive" (Figure 5.17). As we skim through the results, the first thing to notice is, there is no indication from SocialMention as to what words make these posts "positive," as there is in Samepoint. Samepoint at least gave us the words it used to determine sentiment. SocialMention gives no such clue. In a quick scan, most of these do seem like positive mentions. It would be worthwhile to go into several items to confirm the tone of the results. As mentioned earlier, one of the biggest drawbacks to sentiment assignment is the inability for computers to detect sarcasm. Especially when searching "heated" topics – like the Federal Reserve Bank – even the most accurate sentiment gauges are going to be skewed by sarcasm.

Sentiment

positive		97
neutral		447
negative		48

Figure 5.16 Sentiment categories in SocialMention

Mentions about federal reserve bank

Sort By: [Date ▼] Results: [Anytime ▼]   Results 1 - 15 of 95 mentions.

🐦 The Fed says all aspects of the economy is improving except for housing. Trust the Federal Reserve Bank, they've our best interests in mind.

twitter.com/James_H_J/statuses/157472965439655937
34 minutes ago - by @James_H_J on twitter

📘 ActionForex.com Home Markets Top Movers Currency Heat Map Pivot Points Action Bias Vola...

www.facebook.com/profile.php?id=100001310262029&v=wall&story_fbid=274569582596715
2 hours ago - by Qaisar Riaz on facebook

📘 Oggetto: SI' Da: Joe Fallisi Data: 11 gennaio 2012 21.46.30 GMT+01.00 A: libertari@yahoogroups.com FRIDAY, DECEMBER 30, 2011 Do Jews ...

www.facebook.com/profile.php?id=595176700&v=wall&story_fbid=344018352277089
3 hours ago - by Joe Fallisi on facebook

📘 Why is he wrong? Because he is against a private bank, (Federal Reserve), which loans money, (that is printed out of thin air), to the U.S. ...

Figure 5.17 "Positive" sentiment results for Federal Reserve Bank. Note that the fourth result is decidedly not positive

Alternatively, let's look at the negative mentions (Figure 5.18). In this instance, the negative mentions get a little weird sometimes ("THE HUMAN RACE IS 1! WE MUST UNITE TO DEFEAT EVIL!" Actual quote from one of my search results.). But again, in general, the negative sentiment indicators do seem to be relatively accurate. Just as with the positive sentiment results, it would be worthwhile to take a look at several posts to confirm that the results are indeed negative.

Finally, let's take a look at what's being categorized as "neutral" (Figure 5.19). Frankly, I appreciate the fact that SocialMention has a neutral category. To me, this gives more credibility to Social Mention's sentiment evaluation process – because there are

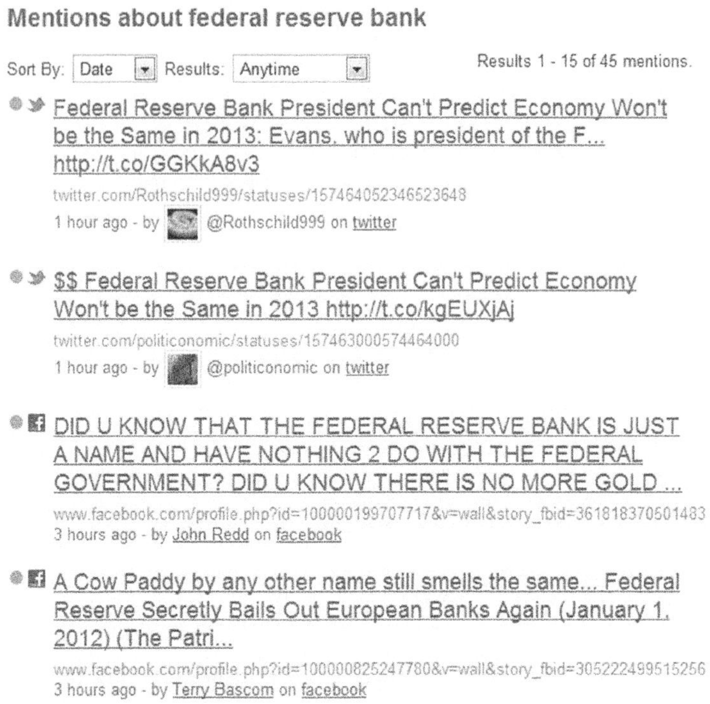

Mentions about federal reserve bank

Sort By: [Date ▼] Results: [Anytime ▼]   Results 1 - 15 of 45 mentions.

Federal Reserve Bank President Can't Predict Economy Won't be the Same in 2013: Evans. who is president of the F...
http://t.co/GGKkA8v3
twitter.com/Rothschild999/statuses/157464052346523648
1 hour ago - by 🖼 @Rothschild999 on twitter

$$ Federal Reserve Bank President Can't Predict Economy Won't be the Same in 2013 http://t.co/kgEUXjAj
twitter.com/politiconomic/statuses/157463000574464000
1 hour ago - by 🖼 @politiconomic on twitter

DID U KNOW THAT THE FEDERAL RESERVE BANK IS JUST A NAME AND HAVE NOTHING 2 DO WITH THE FEDERAL GOVERNMENT? DID U KNOW THERE IS NO MORE GOLD ...
www.facebook.com/profile.php?id=100000199707717&v=wall&story_fbid=361818370501483
3 hours ago - by John Redd on facebook

A Cow Paddy by any other name still smells the same... Federal Reserve Secretly Bails Out European Banks Again (January 1, 2012) (The Patri...
www.facebook.com/profile.php?id=100000825247780&v=wall&story_fbid=305222499515256
3 hours ago - by Terry Bascom on facebook

Figure 5.18 — Screenshot of negative results in SocialMention. I left out the one about defeating evil. Sorry

a number of posts and conversations that *are* neutral in sentiment, or are potentially too ambiguous to assign positive or negative sentiment. When we look at the "neutral" results, we see that the results generally *are* neutral: news items, check-ins, and job postings.

Keywords, users, hashtags, and sources

Let's take a look at the keywords, users, and hashtags associated with our Federal Reserve Bank search in SocialMention.

A lot of the keywords in Figure 5.20 are ones we would expect to be associated with the FRB: banks, national, government, and money, for example. Some interesting ones to note are "debt" and

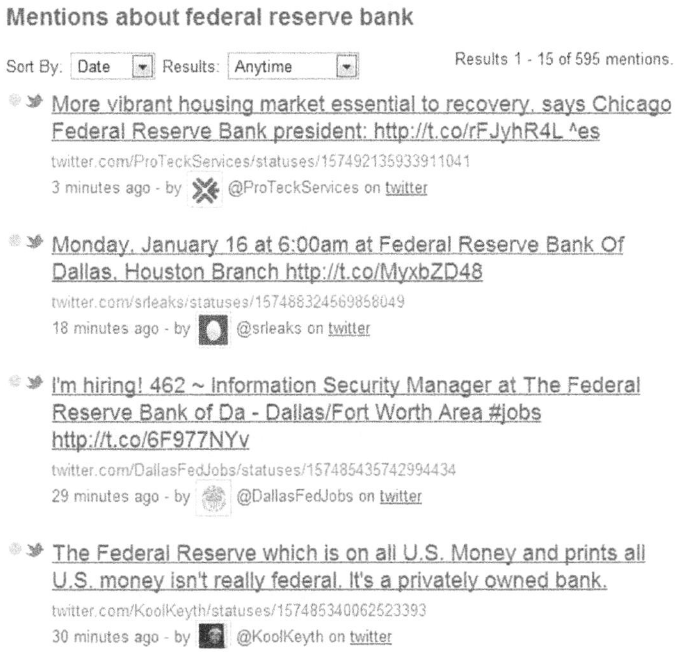

Mentions about federal reserve bank

Sort By: [Date ▾] Results: [Anytime ▾]   Results 1 - 15 of 595 mentions.

More vibrant housing market essential to recovery, says Chicago Federal Reserve Bank president: http://t.co/rFJyhR4L ^es
twitter.com/ProTeckServices/statuses/157492135933911041
3 minutes ago - by ✳ @ProTeckServices on twitter

Monday, January 16 at 6:00am at Federal Reserve Bank Of Dallas, Houston Branch http://t.co/MyxbZD48
twitter.com/srleaks/statuses/157488324569858049
18 minutes ago - by ◯ @srleaks on twitter

I'm hiring! 462 ~ Information Security Manager at The Federal Reserve Bank of Da - Dallas/Fort Worth Area #jobs http://t.co/6F977NYv
twitter.com/DallasFedJobs/statuses/157485435742994434
29 minutes ago - by 🏛 @DallasFedJobs on twitter

The Federal Reserve which is on all U.S. Money and prints all U.S. money isn't really federal. It's a privately owned bank.
twitter.com/KoolKeyth/statuses/157485340062523393
30 minutes ago - by 🦅 @KoolKeyth on twitter

Figure 5.19   "Neutral" sentiment search results from SocialMention

Top Keywords

Keyword	Count
office	172
united	114
banks	110
national	99
central	92
government	91
debt	74
money	72
policy	70
video	70

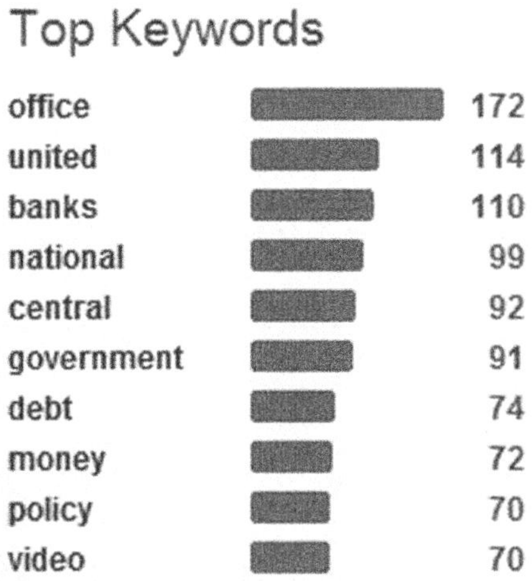

Figure 5.20   Top keywords results from SocialMention

"video." Debt is a term that makes sense in this context, yet because of the negative connotation of it, it may be useful to take a look at the results associated with it (Figure 5.21). And indeed, our results associated with debt provide a lot of great information on the role of the US national debt in relation to the FRB.

Video (see Figure 5.20) is an interesting keyword to note and investigate, simply because it indicates there is a lot of video being posted in relation to this search.

For the "top users" results, the main interest here would be to investigate those people who are writing most about your search (Figure 5.22).

Top hashtag results, as mentioned earlier in relation to CSV files, gives you a quick view of the hashtags being used on Twitter in relation to your search terms (Figure 5.23). Again, this could be a great resource for locating Twitter hashtags on any given topic.

Mentions about federal reserve bank

Sort By: Date ▼ Results: Anytime ▼   Results 1 - 15 of 49 mentions.

● ⊞ Bailout Total $154 trillion - added to the U.S. Public Debt? - 666 Bailout! Federal Reserve Now Backstopping $75 Trillion Of Bank Of Americ...

This story from Bloomberg just hit the wires this morning. Bank of America is shifting derivatives in its Merrill investment banking unit to its depository arm, whi...

www.facebook.com/profile.php?id=100000675824442&v=wall&story_fbid=279364895463809
30 minutes ago - by Paul Decourcey on facebook

● ⊞ Untitled Document

Privately owned US Federal Reserve banks tactics akin to the ones that fostered the subprime mortgages in the United States caused the debt crisis shaking Greece an...

www.facebook.com/profile.php?id=542019575&v=wall&story_fbid=322641427776796
42 minutes ago - by Michael Perillo on facebook

● ⊞ http://www.youtube.com/watch?v=tGk5ioEXIIM Deficit spending, Quantitative Easing & Fractional Reserve Banking are destroying our Country. M...

(PLEASE THUMBS UP/COMMENT/SHARE. LETS GO VIRAL!) Please Buy a DVD @ http://www.infowarsshop.com/The-American-Dream_p_454.html Subtitles/Other Languages @ Lin...

Figure 5.21 Federal Reserve Bank results from SocialMention, narrowed down to the keyword "debt"

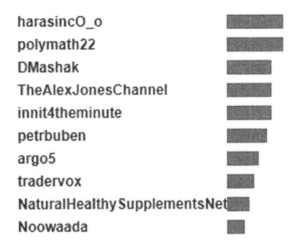

Top Users

harasincO_o
polymath22
DMashak
TheAlexJonesChannel
innit4theminute
petrbuben
argo5
tradervox
NaturalHealthy SupplementsNet
Noowaada

Figure 5.22 Top users results from SocialMention

Top Hashtags

x2e		30
x2c		12
wethepeople		10
etf		10
military		10
asamom		9
militia		9
sgp		9
tcot		9
fastfedfacts		9

Figure 5.23 Top hashtags results from SocialMention

You can think of top sources as another view into what social properties might be best to search further (Figure 5.24). In this example, Digg and Photobucket (interestingly) are the top two sources. However, we can also see that a lot of discussion happens on Twitter and Facebook. Additionally, YouTube shows up as a top source, confirming the "video" keyword we discovered earlier.

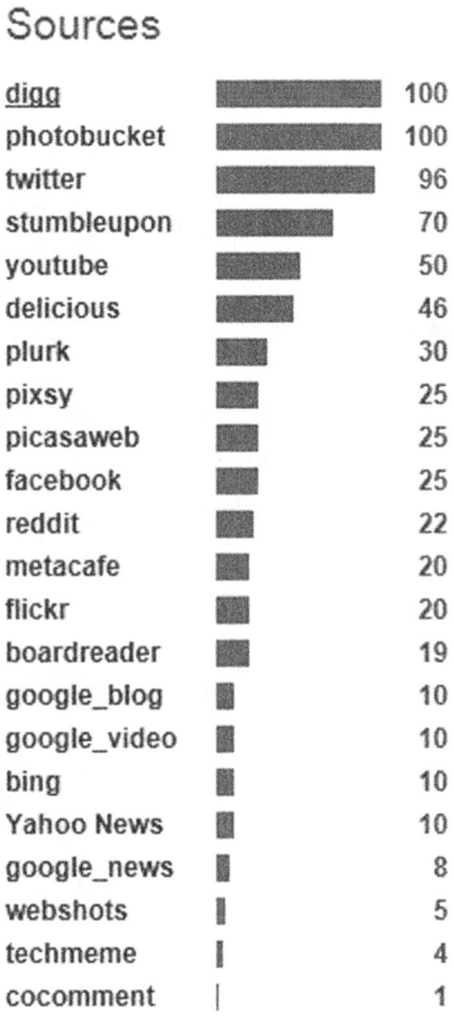

Sources

digg	████████	100
photobucket	████████	100
twitter	███████	96
stumbleupon	█████	70
youtube	████	50
delicious	███	46
plurk	██	30
pixsy	█	25
picasaweb	█	25
facebook	█	25
reddit	█	22
metacafe	█	20
flickr	█	20
boardreader	█	19
google_blog	▌	10
google_video	▌	10
bing	▌	10
Yahoo News	▌	10
google_news	▌	8
webshots		5
techmeme		4
cocomment		1

Figure 5.24 Top sources results from SocialMention

A side note: it may be worthwhile conducting a search at regular intervals to see how the sentiment, keywords, users, and hashtags change over time. Even between one day and the next, you can see changes in what rises to the top. This is (I believe) primarily due to the time-frame of SocialMention search, which covers only the last 30 days. Because of this limited scope, you can see shifts happen fairly quickly.

Finally, now that we've covered some of the unique features in SocialMention, let's move back to the top of our search results page to look at the categories of results (Figure 5.25).

While SocialMention has similar categories to Samepoint (blogs, microblogs, comments), there are a couple of unique categories: events and audio. While it's definitely worthwhile to check out each category to see what's available – especially in light of the filtering features that you can then apply to those categories – let's take a quick look at the unique categories here.

Looking at the "Events" category (Figure 5.26), we see results from Meetup, which is delightful! While the results in this example, at a quick glance, don't necessarily look particularly helpful, this added feature of SocialMention could help you to quickly identify Meetup events associated with any search. For me, this feature both pulls the results, and reminds me to check Meetup – which I frequently forget to do.

For "Audio," in this example, no results come up. And, interestingly, after trying several much broader searches to try to find audio content, I have yet to be able to pull up audio results. Nonetheless, be sure to take a look at the results available here.

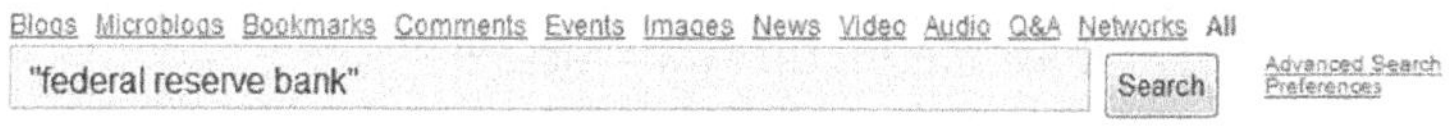

Blogs Microblogs Bookmarks Comments Events Images News Video Audio Q&A Networks All

"federal reserve bank"   [Search]   Advanced Search
Preferences

Figure 5.25   Search box in SocialMention after searching. Note that you have the option to limit results by social tool category

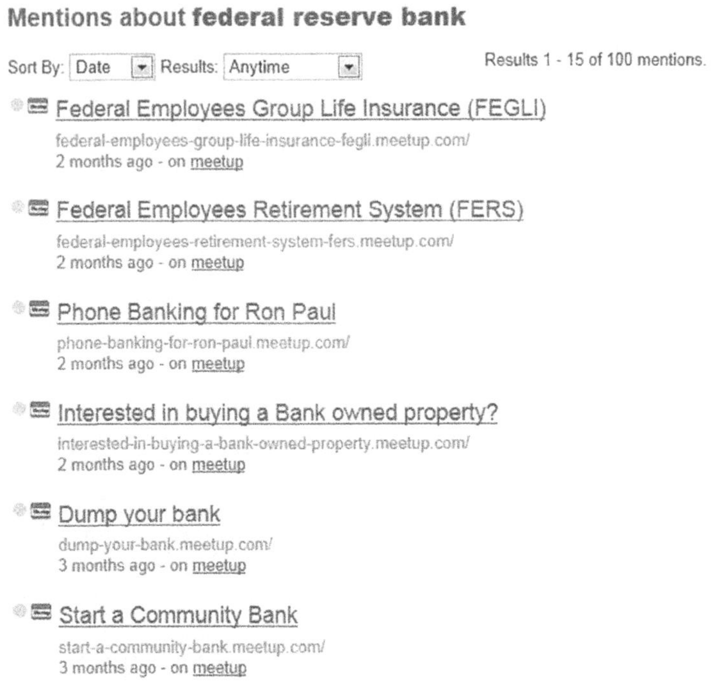

Mentions about federal reserve bank

Sort By: Date ▼ Results: Anytime ▼   Results 1 - 15 of 100 mentions.

✉ Federal Employees Group Life Insurance (FEGLI)

federal-employees-group-life-insurance-fegli.meetup.com/
2 months ago - on meetup

✉ Federal Employees Retirement System (FERS)

federal-employees-retirement-system-fers.meetup.com/
2 months ago - on meetup

✉ Phone Banking for Ron Paul

phone-banking-for-ron-paul.meetup.com/
2 months ago - on meetup

✉ Interested in buying a Bank owned property?

interested-in-buying-a-bank-owned-property.meetup.com/
2 months ago - on meetup

✉ Dump your bank

dump-your-bank.meetup.com/
3 months ago - on meetup

✉ Start a Community Bank

start-a-community-bank.meetup.com/
3 months ago - on meetup

Figure 5.26 Events results from a search for Federal Reserve Bank in SocialMention

As we wrap up this quick view of SocialMention, note, too, that there is an "advanced search" feature that is not immediately visible from the initial search page (Figure 5.27). The advanced search, as of this writing, provides you the ability to do phrase searching, exclude words, filter by location, and limit results to a particular language. The other interesting feature in advanced search is the ability to *exclude* certain users. This may be very helpful after reviewing your results by top users, as there may be particular users that "clutter up" your results.

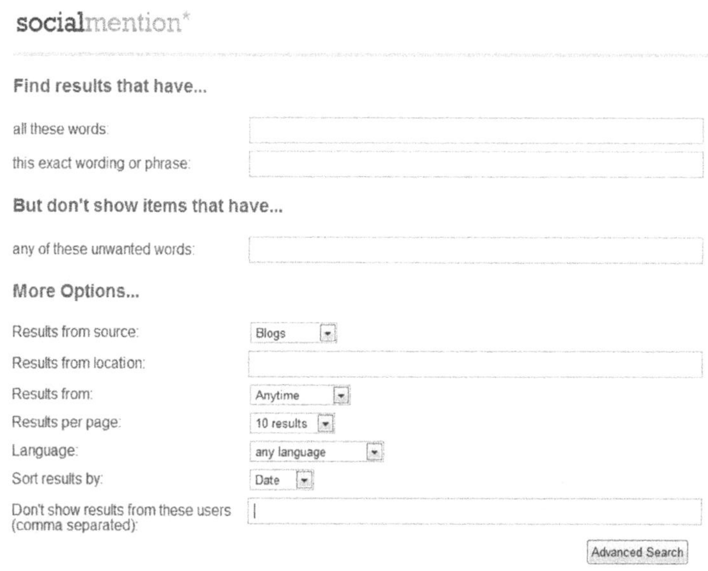

socialmention*

Find results that have...

all these words:

this exact wording or phrase:

But don't show items that have...

any of these unwanted words:

More Options...

Results from source: | Blogs ▾ |

Results from location:

Results from: | Anytime ▾ |

Results per page: | 10 results ▾ |

Language: | any language ▾ |

Sort results by: | Date ▾ |

Don't show results from these users
(comma separated):

[Advanced Search]

Figure 5.27   Advanced search options in SocialMention

Caveats

You might be asking yourself, why would you use anything *but* social search engines, if they search across a variety of social sources?

As we've seen, social search engines are a good place to start a search on any organization. They can often give you a good overview of "where to look next." However, search results for any particular social tool are usually limited to only a certain number of results, and only the most recent results. For these reasons, social search engines can be a good starting-point for your search, but should rarely be your only source.

As I've also emphasized – probably to the point of redundancy – the other big caveat of using social search engines is relying on them for a "true" sense of sentiment. Sentiment tracking is a terrific concept, and an invaluable one for any organization interested in tracking what people are saying about the organization. However, any user of a tool – free or paid – that claims to track sentiment in online tools needs to check carefully into the claims of those tools to confirm the reliability of the sentiment tracking.

A last caveat for SocialMention specifically: As you drill down by keyword or other limiters, be sure to observe in the URL if the limiters are "stacking up" or if they are separate. For example, in using the limiter examples, I looked at my URL:

http://socialmention.com/search?q=federal+reserve+bank&t=all&btn G=Search&filter_keyword=debt&filter_source=digg

The URL indicates that, while I was hoping to limit just by the "debt" keyword, my results were also being limited to just Digg as a source.

Additionally, be sure to look at the number of your search results as you use your filters. My experience has been that my SocialMention searches are sometimes difficult to "reset." Even if I conduct a new search, it seems that my limiters are still in place.

Additional and related tools in this category

A related set of tools in this area are what might be characterized as people tracking tools, which, as a general rule, combine public record information with information derived from social tools such as LinkedIn.

These tools can be very helpful if you are trying to find out if a particular person is using social media, or are trying to gather information on a particular person. Many private investigators are actively using these tools, and frankly, the depth of personal information you can find in some of these tools can be somewhat alarming.

Some of the tools that fall into this category are:

- **YoName:** YoName allows you to conduct a web search, business search, public record search, or people search.
- **Spokeo:** Spokeo searches across a variety of social networks (using name, email, phone, username, or address). Some results are available without a subscription, and some are not.
- **ZabaSearch:** ZabaSearch is more of a straight public records search, but integrates mapping capabilities. ZabaSearch ultimately links into Intelius (*http://www.intelius.com*), which is a background check service.

Tools like YoName and Spokeo are interesting and useful because they allow you to search by email or by user name, among other things (Figure 5.28). So, for example, if you have a user name associated with a person you're researching, a tool like YoName does a pretty good job

Figure 5.28   Search results for "scbrown5" in YoName

of aggregating and finding all the social properties containing that user name.

GlassDoor is another tool I include as an investigative social search tool, though it's distinctly different from the people-search tools. GlassDoor allows users to post information about company salaries, interviews, and reviews anonymously. For the interview section, for example, users may be employees, or may be people who went through an interview and did not get the job (Figure 5.29). Users can rank the difficulty of their interview, provide detail about the process, and indicate whether they received a job offer and whether they accepted the offer.

Due to the anonymity of its users, it certainly is possible that users could submit false or misleading information. Nonetheless, it's fascinating to look at the information available in GlassDoor to get a real insider's view of a company's personnel process.

Ongoing GlassDoor access, as of this writing, requires a subscription. However, you are able to conduct a few "free" searches to get a sense of the information available, prior to being required to subscribe.

Figure 5.29 AT&T on GlassDoor. This screenshot shows interview questions and reviews results

Review

So, ultimately, what were the benefits of using social search engines? What type of information were we able to find?

- A broad view of the "buzz" at the moment on an organization, product, service, or other topic.

- Clues and pointers as to which social platforms to search further.

- Pointers to tools you may not know about, or may have forgotten about.

- A rough indication of "sentiment" of the conversation around your search topic – negative or positive. Be sure to keep in mind all the caveats on sentiment, but also, don't discount sentiment functionality. I believe the functionality and accuracy will continue to improve, and provide a quick view of the tone of conversation.

- Through SocialMention, we were able to find Twitter hashtags for a particular topic.

- A search mechanism for tools that don't have a "built-in" search mechanism, such as Ning. Tools like Samepoint also provide unique search capabilities for US government entities.

This chapter on social search brings our deep focus on particular tools to an end. In the next chapter, we'll take a look at some of the current trends in social tools, some possible directions for the future, and discuss how to keep up with these kinds of tools going forward.

6

The future of social information

Abstract: This concluding chapter looks at several current trends and developments in social tools. The trends and tools are discussed as a way to understand how social tools may evolve and change in the future. Trends such as social product development, gaming and crowd sourcing, the integration of social features into proprietary tools, social capital, content ownership, specialized social networks, and the role of social tools in political and societal change are briefly discussed. The issue of online safety is revisited briefly. Finally, the chapter concludes with tips on staying current on social tools.

Key words: Future of social tools, future of social information, trends, online safety, current awareness, crowd sourcing, resources.

Introduction

As we've seen, there is currently an enormous amount of information available to us via social tools. We've explored the types of information available, and some ways to get at that information. Social tools will continue to be a source of a unique kind of information on organizations, people, and industries. And the amount of information available via social tools will only continue to grow.

Some questions around social tools that seem to linger for many people are:

- Are social tools a fad?
- Will Facebook (or fill in the tool name) be around in five years?
- Are mobile apps the next "social" tools?
- In a world where there seems to be a new social tool released every day – and where even "familiar" tools like Facebook change regularly – how do we keep up with the evolving and changing nature of these tools?

These questions are not easily answered. We can see some trends and patterns in current tools that might tell us where social tools are going in the near future. In this chapter, we'll explore those trends and patterns, and also discuss some ways to keep up with social technologies. We'll also wrap up with some resources that can help you to stay on top of trends in this area.

Current trends and developments

In many ways, the tools we've covered here are only a small start in exploring how these tools can be applied for information and research purposes. We've looked at some of the richest, most widely known, global tools for finding information. In this section, we'll look at some trends in social tools, and what those might mean to the topic of finding information via social tools.

The "already" future

In this section, we'll look at some trends that are already happening in this space that point to potential future trends in these tools – hence, my use of the term the "already" future. I don't claim to have a crystal ball, or to be a "futurist," though I do enjoy thinking about what might be coming in this space. But I think social tools (and the application of social tools) are particularly unpredictable. What I offer here is my best guess at developments we might see in this space going forward.

What are the driving forces behind the explosion of social tools? Though the answer to this question is up for interpretation, I want to highlight three aspects of social tools that I think contribute to the unprecedented global adoption of these tools.

- One aspect is the ease of using the tools. It literally takes a few minutes to set up a Twitter account and start sharing opinions, information, and photos. This ease of use reduces the barrier to using the tools.

- A second aspect is the "equalizing" factor of these tools – the ability for anyone to use them, anywhere there is access to the Internet. The subset of this aspect is the explosion of mobile device access to the Internet, which is fueling the growth of the use of social tools. For many of the tools, there is no "requirement" for participation, and no minimum guidelines to meet (although some tools have a minimum age requirement to create an account). The average person has just as much access as anyone else to these tools. Additionally, travelers, people who have no permanent home, and flexible workers are just as able to maintain an online presence and contribute content as someone who is in the same place all of the time. People are flocking to public libraries in the US and elsewhere to get online, interact, and share their information and opinions. Mobile participation – the ability for people to access and post information to social tools via phones or other devices – is becoming an integral part of how we live.

- A third aspect is that social tools tap into our desire to share information and, I believe, a creative aspect in all of us. I believe people are increasingly finding that they enjoy sharing information, and social tools make it incredibly easy to do so. Additionally, many people are not only sharing information, but creating their own content and sharing that as well. Granted, you likely won't find the equivalent of the *Mona Lisa* online. Yet people are creating and sharing content, some of which is gaining global visibility and use.

I believe all of these factors mean that the overarching *dynamics* of social tools are not going away. The tools may change and evolve, but the dynamic that social tools have created – the ability to create and share content, and to find information almost instantaneously – is here to stay, at least for a while, and at least while the Internet is still widely available. Whether we're still specifically using tools like Facebook in five years' time to do that is impossible for anyone to say.

So, these dynamics will drive the evolution of the use of social tools. What other current trends give us a clue as to where social tools are going, at least in the foreseeable future?

Social product development

The concept of "crowdsourcing" – utilizing a group of people to come up with ideas, discussion, and solutions – has been around for many years already, and is an idea that continues to be utilized and developed. An aspect of this is that many organizations are adopting the idea of crowdsourcing product development and improvement – using a particular set of social tools to gather and rank ideas for product development or improvement.

One example of this is Adobe Labs Ideas (*http://ideas.adobe.com*) (Figure 6.1). The Adobe Lab Ideas site, among other things, provides input forums for a broad spectrum of its products, from Adobe Reader to Adobe Air. Users can go on to the site, see the ideas that have been submitted for product improvements, vote on suggestions, and provide suggestions of their own (Figure 6.2).

Quirky (*http://quirky.com*) is another example of an online product development site, but geared toward inventors. Quirky works in two ways. It allows inventors to submit their product ideas to the Quirky online community. That community then evaluates those ideas, and suggests improvements and changes. The Quirky team then evaluates the idea and decides whether or not to put it into production. Alternatively, anyone can come to the Quirky site to shop for products developed and produced via Quirky. Granted, Quirky has points in the process where it takes in revenue both from inventors and from consumers. Yet the idea – being able to develop and actually bring to fruition a product online, with the help of an online community – is yet another interesting example of social product development.

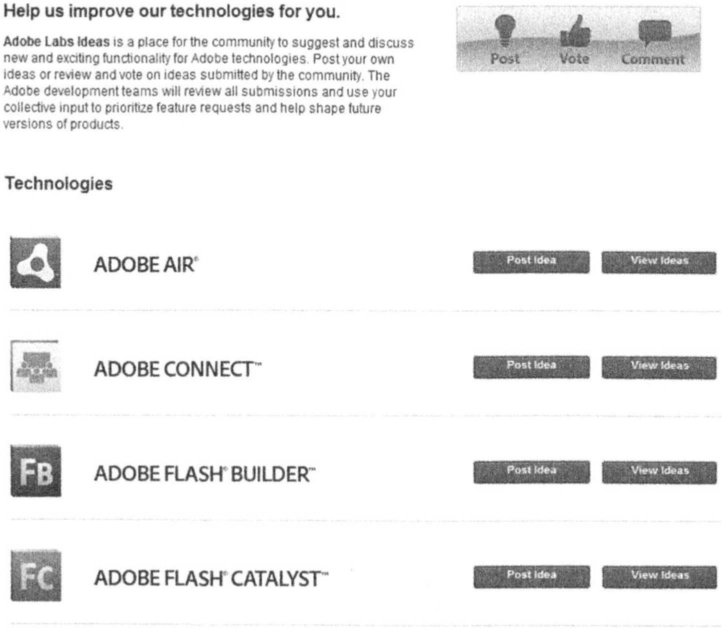

Help us improve our technologies for you.

Adobe Labs Ideas is a place for the community to suggest and discuss new and exciting functionality for Adobe technologies. Post your own ideas or review and vote on ideas submitted by the community. The Adobe development teams will review all submissions and use your collective input to prioritize feature requests and help shape future versions of products.

Post   Vote   Comment

Technologies

ADOBE AIR°   Post Idea   View Ideas

ADOBE CONNECT™   Post Idea   View Ideas

ADOBE FLASH° BUILDER™   Post Idea   View Ideas

ADOBE FLASH° CATALYST™   Post Idea   View Ideas

Figure 6.1   Adobe Labs Ideas site. You can see some of the Adobe products that are available for people to submit ideas

Figure 6.2 The Adobe Air suggestion page. You can see that users can not only submit their ideas, but can also "vote up" or "vote down" ideas. The most popular ideas rise to the top

The use of crowdsourcing is not limited to product development, and is being introduced into more areas of our lives. In 2009, the city of Santa Cruz (California, USA) utilized a crowdsourcing platform in order to make some very difficult budget decisions. When the city staff realized they needed help in determining how to make significant budget cuts, they decided to turn to those directly affected by budget decisions: the people of the city of Santa Cruz. By utilizing a platform similar to Adobe Labs Ideas, the staff were able to gather ideas from the community, and to let the community prioritize and "weigh in" on those ideas, so that the most effective (and hopefully least painful) ideas rose to the top.

While I anticipate that, in the near future, we will see few instances of high-impact decisions being left *entirely* to the community – and I'm willing to be proven wrong – I think we will increasingly see government bodies using social tools to effectively gather and implement the ideas of the community. Whether the governing bodies satisfactorily implement those ideas, of course, remains to be seen.

For researchers, these types of information-gathering mechanisms will be a useful source to indicate product-pain point, faults, customer and community sentiment, and responsiveness of governments and organizations. Looking at platforms like Adobe Labs Ideas, for example, can provide insightful information on Adobe's product development right now.

Gaming and competition in crowdsourcing

Gaming has been around since humans have been social beings. Gaming has naturally translated to the online environment and to participation in social networks. If you are on Facebook, you've likely either seen your friends playing Facebook games (Farmville sound familiar?), been invited into a game, or have participated in a game yourself. Social gaming for entertainment will continue to be a very popular activity.

What I think will be fascinating will be to track how gaming elements will be incorporated into work, organizational, collaboration, and productivity settings. As social tools for collaborating within the organization (such as FMYI) become more widely adopted, a natural evolution will be for gaming elements to begin to be incorporated to drive team-building, networking, and employee productivity and satisfaction. I think you will also start to see mobile elements incorporated into the gaming aspect, as evidenced by the recent use of SCVNGR (*http://www.scvngr.com/builder*) by libraries and museums to build learning scavenger hunts. Businesses are thinking hard about how to apply this kind of dynamic to their use of social tools. In some instances, human resources departments are already utilizing games to help new employees become familiar with the organization. I think you will see more examples emerging of innovative ways of applying social tools and gaming in the organization.

On the crowdsourcing side, Kaggle (*http://www.kaggle.com*) is one example of the application of competitive crowdsourcing. Kaggle specializes in crowdsourced competitions in data science issues. The site allows organizations to post their data, and have data scientists and teams opt in to work on the problem or issue. In exchange for a prize – which can run anywhere from $500 to $3 000 000 as of this writing – the winning person or team provides the algorithms and solutions that best solve the problem. Kaggle also runs a site called Kaggle In Class (*http://inclass.kaggle.com/*), where educators can take advantage of Kaggle's platform and have their students compete on data projects for classroom purposes. These "next-step" ideas and tools in crowdsourcing are changing the way people solve issues and create new products and services. From a research perspective, these tools are not only leading-edge in themselves; they also give some visibility to leading-edge development practices, and next-generation products and challenges. If for no other reason, these types of resources are fascinating to watch.

Proprietary products incorporating information available in social tools

In Chapter 5, we discussed how people-search tools like Spokeo are incorporating information from social tools into public records search results. Increasingly, proprietary tools are incorporating the information available from social tools like LinkedIn and Facebook. One example is InsideView (*http://www.insideview.com*). InsideView is similar to lead-generation tools like ZoomInfo (*http://www.zoominfo.com*), in that it aggregates company and individual contact information. Tools like InsideView also integrate social information, and offer that as a stand-alone product, or the option to integrate the information into a company's Customer Relationship Management (CRM) system. I believe we'll continue to see this integration of social information into proprietary data, because vendors are realizing the value of the type of information that social tools can provide.

Increasing incorporation of social functionality into vendor tools

A related trend is the ongoing incorporation of social functionality into proprietary tools and offerings. By "social functionality," I mean elements such as star rating, reviews, and tagging, as contrasted with social content, such as information from a LinkedIn profile. For example, some public library and other library catalogs are incorporating the ability for users to rate, review, and tag books and other material available in the library. Library catalogs are increasingly replicating the online buying experience of tools like Amazon.com, where customers can rate and review their purchases (Figure 6.3).

Information and content management systems are also integrating these elements. Tools like Intelligence Plaza (*http://www.intelligenceplaza. com/*) and Knowledge XChanger,[1] which allow an organization to acquire and manage internal and external documents, links, and information, also offer features such as commenting, bookmarking, and tagging by the system's users. The vendors of these proprietary tools recognize the value of this type of functionality, and recognize that users are increasingly expecting this kind of functionality, no matter what tools they are using. I believe you will continue to see this "cross-over" of social functionality into proprietary tools.

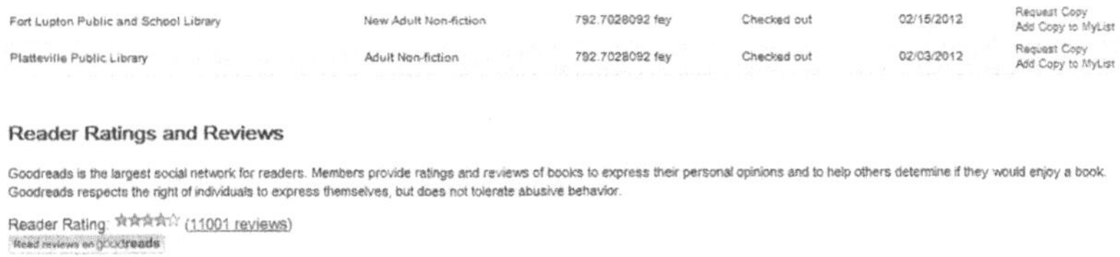

| Fort Lupton Public and School Library | New Adult Non-fiction | 792.7028092 fey | Checked out | 02/15/2012 | Request Copy Add Copy to MyList |
| Platteville Public Library | Adult Non-fiction | 792.7028092 fey | Checked out | 02/03/2012 | Request Copy Add Copy to MyList |

Reader Ratings and Reviews

Goodreads is the largest social network for readers. Members provide ratings and reviews of books to express their personal opinions and to help others determine if they would enjoy a book. Goodreads respects the right of individuals to express themselves, but does not tolerate abusive behavior.

Reader Rating: ★★★★☆ (11001 reviews)
Read reviews on goodreads

Figure 6.3 Example of a library catalog incorporating social elements. In this example, you see a typical listing of holdings in a library for a title, and a review rating for the title, incorporated from Goodreads

What does all of this mean for researchers and information professionals? There are a few implications. Social functionality will provide fascinating views of internal data. Which content is the highest-rated in the organization? From your perspective as a researcher, what does that say about that content or topic? There will be a myriad of ways to mine internal data, thanks to social functionality. Additionally, because you are now more skilled at utilizing social tools for finding information, you will be able to do so more quickly, and easily understand the application of these tools, and be able to teach others in your organization how to utilize them as well.

The growing implementation of the idea of social capital

"Social capital" is a term that has no clear definition – or rather, several definitions that have been put forth in the literature. The way I will define it for our purposes is: gaining recognition as an expert in one or more topic areas in the context of social tools. In this definition, expertise and networking are closely tied. Experts, by sharing credible and authoritative information and insight regularly via social tools, gain recognition – and "social capital" – as experts in the context of those tools.

The way this idea plays out in social tools is that people who are active in a particular topic gain more "capital." Social capital can be gained in a variety of ways, depending upon the tool: by writing about it a lot, tagging content on the topic, sharing content on the topic, receiving comments, "likes," or ratings on the content posted, answering questions on the topic, or by simply being active in a particular forum on the topic.

There are several manifestations of social capital, depending upon the tool. LinkedIn Groups, for example, uses the concept of "influencers" for the week – bringing to the forefront those people who have been most active in the group over the past week (Figure 6.4).

Top Influencers This Week

| MSc | CFC | PRINCE2 |
MOR |

(www.vivaex.com)

Figure 6.4 Top influencers for the Business Forecasting & Planning Innovation group in LinkedIn

In HASTAC (*http://www.hastac.org*), a blogging/posting site focused on the Humanities, Arts, Science, and Technology, those participants who post often gain social capital, and this capital is viewable by other users of the site (Figure 6.5). This feature allows users to quickly identify experts in a topic area, and also provides a reputation "boost" to those experts.

In some tools that offer expertise database functionality, such as Knowledge XChanger mentioned above,[2] users are often able to self-identify as experts and associate themselves with certain topic areas.

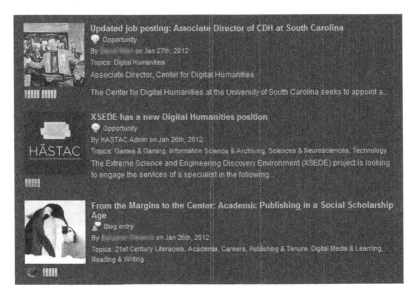

| **Figure 6.5** | Examples of social capital in HASTAC. The bars beneath the images on the left indicate amount of capital, from "lurker" to "super contributor" |

In the example of Knowledge XChanger, the system also uses a social capital functionality to assign "Knowledge Points" to users, further enhancing their social capital status. While the exact algorithm for assigning Knowledge Points to users is proprietary information, the activities of sharing and commenting on content in particular topic areas help users gain Knowledge Points, the social capital "currency" within Knowledge XChanger.

Again, I believe the idea of social capital, as illustrated here, will become more prominent in social tools. For researchers, social capital indicators can help you identify expertise in particular topic areas more quickly and easily.

More ownership of content

Have you looked closely at the Terms you agree to in using Facebook (Figure 6.6)?

While Facebook says "you own all of the content and information you post in Facebook," it also states that you give Facebook "royalty-free, worldwide license to use any IP content that you post on or in connection with Facebook (IP License)."

2. **Sharing Your Content and Information**

You own all of the content and information you post on Facebook, and you can control how it is shared through your privacy and application settings. In addition:

1. For content that is covered by intellectual property rights, like photos and videos (IP content), you specifically give us the following permission, subject to your privacy and application settings: you grant us a non-exclusive, transferable, sub-licensable, royalty-free, worldwide license to use any IP content that you post on or in connection with Facebook (IP License). This IP License ends when you delete your IP content or your account unless your content has been shared with others, and they have not deleted it.

2. When you delete IP content, it is deleted in a manner similar to emptying the recycle bin on a computer. However, you understand that removed content may persist in backup copies for a reasonable period of time (but will not be available to others).

3. When you use an application, your content and information is shared with the application. We require applications to respect your privacy, and your agreement with that application will control how the application can use, store, and transfer that content and information. (To learn more about Platform, read our Privacy Policy and Platform Page.)

4. When you publish content or information using the Public setting, it means that you are allowing everyone, including people off of Facebook, to access and use that information, and to associate it with you (i.e., your name and profile picture).

5. We always appreciate your feedback or other suggestions about Facebook, but you understand that we may use them without any obligation to compensate you for them (just as you have no obligation to offer them).

Figure 6.6 Screenshot of part of the Terms agreement on Facebook, as of January 2012

Is that clear?

The fact is, it's not clear, but it is somewhat clear that Facebook is reserving the right to use some of your content that you post on Facebook in any way it likes.

In March 2012, the controversy surrounding copyright and ownership issues flared up around Pinterest. The flare-up happened on two fronts. In its Terms of Service, Pinterest made even more obvious its ownership of "member-shared" content:

> Subject to any applicable account settings you select, you grant us a non-exclusive, royalty-free, transferable, sublicensable, worldwide license to use, display, reproduce, re-pin, modify (e.g., re-format), re-arrange, and distribute your User Content on Pinterest for the purposes of operating and providing the Service(s) to you and to our other Users. Nothing in these Terms shall restrict Pinterest's rights under separate licenses to User Content. Please remember that the Pinterest Service is a public platform, and that other Users may search for, see, use, and/or re-pin any User Content that you make publicly available through the Service.[3]

Pinterest also stoked an ongoing, larger controversy around users' "pinning" and sharing of copyrighted material. While Pinterest's Acceptable Use Policy forbids the posting of copyrighted material, the main Pinterest page prominently states, **"Pinterest is an online pinboard.**

Organize and share the things you love." For most users of Pinterest, the tendency will be to follow the spirit of the site rather than the Acceptable Use Policy.

Issues such as these – the ownership of content shared on social tools, and copyright infringement – will continue to plague tools like Pinterest, and social tools in general. Because of these types of terms in social tools, more movements are popping up to protect original content that is being shared in social tools.

One example is WhoSay.com (*http://www.whosay.com*). WhoSay.com was developed as a way to help celebrities and other public figures sharing information via social tools to keep ownership of their content. Participation is by invitation only.

On a larger scale, Diaspora (*https://joindiaspora.com/* and *http://diasporaproject.org/*) is a similar initiative, but potentially open to anyone. Again, the goal is to preserve ownership of content shared via social tools.

I believe content ownership issues will continue to drive the use of social media. For researchers, while it hopefully will not restrict access to information available via social tools, it may mean that utilizing certain content found in social tools will require gaining permissions from the creator.

Specialized social networks

Tools like Facebook and LinkedIn aim to be all-inclusive – anyone can join, and you can participate in discussions on any topic. For many reasons, all-inclusive networks work well. They allow for wide-ranging discussion across a spectrum of participants. The emergence of more focused social networks, such as the example of HASTAC shared earlier, indicates a desire to have smaller and more topic-oriented communities.

While I could cite several examples of specialized social networks, I'll share just a few. CapLinked (*http://www.caplinked.com*) (Figure 6.7) and AngelList (*http://www.angellist.co*) are two specialized networks focusing on the venture capital area. Both sites specifically facilitate a place for funders and companies to connect and identify venture capital funding opportunities.

While CapLinked and AngelList are more focused examples, other social networking tools like Edmodo (*http://www.edmodo.com*) are emerging as well. Edmodois a Facebook-like online network that allows students and teachers to connect and collaborate. Edmodo is fascinating

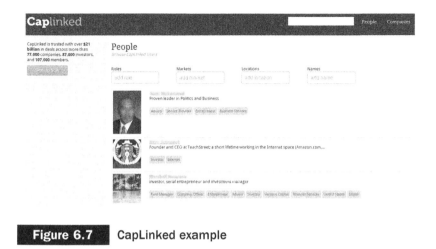

Figure 6.7 CapLinked example

because it incorporates many features for the classroom, including discussion groups, projects, and grading. While products like Blackboard Collaborate[4] are adopting social functionality like Edmodo, Edmodo is a fascinating evolution of the use of social tools for education.

For researchers, I think specialized networks such as CapLinked and AngelList are going to be excellent resources of information. Because of the targeted focus of these tools, they will be invaluable if you are looking for in-depth information on an organization or individual active in a particular focus area. I think the challenge will be in finding the right specialized social networks for our research.

Social networks as an information platform/access model

This concept is a little harder to explain, so I'll do so using the example of First Street (*http://firststreet.cqpress.com*). First Street, produced by CQ Press and SAGE Publications, provides a unique view of political influencers in the United States by drawing upon information from a variety of resources, and presenting that information in a social network interface. In other words, the information First Street draws together is available via a variety of sources. By pulling together that information in a unique way, it utilizes the power and techniques of finding information in a tool like LinkedIn to help make sense of it. Especially in an arena like US politics, where connections are key, presenting the information in a network view is extremely powerful.

First Street is not a free tool. However, I find the concept behind First Street fascinating. I think CQ Press and SAGE Publications have utilized the dynamics of social networks to create a brilliant application that draws upon those dynamics very effectively. I expect that we will see more tools utilizing this kind of "social" interface to make accessing and understanding information easier.

For researchers, keep an eye open for these kinds of developments. I think the value that this kind of tool can offer is obvious; it will be fascinating to see other examples of this as they emerge.

Social networks as a tool for social change

For this final trend, let's look at social tools from a perspective broader than just organization and industry information. The role that social tools have had in social and political change – especially Twitter – is one that cannot be denied. I don't believe that social tools alone make things like the uprising in Egypt or the Occupy movement happen. There are obviously many complex factors in these types of occurrences. However, social tools are playing a role in how people communicate and organize across their usual boundaries. The demographics behind tools like LinkedIn and Facebook are just one testament to how these tools help span geographical boundaries. The tools help people come together in unique ways, and will continue to do so.

For researchers, the ability to track larger movements and topics in the world is invaluable, and not limited to just researchers. I think there are two advantages. One, these tools allow us to identify and track larger issues in the world – societal, regulatory, and otherwise. Two, these tools and applications allow us to see new and unique ways that we can apply the use of the tools to our own purposes. How might we use these tools ourselves to share information? How might we use them to impact on our community? What lessons can we learn?

The emerging and unknown future

I will save myself the embarrassment of attempting to predict the future of social tools. I've outlined what I see as some of the underlying dynamics and current trends that I think may influence what we see in social tools over the next few years.

I do think that mobile access and mobile "apps" will be a strong influence on social tools. First, you will continue to see more and more apps for accessing online social tools (for example, existing apps like the

Facebook, LinkedIn, and Twitter apps, which allow you to access these sites on a mobile device).

Second, you'll continue to see more and more apps available. True, there are already hundreds of thousands of apps available – and there are going to be even more.

Third, I think you'll see more social tools available *solely* via apps. One example that exists today is Path, which I've mentioned earlier. Path is an interesting combination of a limited social network (you connect with up to only 50 people), lifecasting, and a location app like Foursquare or SCVNGR. Foursquare and SCVNGR offer a lot of the same features as Path, but of these three, only Path is available *only* as an app – there is no browser-based version.

Another indication of the future direction of social apps is the popularity of food-, restaurant-, and business-review apps like Yelp or Urbanspoon. Like Foursquare and SCVNGR, these apps have browser-based versions as well, but they are heavily used in their mobile versions. Researchers can currently use these kinds of apps to find reviews and ratings of restaurants and businesses quickly and easily. For doing competitive research in the restaurant business, for example, these tools can be invaluable.

I want to be clear that I don't consider apps in general to be social tools. However, I do think there are apps like Path and Yelp that are social in nature, and have the potential to be sources of great information for researchers.

At this point in time, it's a bit difficult to envision exactly how researchers might mine the increasing amount of information that will be available in mobile apps going forward. I think it will be important to keep a close eye on the apps space, and to look for opportunities for finding important business and industry information available via mobile apps.

What does the future look like? Again, I've provided some of my perspective on some potential directions going forward. Let me wrap up by answering three questions as best I can:

- Will social tools change? Yes, definitely.
- Will the dynamics of social tools change? Yes, but they will also stay the same.
- Will Facebook or Google Plus be around for the next few years? No one knows.

With this perspective in mind, let's take a look at ways you might keep up on developments in social tools for finding business and competitive information.

Keeping up with social technologies

To complete this chapter and to finish the book, I want simply to share some tips on approaching and working with social tools, and some things that I've found helpful to keep up on these rapidly evolving tools.

Taking a strategic vs. tactical approach

Throughout this book, I've tried to provide a combination of a strategic approach to these tools with specific tactical examples. I feel both are important. A strategic approach – understanding how common sets of tools work and the type of information you might look for in those tools – will help you adapt your skills to whatever new tools emerge. The tactical examples give you a concrete idea of how you might go about actually finding that information in a particular tool.

Because the tools change so rapidly, it's difficult to provide tactical examples that won't have lost their relevance by the time this book is published! In my examples, I've tried to be specific without being too detailed (such as saying "click here" and "look on the right side," though in some cases that was impossible to avoid).

I mention this because I suggest you take a similar approach in using these tools going forward. When investigating new tools, try first to get an understanding of what the tool can offer. Who is participating in the tool? What kind of information does it provide, or what kind of information might I try to get out of it? What kind of a social tool is it? Considering these kinds of questions will help you get an understanding of the tool before you even start, and will help inform your search.

Then, dive in. Start playing with it. Try everything, to see what you can discover. Do you find what you expect? What kind of functions and capabilities does the tool offer? What's interesting and unique? This kind of "hands-on," experimental, and playful approach will help build your understanding of the tool, and help you evaluate the usefulness of the tool.

Checking back in with "old" tools

I highly recommend that you regularly check back in with tools you've reviewed in the past, even if you found them not very useful at the time. I've regularly been surprised how much a tool has improved since the last time I looked at it. Additionally, I am regularly and pleasantly surprised by new features in tools like LinkedIn.

And yes, you will check back in with old tools, and some of them *still* won't be very good.

Looking elsewhere: international or non-US tools

It can be easy to slip into searching the same tools over and over again. They work well, we know them, and we can reliably find information in them. It can be easy, too, to assume that since we're searching the "major" tools like LinkedIn, we're getting the full "picture."

I encourage you to regularly take a look at other tools, especially tools that may be popular outside of the US. As we've seen, there are tools like Mixi that are being used by millions and millions of people in Japan. It can sometimes be easy to forget about other resources besides the ones we're used to.

"Expertise" in searching social tools

People can get very good at searching social tools for information. I don't really believe, however, that people can become true experts. One of the challenges of working with social tools and social information is that they are both in a state of constant flux.

Researchers develop expertise in "traditional" tools and databases partly because of the structure of "traditional" tools. They commonly have:

- a structured search mechanism;
- a structured browse mechanism, with a stable and controlled set of key terms;
- relatively reliable and "vetted" information from reliable sources;
- a stable interface and internal structure.

Let's contrast this with social tools, where:

- the search and browse effectiveness and capabilities vary wildly;
- there is lack of a true "federated search" that searches across *all* sources;
- the tools, features, and content are constantly changing;
- all information is potentially questionable.

Because of the relatively stable and standardized nature of "traditional" tools, yes, researchers can develop an expertise in searching them.

I think "expertise" with social tools is of a different nature. It's a willingness to try to look at everything in the tools, and to try different approaches to the tools. It's being willing to interpret the information you find – what does it mean, and what can you conclude? It's a willingness to use the information as a lead-generation tool for further research. It's an acceptance that you may find great information, and you may not find information at all. Most importantly, it's a willingness to experiment and be creative with the tools.

Taking a sensible approach

One of the things that keep me from being overwhelmed in tracking these tools is maintaining a common-sense perspective on it all. Right here, right now, is this tool useful for my research? If the answer is "No," then I move on. For the research I'm doing, do social tools even make sense? If the answer is "No," then I don't include social tools in my research. Remember, social tools are just another tool in your research toolbox.

Being aware of trends, and knowing when to investigate a new tool

I provide some resources below that I find helpful in keeping up on new developments in social tools. Some of these provide a *lot* of information. Though I know there are a few individuals out there who can keep on top of *every* new social tool that comes out, I know that I can't.

So how do you keep on top of it without becoming overwhelmed? Here's what I do.

- **Subscribe to (or regularly check) the sources listed on pages 297–8.** I subscribe to a lot of sources, because I find that social tools are being discussed in a lot of forums. The sources I provide below are absolutely *not* definitive or complete, but they are the ones I've found to be particularly valuable.

- **Scan.** Just as it's almost humanly impossible to keep track of every new social tool that comes out, it's just as almost humanly impossible to read every single article being written on social media tools. As a result, I've become very good at scanning headlines, sources, and articles to understand which ones I should read further. You too will get a sense of this as you become familiar with the sources and what's being written about social tools. Accept the fact, too, that you're going to miss some things.

- **If you see something being mentioned a few times, it's time to check it out**. In some sense, this is a safety net that I trust to keep me from missing important stuff. Social media, by its nature, has a way of bringing back around the news and information that's causing a buzz. If I see a tool being mentioned in a few different contexts – as of this writing, it's been Pinterest – then I know it's time for me to go take a look. Yes, there are some tools that I check out on first mention, because they're either really unique and interesting, or they're big, like Google Plus. But generally, I'll take a closer look when I see a tool coming back into my awareness again.

Stepping away

This may sound strange, but it's very important not to drive yourself crazy with these tools. I really like social tools, but they also drive me crazy sometimes, and I step away from them for a while. I think anyone who's an information junkie worries that they'll "miss something" if they step away from a tool, even for a little bit. Tools that move very quickly, like Twitter, can be especially anxiety provoking, simply due to the sheer amount of information being shared.

The fact is, you're already missing *some* stuff, no matter how closely you're tracking things. If you find yourself getting overwhelmed, give yourself a break. Step away, rebalance, and come back to the tools when you're ready.

Some resources to help

Here are some of my top resources that I've found to be particularly helpful in keeping up on social tools.

- **SmartBrief on Social Media** (*http://www.smartbrief.com/socialmedia*): I find this to be a good source for keeping up to date on trends, rather than individual tools. SmartBrief on social media provides overall trends, updates on tools, and a variety of case studies.
- **Mashable Social Media** (*http://mashable.com/social-media*): Mashable provides a leading-edge look at the social media space, and is a great place to learn about new and emerging tools. The amount of information can be a bit overwhelming, but Mashable is

one of the sources I trust most on this topic. Additionally, it often provides great summaries of new tools, and new developments in existing tools.

- **Social Media Examiner** (*http://www.socialmediaexaminer.com*): Social Media Examiner is focused on the "business" side of social media, helping businesses use it effectively. It provides links to some good reports, and pointers to ways you might find company information on social tools.

- **Social Media Today** (*http://socialmediatoday.com*): Social Media Today provides a comprehensive look at the social media space. It can feel a bit overwhelming, but one of the helpful features of the Social Media Today site is that it breaks out social topics into sub-topics such as Twitter, strategy, search, metrics, and others.

There are many other sources out there, but these are the ones that I find provide me the best news and perspective on working with social tools. Most have multiple ways that you can utilize to stay informed: email, RSS, or via social properties such as Twitter and Facebook.

Of course, I also utilize my Social Information Group Twitter feed to share information on developments, case studies, and trends in social tools. You can find that at *http://twitter.com/socialinfo* or *@socialinfo*.

A final word about safety

Through each chapter of this book, I've tried to give you guidance on making sure you protect your information when using these tools, where necessary. Where appropriate, I've indicated which tools require some kind of "profile" information, and where you can get away with not creating an account at all. In an age of identity theft, people are understandably cautious about putting their personal and identifying information online.

Ultimately, you are the one who decides what information you share online and how comfortable you are online. People who have been victims of identity theft or of online stalking obviously have good reason to be wary of putting any kind of personal information online. The number one consideration is to protect yourself. Be sure to take into account all of the factors that come into play in your situation, and make sure that your "presence" online serves your needs.

Conclusion

As you've likely realized, I really enjoy using these tools for a variety of reasons. At a very basic level, I love the experimental and playful nature of them. For research purposes, I love that I am regularly surprised by the information that I find. It's amazing and delightful to discover a new and unique tool, or a new feature of a tool I already know. These are the things that keep me deeply enthusiastic about social tools, and excited about how social tools will continue to evolve. I hope the approaches and tactics I've covered in this book will be helpful to you in your research and information gathering, and that you share some of my enthusiasm in using them.

I encourage you to connect with me – I'd love to see you online! Though I have a variety of social presences, here are the best ways to connect with me:

- LinkedIn: *http://www.linkedin.com/in/scottrbrown*
- Twitter: @socialinfo or @scbrown5
- Email: scott@socialinformationgroup.com

Good luck in your searching, and have fun!

Notes

1. Comintelli (2012) Knowledge XChanger. *Comintelli*. Available from: *http://www.comintelli.com/website/website.cfm?infoelementid=498* [Accessed 25 April 2012].
2. See note 1.
3. Pinterest (2012) Terms & Privacy. *Pinterest*. Available from: *http://pinterest.com/about/terms* [Accessed 2 April 2012].
4. Blackboard (2012) Overview. *Blackboard Collaborate*. Available from: *http://www.blackboard.com/Platforms/Collaborate/Overview.aspx498* [Accessed 25 April 2012].

Appendix 1: resources

This resources section is intended to point you to additional information and guides on some of the major tools discussed in this book.

LinkedIn

- LinkedIn Learning Center: *http://learn.linkedin.com*. This is LinkedIn's official site for learning about the functionality of LinkedIn, and different ways to use LinkedIn, depending on your role: journalist, small business, job seeker, business development, etc.
- LinkedIn Blog: New LinkedIn Features: *http://blog.linkedin.com/topic/new-linkedin-features*. This blog category on LinkedIn's blog will keep you up to date on new developments.
- Boolean Blackbelt: *http://www.booleanblackbelt.com*. Written by Glen Cathey from the perspective of a recruiter, this blog provides fantastic search tips for finding people in LinkedIn and other social tools.

Facebook

- Facebook Basics: *http://www.facebook.com/help/basics*
- Facebook Family Safety Center: *http://www.facebook.com/safety*

Google Plus

- A quick look at Google+: *http://www.google.com/intl/en/+/learnmore*
- Google+ support (including "how tos"): *http://support.google.com/plus*

Twitter

- Twitter basics: *https://support.twitter.com/groups/31-twitter-basics*. Good overview from Twitter, both for setting up your Twitter feed and for finding people to follow.
- The Twitter Guide Book from Mashable: *http://mashable.com/guidebook/twitter*

Flickr

- Flickr: Explore: *http://www.flickr.com/explore*
- Watch the World with Flickr: *http://www.flickr.com/tour/#section= watch-the-world*. Part of the Flickr Tour, this page gives you some guidance on the different ways to access images.

Picasa

- Picasa: Explore: *https://picasaweb.google.com/lh/explore*

YouTube

- YouTube Help: *http://support.google.com/youtube*. This site has links to a variety of information on using YouTube for posting and finding videos.
- YouTube Essentials: *http://www.youtube.com/t/about_essentials*

iTunes

- iTunes: Tips for Podcast Fans: *http://www.apple.com/itunes/podcasts/*

Appendix 2: tools

This is a selected list of tools in each of the ten social tool categories outlined in Chapter 1. *This is not a comprehensive list.* It does include most tools mentioned in the book. For an extensive list of social networking sites, check Wikipedia: *http://en.wikipedia.org/wiki/List_of_social_networking_websites*.

Networking

The primary focus of these tools is connecting with others. These are the most social of social tools. Examples include:

- Badoo (*http://www.badoo.com*)
- Bebo (*http://www.bebo.com*)
- Facebook (*http://www.facebook.com*)
- Friendster (*http://www.friendster.com*)
- Google Plus (*http://plus.google.com*)
- Hi5 (*http://www.hi5.com*)
- LinkedIn (*http://www.linkedin.com*)
- Meetup (*http://www.meetup.com*)
- MerchantCircle (*http://www.merchantcircle.com*)
- Mixi (*http://mixi.jp*)
- Multiply (*http://multiply.com*)
- MySpace (*http://www.myspace.com*)
- MyYearbook (*http://www.myyearbook.com*)
- Netlog (*http://www.netlog.com*)

- Ning (*http://www.ning.com*)
- Orkut (*http://www.orkut.com*)
- Perfspot (*http://www.perfspot.com*)
- Plaxo (*http://www.plaxo.com*)
- Qzone (*http://qzone.qq.com*)
- Tagged (*http://www.tagged.com*)
- Vkontakte (*http://vkontakte.ru* or *http://vk.com*)
- Xing (*http://xing.com*)
- Zorpia (*http://www.zorpia.com*)

Publishing

These tools allow single or multiple authors to publish their writing. Typically, entries are written in a personal or journalistic format and style.

- **Blogs,** a form of personal and professional online publishing. Examples include:
    - WordPress (*http://www.wordpress.com* or *http://www.wordpress.org*)
    - Blogger (*http://www.blogger.com*)
    - Typepad (*http://www.typepad.com*)
    - Tumblr (*http://www.tumblr.com*)
    - Pinterest (*http://www.pinterest.com*)

Blog search and directory tools include:

    - Bloglines Local (*http://www.bloglines.com*)
    - Google Blog Search (*http://www.google.com/blogsearch*)
    - Icerocket (*http://www.icerocket.com*)
    - Technorati (*http://technorati.com*)
- **Microblogs,** which typically have a limit on the length of your entry. Examples include:
    - Sharetronix (*http://sharetronix.com*)
    - Twitter (*http://twitter.com*)
    - Yammer (*http://www.yammer.com*)

- **Twitter account directories.** To discover some key Twitter topic feeds quickly, you can utilize Twitter feed directories such as:
  - Listorious (*http://listorious.com*)
  - WeFollow (*http://wefollow.com*)
  - Twellow (*http://twellow.com*)
- **Twitter analysis tools**
  - Mirror.me (*http://mirror.me*)
  - NearbyTweets (*http://www.nearbytweets.com*)
  - Trendsmap (*http://www.trendsmap.com*)
  - Tweet Topic Explorer (*http://tweettopicexplorer.neoformix.com*)
  - Tweetgrid (*http://www.tweetgrid.com*)
  - TweetReach (*http://www.tweetreach.com*)
  - Twtrland (*http://www.twtrland.com*)
  - Wordle (*http://wordle.net*)

Social search engines

Social search engines primarily pull information from social sites, though most will often include information that isn't "social." Examples include:

- Addictomatic (*http://www.addictomatic.com*)
- CrowdEye (focuses specifically on Twitter search) (*http://www.crowdeye.com*)
- Samepoint (*http://www.samepoint.com*)
- SocialMention (*http://www.socialmention.com*)
- Topsy (*http://www.topsy.com*)
- WhosTalkin (*http://www.whostalkin.com*)
- Yauba (*http://www.yauba.com*)

Related tools include "people search" tools and others. Examples include:

- Glassdoor (*http://www.glassdoor.com*), focused on the interview and hiring experience within companies
- Pipl (focuses on information on individuals in social sites) (*http://www.pipl.com*)

- Spokeo (*http://www.spokeo.com*)
- YoName (also focuses on information on individuals in social sites) (*http://www.yoname.com*)
- ZabaSearch (*http://www.zabasearch.com*)

RSS and news feeds

RSS is generally accepted to be an acronym for "Really Simple Syndication." In practice, RSS feeds provide an automatic way to get the latest news from a site or a resource. Examples of RSS aggregator sites and tools include:

- Google Reader (*http://www.google.com/reader*)
- FeedBlitz (*http://www.feedblitz.com*)
- NetVibes (*http://www.netvibes.com*)

Video/audio/images

These tools primarily provide places to share and find video, audio, or images. Examples include:

Video

- Bing Video (*http://www.bing.com/videos*)
- Blinkx (*http://www.blinkx.com*)
- DailyMotion (*http://www.dailymotion.com*)
- Hulu (*http://www.hulu.com*)
- VEVO (*http://www.vevo.com*)
- Vimeo (*http://www.vimeo.com*)
- Yahoo! Video (*http://video.yahoo.com*)
- YouTube (*http://www.youtube.com*)

Podcasts and videocasts

- iTunes (*http://www.apple.com/itunes/podcasts/*)
- Podcast Alley (*http://www.podcastalley.com/*)

- Podfeed.net (*http://www.podfeed.net/*)
- Podfreaks (*http://podfreaks.com/*)
- Videopodcasts.tv (*http://www.videopodcasts.tv/*)

Images (including slides and documents sources)

- Flickr (*http://www.flickr.com*)
- Photobucket (*http://photobucket.com*)
- Picasa (*http://picasaweb.google.com/*)
- Scribd (*http://www.scribd.com*)
- SlideShare (*http://www.slideshare.net*)
- SmugMug (*http://www.smugmug.com*)

Collaboration

Collaboration tools help people work together. While many social tools naturally have collaboration features, these tools focus primarily on facilitating collaboration in sharing information.

- **Social bookmarking tools** allow you to tag articles, links, websites, and other online sources with keywords to make them more findable. Examples include:
  - Delicious (*http://www.delicious.com*)
  - Digg (*http://digg.com*)
  - Diigo (*http://www.diigo.com*)
  - Evernote (*http://www.evernote.com*)
  - Instapaper (*http://www.instapaper.com*)
- **Wikis** provide a simplified interface for a group of users to create online pages of resources. They usually allow users to create a hierarchy of and structure for information, to create web pages on the wiki, and to include both online links and documents. Examples include:
  - PBworks (*http://www.pbworks.com*)
  - Zoho (*http://www.zoho.com/wiki/*)
- **Other examples include**
  - FMYI (*http://www.fmyi.com*), an internal collaboration platform

Communication

These tools help users communicate via text, voice and/or video. Examples include:

- AOL Instant Messenger (*http://www.aim.com*)
- ooVoo (*http://www.oovoo.com*)
- Skype (*http://www.skype.com*)
- Windows Live Messenger (*http://explore.live.com/windows-live-messenger*)
- Yahoo! Messenger (*http://messenger.yahoo.com*)

Location

These tools have an emphasis on location. Examples include:

- FourSquare (*http://www.foursquare.com*)
- SCVNGR (*http://www.scvngr.com*)
- Path (*http://www.path.com*) – a more limited, personal networking tool
- Urbanspoon (*http://www.urbanspoon.com*)
- Yelp (food-based) (*http://www.yelp.com*)

Games and virtual worlds

These are primarily just for fun! Examples include:

- Friendster (*http://www.friendster.com*)
- Second Life (*http://secondlife.com*) – though Second Life in itself is not a game, it can have some gaming elements in-world.
- World of Warcraft (*http://us.battle.net/wow*)

Lifecasting

Lifecasting can encompass live video streaming, and can be taken to the extent of "always on" broadcasting of your life. Examples include:

- Justin.tv (*http://www.justin.tv*)
- Livestream (*http://www.livestream.com*)
- UStream (*http://www.ustream.tv*)

Bibliography

Alpeyev, P. and Eki, Y. (2011) Facebook may not be dominant in Japan, Zynga says. *Bloomberg Business Week*, 7 February. Available from: *http://www.businessweek.com/news/2011-02-07/facebook-may-not-be-dominant-in-japan-zynga-says.html* [Accessed 17 January 2011].

Apple (2011) What is iTunes? *Apple*. Available from: *http://www.apple.com/itunes/what-is/* [Accessed 18 December2011].

Arrington, M. (2008) Twitter saves man from Egyptian Justice. *Techcrunch* (16 April). Available from: *http://techcrunch.com/2008/04/16/twitter-saves-man-from-egyptian-justice/* [Accessed 25 April 2012].

BBC News (2011) Google+ social network lets firms have their own pages. *BBC News*, 7 November. Available from: *http://www.bbc.co.uk/news/technology-15625577* [Accessed 18 January 2012].

Bertelsmann (n.d.) About. *BertelsmannStiftung FutureChallenge*. Available from: *http://futurechallenges.org/about/* [Accessed 18 January 2012].

Blackboard (2012) Overview. *Blackboard Collaborate*. Available from: *http://www.blackboard.com/Platforms/Collaborate/Overview.aspx498* [Accessed 25 April 2012].

Blinkx (n.d.) History. *Blinkx*. Available from: *http://www.blinkx.com/about* [Accessed 8 November 2011].

Builtwith.com (2012) WordPress usage trends. *Built With Technology Usage Statistics*. Available from: *http://trends.builtwith.com/blog/WordPress* [Accessed 18 January 2012].

Burson-Marsteller (2011) 2011 Fortune Global 100 social media study (15 February) *The Burson-Marsteller Blog*. Available from: *http://www.burson-marsteller.com/Innovation_and_insights/blogs_and_podcasts/BM_Blog/Lists/Posts/Post.aspx?ID=254* [Accessed 8 August 2011].

Burson-Marsteller (2011) The global social media check-up 2011 (15 February). Available from: *http://www.slideshare.net/BMGlobalNews/bursonmarsteller-2011-global-social-media-checkup* [Accessed 8 August 2011].

CMU (2011) Bertelsmann CFO confirms BMG's acquisition intent. *theCMUwebsite.com*, 30 March. Available from: *http://www. thecmuwebsite.com/article/bertelsmann-cfo-confirms-bmgs-acquisition-intent/* [Accessed 18 April 2011].

Coca-Cola Company (2012) The Coca-Cola Company. *YouTube.* Available from: *http://www.flickr.com/groups/thecoca-colaco/* [Accessed 25 April 2012].

Comintelli (2012) Knowledge XChanger. *Comintelli.* Available from: *http://www.comintelli.com/website/website.cfm?infoelementid=498* [Accessed 25 April 2012].

DailyMotion (n.d.) About us. *DailyMotion.* Available from: *http://www. dailymotion.com/us/about* [Accessed 6 November 2011].

Dant, A. and Richards, J. (2011) Behind the rumours: how we built our Twitter riots interactive. *The Guardian DataBlog*, 8 December. Available from: *http://www.guardian.co.uk/news/datablog/2011/dec/08/twitter-riots-interactive* [Accessed 28 December 2011].

Edmodo (2011) About. *Edmodo.* Available from: *http://about.edmodo. com* [Accessed 26 January 2012].

Facebook (2012) About. *Facebook.* Available from: *http://www.facebook. com/#!/facebook?sk=info* [Accessed 18 January 2012].

Facebook (2012) Statement of rights and responsibilities. *Facebook.* Available from: *http://www.facebook.com/legal/terms* [Accessed 26 January 2012].

Facebook (2012) Statistics. *Facebook.* Available from: *http://www. facebook.com/press/info.php?statistics* [Accessed 18 January 2012].

Facebook (2012) Timeline. *Facebook.* Available from: *http://www. facebook.com/press/info.php?timeline* [Accessed 12 January 2012].

Fisch, Karl. (2008) Did you know? Music industry remix. *The Fischbowl.* Available from: *http://thefischbowl.blogspot.com/2008/08/did-you-know-music-industry-remix.html* [Accessed 18 January 2011].

Flickr (2011) About Flickr. *Flickr.* Available from: *http://www.flickr. com/about/* [Accessed 11 December 2011].

Google (n.d.) A quick look at Google+. *Google.* Available from: *http:// www.google.com/+/learnmore/* [Accessed 28 January 2012].

Guardian (n.d.) Sir Philip Green. *Guardian.* Available from: *http://www. guardian.co.uk/business/philip-green* [Accessed 30 January 2012].

Hernandez, V. (2011) Facebook tops 800 million members. *International Business Times* (5 October). Available from: *http://au.ibtimes.com/ articles/225185/20111005/facebook-members-exceed-800-million-mark.htm* [Accessed 11 January 2011].

History of Computing Education Trends: The Emergence of Competitive Intelligence, IFIP, International Federation for Information Processing, 2008, Volume 269/2008, 113–127, DOI:10.1007/978-0-387-09657-5-7.

Is Google+ a plus for information pros? (2011) *The Information Advisor*, 23(9), pp. 1–3, 8.

Johansmeyer, T. (2011) 20 million Twitter accounts … but how many are active? *Social Times* (3 February). Available from: *http://socialtimes. com/200-million-twitter-accounts-but-how-many-are-active_b36952* [Accessed 8 September 2011].

Koht, P. (n.d.) City of Santa Cruz offers blueprint for solving CA budget crisis with social media. *O'Reilly Gov 2.0 Online Conference.* Available from: *http://en.oreilly.com/gov2fall09/public/schedule/ detail/11269* [Accessed 28 January 2012].

Kremerskothen, K. (2011) 6,000,000,000. *Flickr blog* (4 August). Available from: *http://blog.flickr.net/en/2011/08/04/6000000000/* [Accessed 6 November 2011].

Learmonth, M. (2011) With Facebook in crosshairs, Google+ opens for business. *AdAge Digital* (7 November). Available from: *http://adage. com/article/digital/google-open-business/230862* [Accessed 18 January 2012].

Lenier, B.M., Cerf, V.G., Clark, D.D., Kahn, R.E., Kleinrock, L. et al. (n.d.) Brief history of the Internet. *Internet Society.* Available from: *http://www.internetsociety.org/internet/internet-51/history-internet/ brief-history-internet* [Accessed 28 January 2011].

Levy, S. (2010) The 'path' to social network security is lined with 50 friends. *Wired* (15 November). Available from: *http://www.wired.com/ epicenter/2010/11/the-path-to-social-network-tranquility-is-lined-by- 50-friends/* [Accessed 22 January 2011].

LinkedIn (2012) About us. *LinkedIn.* Available from: *http://press. linkedin.com/about* [Accessed 18 January 2012].

Malik, O. (2011) Vimeo has 150,000 paying subscribers. *GigaOm* (6 November). Available from: *http://gigaom.com/video/vimeo-has- 150000-paying-subscribers/* [Accessed 8 November 2011].

Maloy, S. (2011) WhoSay returns social media copyright back to celebrities. *Billboard.biz* (1 July). Available from: *http://www.billboard. biz/bbbiz/industry/digital-and-mobile/whosay-returns-social-media- copyright-back-1005260532.story* [Accessed 26 January 2012].

Marcus, S. (2010) A brief history of 9 popular blogging platforms. *Mashable Social Media* (6 August). Available from: *http://mashable. com/2010/08/06/history-of-blogs/* [Accessed 8 August 2011].

McBride, T. and Nief, R. (2012) The Mindset List. *Beloit College*. Available from: *http://www.beloit.edu/mindset/* [Accessed 17 January 2012].

Meetup (n.d.) About Meetup. *Meetup*. Available from: *http://www.meetup.com/about/* [Accessed 8 November 2011].

Monoyios, K. (2012) Pinterest's Terms of Service, Word by Terrifying Word. *Scientific American Blogs* (19 March). Available from: *http://blogs.scientificamerican.com/symbiartic/2012/03/19/pinterests-terms-of-service-word-by-terrifying-word* [Accessed 2 April 2012].

MySpace (2011) About us. *MySpace*. Available from: *http://www.myspace.com/Help/AboutUs* [Accessed 4 April 2011].

Natalie (2011) Facebook photo trends [INFOGRAPHIC]. *Pixable Blog* (14 February). Available from: *http://blog.pixable.com//2011/02/14/facebook-photo-trends-infographic/* [Accessed 6 November 2011].

Net Impact (2011) About us. *Net Impact*. Available from: *http://netimpact.org/about* [Accessed 2 September 2011].

Nickson, C. (2009) The history of social networking. *Digital Trends* (21 January). Available from: *http://www.digitaltrends.com/features/the-history-of-social-networking/* [Accessed 27 January 2011].

Nielsen.com (2011) September 2011: Top U.S. online destinations for video). *NielsenWire* (3 November). Available from: *http://blog.nielsen.com/nielsenwire/online_mobile/september-2011-top-u-s-online-destinations-for-video/* [Accessed 8 November 2011].

Orkut (n.d.) MembersAll. *Orkut*. Available from: *http://www.orkut.com/Main#MembersAll* [Accessed 28 January 2012].

Pinterest (2012) Terms & Privacy. *Pinterest*. Available from: *http://pinterest.com/about/terms/* [Accessed 2 April 2012].

Plaxo (2012) About Plaxo. *Plaxo*. Available from: *http://www.plaxo.com/about/index* [Accessed 29 January 2011].

Sawyers, P. (2010) Brazil's nuts about social networking and Orkut best watch out, Facebook is on the rise. *The Next Web* (16 October). Available from: *http://thenextweb.com/socialmedia/2010/10/16/brazils-nuts-about-social-networking-and-orkut-best-watch-out-facebook-is-on-the-rise/* [Accessed 21 December 2011].

Scribd (n.d.) About. *Scribd*. Available from: *http://www.scribd.com/about* [Accessed 18 January 2012].

Sherman, A. (2011) 4 U.S. government agencies getting social on YouTube. *Mashable Social Media* (14 October). Available from: *http://mashable.com/2011/10/14/government-youtube/* [Accessed 11 November 2011].

SlideShare (n.d.) Why you should use SlideShare? [*sic*] *SlideShare*. Available from: *http://www.slideshare.net/about* [Accessed 8 January 2012].

SmugMug (2012) We followed our hearts. *SmugMug*. Available from: *http://www.smugmug.com/about/story/* [Accessed 11 November 2011].

Social Mention (n.d.) About. *Social Mention*. Available from: *http://socialmention.com/about/* [Accessed 11 January 2012].

Sullivan, D. (2004) Google releases Orkut social networking service. *Search Engine Watch* (21 January). Available from: *http://searchenginewatch.com/3302741* [Accessed 22 January 2011].

Sullivan, D. (2012) Google's results get more personal with "Search Plus Your World". *Search Engine Land* (10 January). Available from: *http://searchengineland.com/googles-results-get-more-personal-with-search-plus-your-world-107285* [Accessed 26 January 2012].

Swallow, E. (2010) 15 excellent corporate blogs to learn from. *Mashable Business* (13 August). Available from: *http://mashable.com/2010/08/13/great-corporate-blogs/* [Accessed 28 August 2011].

Thompson, C. (2006) The early years. *New York* (12 February). Available from: *http://nymag.com/news/media/15971/* [Accessed 19 May 2011].

Twitter (2011) #numbers (2011). *Twitter blog* (14 March). Available from: *http://blog.twitter.com/2011/03/numbers.html* [Accessed 6 September 2011].

Twitter (2012) The Twitter glossary. *Twitter*. Available from: *http://support.twitter.com/entries/166337-the-twitter-glossary* [Accessed 25 April 2012].

Twitter (n.d.) LA Times Fire News. *Twitter*. Available from: *http://twitter.com/LATimesFires* [Accessed 30 January 2012].

USAID (29 June 2010) Coffee in Rwanda. *USAID Rwanda*. Available from: *http://www.usaid.gov/rw/our_work/programs/coffee.html* [Accessed 16 January 2012].

Vimeo (n.d.) About Vimeo. *Vimeo*. Available from: *http://vimeo.com/about* [Accessed 8 November 2011].

Vodaphone (2011) About us. *Vodafone*. Available from: *http://www.vodafone.com/content/index/about/about_us.html* [Accessed 11 December 2011].

Wauters, R. (2009) China's social network QZone is big, but is it really the biggest? *TechCrunch* (24 February). Available from: *http://techcrunch.com/2009/02/24/chinas-social-network-qzone-is-big-but-is-it-really-the-biggest/* [Accessed 22 January 2011].

Wikipedia (2012) List of social networking sites. *Wikipedia*. Available from:*http://en.wikipedia.org/wiki/List_of_social_networking_websites* [Accessed 25 April 2012].

Xing (n.d.) Xing AG. *Xing*. Available from: *http://corporate.xing.com/no_cache/english/company/xing-ag/* [Accessed 30 January 2011].

Yee, A. (2011) Gulf to help EU as Syrian oil banned. *The National* (4 September). Available from: *http://www.thenational.ae/business/energy/gulf-to-help-eu-as-syrian-oil-banned* [Accessed 25 April 2012].

YouTube (2012) About YouTube. *YouTube*. Available from: *http://www.youtube.com/t/about_youtube* [Accessed 11 November 2011].

YouTube (n.d.) Statistics. *YouTube*. Available from: *http://www.youtube.com/t/press_statistics* [Accessed 8 November 2011].

Index

Lightning Source UK Ltd.
Milton Keynes UK
UKOW06f2130160715

255290UK00005BA/74/P